RESERVATION RESTLESS

Jim Kristofic

RESERVATION

RESTLESS

University of New Mexico Press / Albuquerque

ISBN 978-0-8263-6113-4 (cloth)
ISBN 978-0-8263-6114-1 (e-book)

Library of Congress Cataloging-in-Publication data
is on file with the Library of Congress.

Jacket photographs by Jim Kristofic
Composed in Realist Sans and Minion Pro

FOR RICK

He was a man, take him for all in all,
I shall not look upon his like again.
Hamlet / act 1 / scene 2

CONTENTS

ACKNOWLEDGMENTS

You're reading this book because enough people thought it would be a good idea and supported it. And so I thank them for helping me to think and write about a place and a people who have given so much to the world.

Thanks to Mom, who gave me life in the West and never refused to buy books.

Thanks to Dad, who taught me that nothing happens overnight. And thanks to all my relatives for their incredible support and loyal kindness. May I repay it in full someday.

Thanks to my brother, Darren, for being my best friend and my worst enemy. I love you, bro. Thanks to my younger sister and brother, for being people who I've always admired. And who I still admire today.

Thanks to Nolan, for being a good model of what a cunning, funny, hardworking man can be. I admire you.

Thanks to all my friends and extended family in Ganado, who gave me a chance and who taught me to live the braver life.

So much thanks to Martha Blue, Ed Chamberlain, Kathy Tabaha, and David Brugge, whose expertise helped me see around corners and whose wisdom helped this book grow toward a greater sense of meaning. Thanks to Ailema Benally, Lyn Carranza, and Tina Lowe at the Hubbell Trading Post National Historic Site, who have inspired and encouraged me during the writing of this book.

My thanks to the staff at Hubbell Trading Post National Historic Site, who welcomed me so graciously and allowed me a peek into the rough-

and-tumble Western world of traders and missionaries, a world that people should never forget.

Thanks so much to the staff at Earthship Biotecture for their mentoring spirit and positive attitude as I came to Taos, New Mexico. I greatly admire you all.

A deep thanks to Whitney Nieman and Ken Eske for giving me a beautiful place where I could write the many drafts of this book. I can never repay you.

I salute the excellent and dedicated staff of Taos High School and Taos Municipal Schools. You inspire me to do my best in all things.

A great thanks goes to former Executive Editor Clark Whitehorn and the University of New Mexico Press for taking a chance on this book. I also thank the anonymous reviewers for their input.

And to the people who live in Ganado, Arizona, and Taos, New Mexico: I envy you. You live in the most beautiful, terrible, and wonderful places on earth.

This is a work of memory. I have set down my own impressions and interviewed friends and family to fact-check those impressions. Any errors or mistakes are unintentional. Names have been altered or changed to protect the innocent and the guilty; there are many traditional taboos surrounding the use of names, and you'd better believe I respect their power. But memories are subjective. Different people may remember some things differently.

Map of *Diné Bikeyah*, Navajo country.
Illustration by Nolan Karras James.

EMERGENCE PLACE

HESPERUS PEAK

Dibe Natsaa

RIO GRANDE

SAN JUAN MOUNTAINS

BLANCA PEAK
Sis Naajini

LA PLATA
MOUNTAINS

SAN JUAN RIVER

DINE TAH

WHEELER PEAK

NARBONA
PASS

SPRUCE HILL
GOBERNADOR KNOB Ch'óol'íí

LARGO CANYON

DINE TAH

HUERFANO MTN.
Dzil Náhoodílii

CHACO PLATEAU

TAOS

CHACO CANYON

JEMEZ Mts.

BLACK
RANGE

• SANTA FE

REDONDO PEAK

SKY REACHING
ROCK

SAN MATEO MTS.

• GALLUP

PLATEAU

ZUNI MTS.

MT. TAYLOR
TSOODZIL

• ALBUQUERQUE

ZUNI

RAMAH

GRANTS •

LUGUNA

RIO GRANDE

PROLOGUE / RAINBOW WALK

This all started with my Mom's Indian Dream.

She moved my brother and me to Indian Country in the Southwest. We grew up in the small town of Ganado, Arizona, on the Navajo Reservation. There, I was a *bilagáana* (white boy) who had to adapt or die. I chose to adapt, and it became a beautiful life for me in that small valley the Diné people who lived there called *Lók'aahnteel* (The Place of the Wide Reeds). I wrote about these years in a book titled *Navajos Wear Nikes*. While I was there, I gained a Diné stepfather named Nolan Manygoats and a sister, Yanabah, and brother, Glen.

When I entered high school, my mom moved us again, to Page, Arizona, where she took a new job with the Navajo Generating Station, the largest coal-burning power plant in the United States, which vented the dreams of a city and the sins of a nation into the sky. In that stark desert country, I would ask new questions I hadn't asked in *Navajos Wear Nikes*. Or perhaps the place asked those questions through me. I once asked why we decide to call a place our home. Now I would ask why we decide to leave that home, to choose restlessness (or let it choose us), to range into strange experience, and to emerge forever changed.

When I had spare time between feeding our fifteen paint horses, fixing fences, building corrals, shoveling manure, watering our flailing apple and pear orchard, and watching my younger sister and brother, Yanabah and Glen, I got restless. So I gave my body to the desert along the Grand Staircase–Escalante National Monument. I used two plastic soda bottles to do this.

I tied at their necks braided yellow and orange plastic hay twine. This way, I could fill them at the kitchen sink and sling them over my back and let the rope carry their weight over my shoulder.

Then I would pick a direction and walk out.

Some days I took my .22 Marlin range rifle and hunted jackrabbits and ground squirrels. I got good enough to hit them on the run, and I would slit their bodies with my pocketknife and let their blood drain onto the sand on the walk back home. Then I fed them to my dogs.

Some days I'd follow tracks for hours. Sometimes it was toward the east, where *Naats'iis'áán*, the Head of the World, raised its broad, ten-thousand-foot cap above the edge of a gray mesa. The Americans named it Navajo Mountain. The Diné said it was the head of a war god lying on his back, defending the borders of their homeland from invaders. Others from the area say it is the head of a woman, strong as pollen, whose legs are *Balakai* mesa. I have heard both stories of what *Naats'iis'áán* is supposed to be. I like to think it is both, just as each of us is both man and woman in the Diné teachings.

I played football with guys who'd been raised on the steppes of that mountain. Their ancestors had used the slithered gray canyons around the mountain to hide from the cavalry during the war with the Americans. When most of the tribe had been corralled and arrested at Fort Defiance and pressed into the Long Walk to Fort Sumner, they stayed behind and survived, always in view of *Naats'iis'áán*. That Female Pollen Mountain. That ancient war god.

They never surrendered.

It hadn't been easy. From the nearly hundred miles of distance, Navajo Mountain's pale sandstone ridges seemed coated with pebbly black paint gleaming in the late morning light like truck-bed liner. But I knew that trick of light on any mountain in the West. The black paint was actually groves of tall ponderosa and piñon pines. Bears and mule deer and elk would sleep in the tall grass in the shadows of those trees.

And to their keen eyes, the desert where I stood seemed like brown smear to the blue horizon. No one saw the sagebrush, yucca, and mounds of dark green ephedra rising like small coral reefs from the sand. Small patches of gray moss clung to the sides of the reefs, waiting for rain that turned them green as any hill in Ireland, then dried to gray and waited for their next drink from the sky. The scarlet globe mallow, with those red-orange blooms like sunset that prophesies storms, grew on dunes next to the white flowers

of the desert morning glory that tossed like white tissue paper with the warming breeze on the edges of its pale green and pink stems.

American soldiers used the mountain to try to kill the Diné. An American officer had the idea to use a heliograph, a large mirror that could flash the light of the sun into coded messages relayed to their Ute and Puebloan scouts to better direct the soldiers to where to find the families and murder them.

The officer ordered troops to take axes to the tallest and oldest trees on the mountain. From the height of the denuded slope, the army officers used a spyglass to spot bands of Diné ranging on the desert floor below. They then set up the mirror of their heliograph and flashed messages to the troops. Some say they would flash the messages as far as Fluted Rock, near Ganado.

The soldiers tried to use the mountain to defeat the Diné. But the heliograph didn't work. The winds often knocked it over. The sun wasn't always at the right angle. *Naats'iis'áán* had protected them. Today, the people who live near *Naats'iis'áán* know that the summit is spiked with steel girders of radar and radio towers. One of those towers is built over a sacred spring. The severed stumps of those *ndíshchíí' tso*—those giant ponderosa pines—are still up there. So are the memories.

Some days the tracks led north, toward the blond and gray mesas of the Grand Staircase. The towns along the stretch of state route 89 where we lived had sprung up around those mesas to house and cater to the miners who would dig into those ancient sea and swamp beds that now held the largest low-sulfur coal reserve in the world. But when President Clinton declared the area a national monument (and effectively closed down all mining operations), he left the residents of Big Water, Church Wells, and Clark Bench with a network of graded roads, some surveyed homesites, and ample room for bouncing around in the desert in their ATVs.

We lived in Church Wells. Church Wells had only one local business: a pay phone near the highway. And that stopped working about a year after we lived there.

It gave me and my family enough room to explore the dry washes and gray canyons, to look for coyote dens and pronghorn grazing grounds, to watch for the constellations after the sun walked down into red and orange fields of burning copper nearly every night. Some cool autumn days we would drive out to a patch of fine gray soil people called "The Moon." We'd take our shoes off and walk out into the ground that puffed and swallowed our feet like baby powder. That cool dust beneath had settled after fifty

millennia of brachiopods and bivalves spent their time living and birthing and dying and taking in the sun before a strange shift in water oxygen levels wiped them from the planet like an absent-minded teacher erasing chalk from a blackboard.

My brother and I found places in Cottonwood Canyon where you could walk out into that fine soil, trowel your hand down into that cool layer of gray powder, and come up with a handful of ancient seashells.

When the tracks led south, I walked to the rocky highlands that stretched to the Kaibab National Forest along the North Rim of the Grand Canyon. I would travel that country of lichen-pocked boulders, rain-smoothed rock ridges, and juniper groves with my stepdad and brother to haul firewood in the back of our Dodge Dakota pickup. Or we'd haul down slabs of sandstone to line our garden and patio. The desert constantly reclaimed these with new dunes of sand. In that high country, we would follow coyote tracks and watch the yellow caps of blackbirds and warblers migrating south. We'd follow the flight paths of golden eagles as they circled up in arcs with the thermals over the desert and scouted for jackrabbits and ground squirrels.

On the day that made me want to write this book, I walked east, the White Shell direction.

I threw the soda bottles over my shoulder. I strapped my Leatherman to my belt. Our Rottweiler mutt, Tilly, our dog since a puppy in Ganado, Arizona, fell in next to me as we walked between the shallow reefs of ephedra and sagebrush and yucca.

I slipped easily through the spot in the barbed-wire fence about a mile from Church Wells. Tilly took her time stooping and dragging her back legs under the fence.

In the years before I emerged into adolescence, Tilly would sprint at any barbed-wire fence and jump it without breaking stride. But the gray hair on her orange and black muzzle told her age. That dogs age faster than humans is my most immediate argument for the cruel nature of the cosmos. She and I had roamed through nearly every wash and bosque, had drunk out of each stream, and had run over every mesa and ridge in a five-mile radius of our adobe home in Ganado by the time my family moved.

At any lake or beach, I could throw a stick into the water for Tilly to fetch. I would dive into her wake and grip the hair between her powerful shoulders as she towed me out through the water. Then we raced each other back to the land, stroke for stroke. She usually won. I felt she and I were on

the same path, walking side by side. But the cosmos had other plans. She was going to finish her walk before me, no matter what I did.

A low rumble fanned across the sky from a sheet of gray clouds pushing over the mesas of the Escalante. The sort of summer monsoon storm that would gallop in from nowhere and drench the pale sandstone until it shined dark as a flint arrowhead and the dry arroyos bled muddy water until the sand could drink no more. These storms. Fast. Once, when Glen and I weeded the tomato plants under the aluminum roof of our *cha'oh*, the shade house, we both shot straight up. We thought someone was shooting an assault rifle next door.* The sky was blue. The sun shined to make you squint. We never saw the patch of storm that had opened up directly over us and sent a shower of hailstones that shimmered like falling crystal and dented the metal roof. About five minutes later, the storm stopped. Glen and I picked through the hailstones shining on the sand around the *cha'oh*. They were clear as glass and shaped like .45 caliber bullets. The thermometer mounted on the post of the *cha'oh* read ninety-six degrees. The hailstones had melted into a white mist before we could run inside and tell anyone what had happened.

This storm growling in from the northeast seemed no different.

Tilly fell in slowly behind me as we sidestepped a cactus and walked toward the arroyo. She accepted that her days of tearing ass after rabbits were over. Such dignity.

The sun had walked down from the top of the summer sky when we reached the sandy arroyo. I had never seen it named on any map. But I knew it held the scattered rabbit bones and gray-blond hairs that marked coyote dens. The *ma'ii* (coyotes) had settled in rocks that caught the shade for most of the day. Their tracks wrote on the sand in that disciplined perfect step, where one track falls neatly into the other.

By our third weekend living in Church Wells, I had named the place Coyote Canyon.

Whenever something weighed hard against my mind, I came to Coyote Canyon. The red ants ran along the stems of grama grass and sagebrush and taught me the smallness of my life drama against the movement of the larger world. When I first fell in love with a girl, I came to Coyote Canyon. When I wanted to write a letter to forgive my dad for abandoning us as

* Considering my neighbors in Church Wells, this was a rational possibility.

kids, I came to Coyote Canyon. When I was asking questions of God and the cosmos and feeling all those strong first realizations of an adolescent life into which my body seemed to be dragging me (whether I liked it or not), I took to the canyon like some zit-faced prophet wandering into the desert wilderness.

My stepdad often did the same thing whenever he felt restless. He also took Tilly with him. The things to which our dogs must bear witness.

The coyotes felt the same. They ranged in a circle, always turning north, then looping back into the arroyo. Some days, Nolan would be washing dishes in the middle of the day, and he'd look up and see a coyote trotting off with one of our roosters dangling in its mouth. We'd learned not to leave our small dogs out at night. I knew that some of those bones at the edges of the dens were probably theirs.

Clouds passed across the sun. The air cooled.

Tilly cocked her head. A gray shadow flitted up and out of the sandstone walling the arroyo. I wondered how long the coyote had been watching us. I ran up along its trail. Tilly huffed and limped behind me. That gray sheet of cloud had dropped its hair and sent a long, pale shower of rain down into the basin that would run to Big Water and then to Lake Powell. The top of the cloud coiled out toward the south and threw a shadow over the town of Big Water in the sloping distance.

"Tilly, *hágo*." Tilly, come here.

I looked to the sky and held my breath.

The sun—*Jóhonaa'éí*, that great ruler of the day who walks his red crystal shield across the sky—had combed his light through the pale hair of water dropping to the ground. The bow of *nááts'íílid*—the rainbow—arced across the sky. One end punched into a small dip in the hills to the north. The other dropped bent to the arroyo. It was maybe forty yards away.

"Are you kidding me?" I said.

I walked to the rainbow. It seemed to shine brighter. Thirty yards. Ten.

I could see the end of the rainbow fixed into the sand of the arroyo.

"Well, the Holy People are out walking today," I said to Tilly, petting one of her ragged ears that still swelled with scars from dogfights long ago.

Science textbooks told me I was seeing a refraction of white light through the prisms of rain droplets or ice crystals. But I also knew the *Diyin Diné*—the Holy People—used rainbows to travel and to communicate with *Nohokaa' Diné*—Five-Fingered Earth Surface People—like me.

I stepped closer to the band of rainbow, wide as two pickup trucks parked beside each other. The red and orange and yellow and green and blue and violet pattern draped like a blanket into the sand.

I squinted.

My stepdad told stories of the Hero Twins who had fought the monsters in this world using rainbows to move faster than eagles across the sky, rainbows that moved them into higher ways of thinking and feeling. They were *atiin diyinii*—trails of holiness, of power. Beauty trails.

I walked toward the *náátsʼíílid*. That trail of beauty.

The colors faded into a mist like a sheet of mica. The air shifted clear. I turned. The colors of the pattern glowed behind me.

I walked through them again. They disappeared.

I walked through them again. They vanished within touching distance.

The other end of the rainbow faded in the north. The rain slowed and seeped into the earth. The rest was going back up into the sky.

I walked through the rainbow again, to the east. The colors faded into air as clear as crystal.

Tilly looked at me and cocked her head, as to say, "Are you all right?"

"Yeah," I said. "Yeah, I'm all right, girl."

A cool breeze blew over my arm. Beads of rain clung to my hands. I hadn't noticed them. My feet felt rooted into the earth.

"Did that just happen?"

Tilly limped to me. Her warm tongue licked the cold rain from my hands.

We walked up the arroyo together. A jackrabbit shot out of a pocket between boulders and skittered up onto the flats. A breeze ruffled the white silk of the desert morning glory by the edge of the arroyo. A semitruck left a Doppler roar as it sped north toward Kanab on Interstate 89.

I unslung the water bottles, cupped my hand, and gave Tilly a drink. The dog always drinks first. Company policy.

We reached the single-wide trailer my family had parked on our four acres of desert. I sat on the mattress my brother and I shared in our room and bent over my notebook to finish my math homework. I doodled rainbows in the corners while I thought out the geometry problems. Tilly walked under the trailer and curled up in the shade.

A few hours later, I walked out to water the trees at sunset and listened to the leathery flaps of bats singing their subsonic chants to hunt moths and gnats in the orange and blue air.

The rainbow in the arroyo. Water falling from the hose.

When my mom got back from her weekend shift at Page Hospital, I didn't tell her what had happened. I didn't tell anyone.

But I told Lyle Parsons.

Lyle Parsons was my English teacher at Page High School. I parachuted into his class after the holiday break. I turned in the sort of English work that I'd been used to doing in Ganado. It wasn't long before I was earning Ds.

So I walked over the scuffed green carpet to Mr. Parson's battered steel desk in the corner of the classroom. He rested at ease in his jeans and Western shirt and white sneakers. His black and gray hair swept back from his tall, sun-tinted forehead. His raptor's gaze from behind his dark-tinted glasses reminded me of a hippie version of Richard III. One of the students in the class had said he looked like a Jewish Bob Dylan.

"Um . . . I think Bob Dylan *is* Jewish," I said.

"Whatever, fag," the student deftly retorted.

Mr. Parsons folded his hands and raised one dark eyebrow at my approach.

"Yes, Mr. Kristofic?" he asked.

"Why do I have a bad grades on my assignments?" I asked.

"Too brief," he gruffed. "You need to write more."

"That's it?" I asked.

"Yes," Mr. Parsons said. "That's it."

I took his advice.

Our short visits turned into after-class conversations. These after-class conversations eventually stretched into after-school conversations. He and I started a literary seminar between us so I could earn extra credit, and I was reading books off the University of Arizona recommended reading list by Spenser, Milton, Orwell, Tolkien, and Conrad.

What I had seen in the arroyo wasn't in any of those books. I told Lyle Parsons about walking through the rainbow.

"Is that even physically possible?" I asked.

"Well, if you put your thumb over a hose and spray the water up in the air, you can see some rainbow in the spray. And that's just a few feet away from you. So it's possible. Rainbows are special. They are powerful. *Look out, man.*"

Lyle talked about how something in us made us look at rainbows. The Israelites in the poetic histories of the Bible had seen promises from God in their rainbows.

The Israelites usually spotted rainbows after a long journey into the wilderness of strange experience—whether it was surviving a world-engulfing flood or walking through a den of lions. The Navajo had seen the rainbow as a guide toward safe journeys. I thought about my own desire to move out into those wildernesses, those places I didn't know but wanted to know. I wanted to get out there. I was *restless*.

"Well, you're not alone there," Lyle said. "Everybody feels like they need to get the hell out of wherever they are. Sometimes they need to get out of their own damn bodies."

But those damn bodies seemed eager for journeys into strange places, to return, and to change what they had considered normal.

"Well," Lyle said. "That's Joseph Campbell's journey right there. The call, the crossing of the threshold, and the return."

I called it "the Emergence."

I told Lyle how the Diné had always been a restless people. If you believe their traditional creation stories, they moved through many worlds and changed the forms of their bodies many times. In the First World, the people were *Nílch'idine'é*, a people almost like spirits, who lived in darkness in the land of *Tó bił dahisk'id* (The Place Where the Waters Cross) with the Insect People and the Bats and other people like *Ch'al* (Frog) and *Táłtł'ááh 'alééh* (Great Blue Heron). These people then emerged into the Second World, a Blue World, where they sent out the Insect People and the Locusts to scout the land. They came to a place where the Swallow People lived.

They emerged out of this world to the Third World, a Yellow World, where they met the Grasshopper People. They emerged through this world again into the Fourth World, where they met the *Kiis'áanii* (People Who Live in Upright Houses, or the Puebloan People) for the first time. From them, they learned to grow corn and pumpkins and beans. They began to hear the voices of the *Haash'chééh Diné* (Great Ones) for the first time. These were the people who spoke only in gesture but were still understood; they traveled on rainbows and commanded the winds, and their voices could be translated only by the Insect People. These Holy People created a cleaner and more intelligent people they called *Áltsé Diné* (First People). These First People ranged again and survived a flood and emerged up through a giant reed into the Fifth World, the Glittering World. Our world. Here, the people changed again into the *Nahook'aa Diné* (Five-Fingered Earth Surface People). They split into clans, and they are these people who today

live and farm and herd sheep and work at Taco Bell and get degrees in welding and law and medicine and dietary science and have their children in *Diné Bikéyah*.

"Sounds almost like Darwinian evolution to me," Lyle said. "Like genetic memories passed on. The Flood. That appears in the stories of the Hebrews, the Assyrians, the Greeks, and the Mayans. Sounds like a real human history."

"Yeah, but if you believe the anthropological story of the Navajo people, they traveled out of Siberia and ranged across the Bering Strait with large groups of Athabascan people who spoke the same language," I said. "Eventually, some broke away down into modern Canada. They ranged south, following the backbone of the Rocky Mountains down into the United States. Well . . . we call it that now, but it was the same sort of landscape then. And then they came into the Southwest. They were a strong, tall people. They had these bows they built with sinew glued into the backs of the wood to increase the power of their arrows."

"So these guys were conquerors?" Lyle asked. "Like the Americans?"

I shrugged. "Not exactly. When you move around in the Southwest, you meet a lot of Native Americans," I said. "Go back East sometime where my relatives live in the Ohio River Valley and near Pittsburgh. There are a lot of Native American names for places. But there aren't any Native people. That's the American way of conquering."

Lyle kicked back his head and laughed. "Ah, shit, man," he said. "What are they teaching you in school these days? Be careful, Mr. Kristofic. You keep talking like that, and you're going to be walking through rainbows the rest of your life."

His grin widened, that smile that made him look my age.

The Diné had met the Puebloan people when the Spanish lanced into the north. The Navajos took any Puebloan refugees into the mountains of northwestern New Mexico. In the safety of the mountains, the Navajo learned farming, basketry, and weaving from them. They also stole and traded sheep, goats, and horses from the Spanish. They interbred with the Puebloan people. They interbred with the Spanish. They changed forms. They herded their new livestock. This livestock walks the grasslands and grocery store parking lots of Navajo country today.

Many Navajo families think nothing of driving on a weekend more than six or seven hours at a stretch to spend a day in a large town like Flagstaff, Albuquerque, or Durango, then driving all night to return to the Reserva-

tion. Navajo families range far from their homes to work jobs all over the Southwest while still maintaining strong ties to their lands.

They like to get out there. They are *restless*.

There was something in me that felt this, too. Some of my best memories were of walking out with Yanabah and Glen and Nolan and looking out over the arroyos and junipers and piñons and sagebrush and ponderosa pines. *Ayóó nizhóní* (so beautiful).

It had something to do with this desire to move. To leave the ground of what we thought was real, to walk along the arc of *nááts'íílid* into a strange reality, and to emerge to put our feet back on our Mother Earth, *Nahasdzáán*, again.

I'm still trying to understand what I really saw in that rainbow that day in Coyote Canyon. The best way to explain it is how my Navajo relatives taught me to explain things. Not with statements, but with stories.

Here are some of them.

LION PATH

In the winter of my senior year at Page High School, a neighbor came to the Friday shift at the Navajo Generating Station, where my mom worked as the on-site nurse, and told her he'd seen a mountain lion.

I filled up the bottles. Clayton Sterling agreed to come out to Church Wells and track the lion with me before any winds pushed the trail away.

He was the only one of my high school friends who thought it seemed like a good idea.

When I'd first moved to Page, I kept to myself. After school, I would walk to the library and read until my mom got off work at six o'clock. I ate my lunch alone in the city park and read Stephen King and Robert E. Howard paperbacks on the picnic tables, made no friends, and gave away at least ten dollars in spare change to the drunks lounging on the grass.

Clayton ran cross-country with the other wiry kids and seemed to love doing it. The Navajo runners made jokes about Clayton being the Pale Horse. Clayton was a tall, skinny kid with red hair and freckles spotting his high cheekbones. He also had blue eyes. And he was left-handed. Once we became friends, I would call him my Genetic Freak Friend.

He also carried his King James Bible from class to class. Other days, he'd wear a hat that read "I Love Jesus" in white gangsta font over the bill. But he never approached me about whether I'd "accepted Jesus Christ as my Lord and Savior," whatever the hell that meant.

In our junior year, we helped each other through our advanced biology class. I took him out to the rocky country to the south of Church Wells, where we collected specimens of desert morning glory, scarlet globe mallow, hoary

aster, locoweed, and Indian paintbrush and set them in between sheets of newspaper and cardboard in our plant presses we'd built with scrap wood and tension straps for our spring semester project. That day, the fuel pump failed on the Dodge Dakota about five miles from the highway.

"Well," Clayton said, stepping out of the cab, "looks like it's a new type of adventure."

I smiled. We shouldered our packs. He and Tilly and I walked the rest of the way down the sloping juniper country and onto the sagebrush plain of Church Wells.

So Clayton came to track the mountain lion. He drove to Church Wells that Saturday morning in his parents' white van just as I was spooning hot oatmeal and apples into Yanabah and Glen's breakfast bowls. I walked into our room and told Darren where I was going. He nodded and went back to playing his video game. I threw another juniper log into the wood stove and yelled to Darren that I'd be back before sunset. We threw our packs into the back of the Dodge Dakota pickup and hoped the fuel pump wouldn't fail again (which it seemed to love to do).

We drove the single paved road at the center of Church Wells, buzzed over the cattle guard at the north fence line, and rumbled down the dirt road toward the gray mesas of the Escalante country. The neighbor said he'd seen the lion moving off that way.

He also thought the lion had a large cub with her. That was good news. With a cub, she'd be moving slower, and we'd maybe have a chance to catch her trail on the cold desert sand.

The winter light angled and shaded the world in hard yellow light against the clean blue sky as we got out of the truck. The door panel groaned from when Nolan had slid down into a ditch and crashed into a barbed-wire fence after a near-hit with a cow while driving at night near Piñon, Arizona. The impact crimped the door so that it only opened halfway. But that was enough.

We locked the truck and walk the gentle slope of sand and sagebrush that I knew would eventually lead us to the top of the humpbacked mesa where my neighbor claimed he saw the lion. Our feet gained traction on the frosted sand as we climbed the slope.

To the west, the gray slot canyons of Jurassic-era sediments arched out in those swerves like tree roots. That architecture of water and gravity. My family and I had hiked down in those canyons. We'd found small springs there. We'd found bobcat and deer tracks.

About halfway up the mesa, a black shadow glided past. It was fast. It was big. In the country around Church Wells, you saw ravens flying every

fifteen minutes. I knew how ravens moved, how their feathers folded to a neat, curving, triangular edge. And every cellular memory inherited from my long-ago ancestors—perhaps those *Nílch'idine'é* in that second Blue World—that taught me to flinch under every bird's shadow knew that this was no raven.

The dark bird screamed and flashed overhead. It banked against the cold winter sun. Its black feathers glimmered to brown. A blond hood crowned its head. White feathers blazed the edge of its six-foot wingspan. Its talons glinted against its chest.

A golden eagle. *'Atsá*.

It circled back, tucked its wings, and dived. Clayton and I yelled and dropped to our knees. I could hear its feathers cutting the air. If I'd been carrying a walking stick, I could have raised it overhead and hit *'Atsá* as it buzzed overhead.

'Atsá banked east, landed on a small hoodoo of rock, opened its feathers to catch some heat from the sun, and watched us.

Eagles speak the language of bodies. Clayton and I walked a circle around the eagle in a way that said, "You made your point. We're no threat to you. It's your world."

'Atsá seemed to understand. It watched us until we crowned the slope of the mesa. Wherever it had built its nest, we were far enough away from it now. *'Atsá* hopped from the hoodoo, flashed its wings, and rejoined the thermals to return to the hunt that has always been the dance of its survival.*

We had reached the top of the mesa. Clayton looked over the red and orange buttes and canyons running up to the roots of the gray mesas in the distance. These mesas were called the Gray Cliffs by geologists at universities we'd never visited. They fanned out like hundred-mile steps on an expansive staircase that led from the Vermillion Cliffs near Lee's Ferry in Marble Canyon to the White Cliffs in the distance, then to the Gray Cliffs and Kolob Terrace, and then to the Pink Cliffs, until they summited

3

* One part of me thought this. But another part of me thought about how traditional Diné people said that birds were always messengers for *Nílchi*, the spirit or Holy Person who looked out for the Diné and the Hero Twins and Changing Woman. Birds live in the sky, and they move from the earth to the sky, where the Great Ones walk. They communicate with them, and birds' feathers can be used to call the attention of the *Diyin Diné*. Birds were the intercessors. Some say the Eagle is like Christ sitting at the right side of the Navajo god, The Sun. So another part of me thought that *'Atsa'* or *Nílchi* was saying, "You. You're on the right path. The lion moved this way. I yelled at her just like I'm yelling at you!"

nearly two hundred miles to the north at the Aquarius Plateau near Bryce Canyon, where we always took my visiting family. These cliffs had been built by sand dunes more than a half-mile tall that had blown and built and hardened on the shores of Pangaea, when dinosaurs walked the land and all the continents were bunched like a defiant fist against the planet's oceans.

The dunes remained through the Jurassic period, but in the Cretaceous, everything was submerged under the Carmel Sea and then totally flooded by the Western Interior Seaway, a massive inland sea that had once stretched from the Arctic Ocean to the Gulf of Mexico. Soon after the dinosaurs died, the earth's crust bent and twisted under volcanic fires. The Rocky Mountains lifted up like the spine of some powerful awakened colossus. The water of the seaway either ran into the ocean or stayed behind and formed worlds of lakes. A short time later—just forty million years—the mountains formed. The winds eroded away some of their dunes. The land dried out once the Sierra Nevada mountains pushed up into the clouds and captured whatever Pacific Ocean moisture had been drifting into modern-day Utah. And so it has been since.

"I don't know how anyone can look at this and think there isn't a God," Clayton said.

My teenage mind had just started reading about the creation of the world in a book by Carl Sagan that I had found in a used bookstore in Cedar City, Utah, after we'd traveled to visit a horse trainer.

The title was *Shadows of Forgotten Ancestors*.

I had read Sagan's book and seen the same patterns playing out. Life had been this gradual emergence. Forms changed into other forms. Life was meant to create life. It seemed its pleasure to do so.

We were all an Emergence People.

So when Clayton saw God in those canyons, I couldn't debate him. I didn't know if the God of the Israelites had ever really visited the lands of the Diné or the Puebloan people. But the Creator was here. And if not the Creator, then the mechanisms of the Creator. Water and gravity making things. Water and gravity in that meandering dance that shaped the swerves of those canyons as surely as it shaped the swerves of the veins in my hands.

But these were the foolish thoughts of a teenage mind.

I wiped my runny nose on the sleeve of my Carhartt coat.

"Yep," I said. "Good country."

We walked the rocky spine of the mesa.

"So do you think we're really going to find this trail?" Clayton asked, swigging some water.

"Wouldn't have come up here if I thought we couldn't find it."

"Well, what do you want to do?"

"If I were a lion and I was headed up north," I said, indicating the way with my hand, "I'd follow this ridge. Path of least resistance."

Clayton nodded, and we walked east and north up along the rock. I knew the mountain lion had probably decided to leave the forest country of the Kaibab near the North Rim of the Grand Canyon and crossed down that smooth rock country where we had gathered firewood. She was moving with her cub down across the basin and would range up toward the Cedar Mountains to the north of the gray drainage of the Escalante. Maybe she was simply following the migration of elk and mule deer. Maybe she was using the stock tanks for water on her way toward the Paria River. Maybe she'd smelled a cow carcass and had a feed for her and the cub. Maybe she was just restless and felt like she needed a change. Maybe she was curious about the lights of the small community and decided to skirt its borders, maybe hoping to catch and eat a jackrabbit or a small dog or cat.

Either way, she was moving from one set of mountains to another. From one island of green life to another. And here Clayton and I were in the middle, walking around in the gray cemetery of an ancient seabed.

As we moved along the trail, I watched each piece of eroded sandstone, every patch of flat sand near each small rabbitbrush and cactus.

Whenever I spotted a cactus, I was also remembering the words of Lyle Parsons.

My senior year, I took Lyle's English class at the local Coconino County Community College. I sketched analyses of Edgar Allan Poe's short stories and James Wright's poetry. My mind ranged through biographies of Albert Einstein and Sandra Cisneros, the essays of Isaac Asimov and Annie Dillard, and the dramas of Shakespeare and Shaw. I learned that geniuses who understand the cosmos can also be compassionate enough to understand people, that revelation often comes from unexpected places, and that some stories really have no "good guys."

Since I'd met Lyle Parsons, I had migrated in that cycle of driving home from football practice in the yellow cascade of an Arizona sunset, of throwing hay to our paint horses, of feeding our dogs and checking on our pigs, of watering the cottonwoods and fruit trees around the trailer. Near the end of the night, I sat on edge of my mattress in the small bedroom that my brother and I shared and balanced my English textbook and my notepad over my lap. There, I started my training as a writer. I wrote my homework essays. I eventually wrote my own short stories. Then I'd type them in the

computer lab in the high school library because my family didn't have a computer at home.

I remembered Lyle's story of hunting while Clayton and I were out walking the trail. It reminded me of why I hadn't brought my rifle with me that day.

Lyle Parsons had moved from the bayous of Louisiana to the Sonoran Desert at the same age I was when I moved from the green woods of Pennsylvania to the desert valley of Ganado. One of the last things he'd done in Louisiana was to paint the eaves of his parents' house before they moved. After he finished the work, his parents paid Lyle fifteen dollars.

When his family arrived in the suburbs of Tucson, Arizona, Lyle used the money to buy a longbow and a quiver of arrows. He had always idealized Davy Crockett and Daniel Boone. He wanted to leave home and go north and homestead in Alaska as soon as he could drive. Something made him want to migrate. Something made him restless against the reality his society was suggesting that he spend the rest of his life living.

I could understand that.

So he and a friend went out into the desert. Slung over Lyle's back were that new bow and a small quiver of arrows. They ditched their bikes in a dry arroyo and stalked between the manzanita and creosote with arrows at the ready.

When a desert cottontail shot out of a clump of ocotillo, the boys drew their bows and shot. Lyle imagined himself a fur-clad, hawk-eyed frontiersman when his arrow punched through the rabbit's back leg. This feeling lasted about a second.

The rabbit screamed. It lurched and jumped blindly and landed in a large patch of prickly pear cactus. The animal thrashed and kicked as the cactus needles pierced its ribs and neck and eyes. It quivered and screamed and jerked in the cactus.

His friend stepped forward and put one more arrow through the rabbit's neck. That stopped the screaming, and the rabbit lay contorted and bleeding in the cactus.

Lyle had just watched. Horrified.

"It sounded like someone was burning a goddang baby," he said. "One of the worst sounds I've ever heard. It haunts me to this day."

A week later, Lyle sold the bow and arrows for fifteen dollars. He used the money to buy a green Norma guitar from a pawn shop in Tucson. He practiced every day. He got pretty good. He played with two or three bands in high school and in college, where he earned degrees in English and

psychology from the University of Arizona. After his graduation, he ended up playing professionally with a country band called Medicine Wheel that toured the bars and honky-tonks from Texas to Canada. He hung out with Alice Cooper back when his band called themselves the Spiders. He played with Link Wray. He migrated between gigs and girlfriends for nearly twenty years before he decided to stop.

Then he found a job in Page, Arizona, working at the power plant. He also worked as a mechanic. He liked the money, but it didn't have the mental stimulation he'd felt in college. So he went back to the classroom at the local high school, where I met him a few years later.

That was where I told him the story of the first time I went out hunting with my .22 Marlin range rifle.

I jogged into a little reef of ephedra, and a jackrabbit the size of a small dog shot straight out and hopped clear of a sagebrush at a dead run. I fired once. The .22 made a little gassy pop and the stock tapped my shoulder. I missed. The jackrabbit kept running.

I cleared the bolt and fired just as the jackrabbit leaped over a tall sagebrush. He cartwheeled forward, and sand flew up. The jackrabbit's gray and brown body lay stretched and surprised. His wet eye reflected the blue sky. It didn't blink.

I knew I should have been proud of what I'd done. I'd always been a good shot whenever I went shooting with my friends. And I'd always won the shooting medals at Boy Scout camp. I'd just hit this jackrabbit on the run from more than fifty yards away.

I was not proud. The gray and black hairs moved in the breeze like the pelt of a wolf. I thought how his white hairs along his rump looked soft as blown snow. How his hair between his ears was slightly blond. How his ancestors had whittled and shaved down their bodies into these running spirits that could cover more than twenty feet in a jump. I would never know the speed his ancestors had given him.

And I'd taken all that with a small piece of lead no larger than a pencil eraser, which probably cost less than two cents to manufacture in some ammo plant in Missouri.

I lifted his stiff head. His other eye was full of blood. A neat hole behind his head revealed my shot. The bullet had come out of his eye. He'd hit the ground without a sound.

I gutted the rabbit with my Leatherman and left half his body for the coyotes. I gave the other half to my dogs.

When I came back the next day, I found only a small patch of blood in the sand. The desert didn't know how to waste. I couldn't say the same for myself.

"Yeah, hunting is something you should only do when you have to," Lyle had said after I'd told him the story. "In the ancient cultures, you had to become one with the animal before you took its life just so you could find it and track it. Then the animal became part of you when you ate it and took it into your body. We've pretty much screwed that up."

"Well," I said, "at least the rabbits taught us what we didn't want to do."

Lyle Parsons lifted his lips. It was almost a smile.

Clayton and I turned a small corner in the spine of rock on the mesa when we saw it.

Next to a clump of sagebrush lay a paw print the size of a softball. No claw marks at the edges of the paws, like a dog. The prints did not overlap. The animal had been walking in perfect step, each print falling into the other in a regular cadence that was almost a dance to some inner music. These prints didn't belong to someone's large dog out for a midnight run after jackrabbits. These tracks had focus. They had purpose.

"That's a mountain lion," I said, touching the edges of the tracks to check the looseness of the sand. They were firm. It hadn't been very long since she'd been here.

"Holy crap!" said Clayton. "What are the odds of us finding this?"

"I know, right?" I said, smiling. "Come on, let's go."

We followed. We found a smaller set to the right of the lion's trail. So it was true: she had a cub traveling with her. We moved along the trail, sometimes striding and sometimes jogging. We'd found the one thing in that desert that we'd wanted. If you'd followed our tracks, they were the trail of wild, running teenagers. That same focus, that purpose, had not come yet.

We ranged to the middle of the mesa, where that wide bridge of land extended out onto those gray sagebrush plains toward the distant mesas that led up to Escalante and toward those lush, green mountains.

As we got closer, the tracks grew tighter. We turned a large clump of sagebrush. The tracks ended.

The sand dropped into a small, smooth impression large enough to hold a sleeping mountain lion.

"She and the cub slept here," I said. "This is where she bedded down."

"You sure?" Clayton asked.

I knelt and plucked a thin, pale clump that had snagged in the sagebrush.

It was a small patch of blond and white hair. Mountain lion hair. It weighed as much as any ghost.

I held it up for Clayton.

"Dude," he said.

"Yeah," I said. "I know."

Clayton took the hairs from my extended hand. "Just beautiful. What should we do with them?"

"Give 'em back to the desert," I said. "The lion did."

Clayton loosened his fingers, and the hairs slipped away like thistledown on the cold wind.

"You good to keep going for a while?"

Clayton nodded and checked his water. "Let's walk."

We stepped north toward the small land bridge of the mesa, following the softball-sized prints in the sand. Our strides grew longer over the yucca and sagebrush. We were on the lion's trail, sensing its wandering energy left behind like some psychic scent. Years later, I would read about how this is where reading and writing really began. Not in some marble temple. Not in some dusty sanctum of a monastery. Not in some oak-paneled library at Oxford. But right here. Tracking the trail of animals while ranging in the wilderness.

This is where narrative intelligence started in humans. Our ancestors read the prints in the earth, like words on a page, and they made sense of things. We use our imaginations. We don't have noses like dogs. We can't pick up scent trails. But our almond-shaped eyes are unique. We see three dimensions. We see elaborate color combinations. The brown-and-white-speckled fawn cannot curl up and hide from our sight in a field of green grass. We see *depth*. We create a story. We imagine the beginning, then a middle, then an end. We can anticipate and reason. We can repeat truth and elaborate fiction.

Beginning. The lion ranged past Church Wells. She probably came there for water. Middle. She used this rocky incline up the mesa because it was the path of least resistance. She moved along the spine of the mesa toward that gently sloping land bridge. She bedded down for the night. Now Clayton and I were looking for the end. We were tracing that story. We were looking for that next step along the holy trail. We couldn't slow down.

Our ancestors emerged into the world with this new kind of narrative intelligence. This ability to infer. They were never the same. And then they gifted it to us. Clayton and I were feeling that gift now, like we'd just stepped into a beautiful story.

Writing and reading were born of restlessness.

As we crossed the land bridge and walked out onto the sagebrush plains, we detected movement ahead and dropped to our haunches.

We lifted our heads like dogs scenting the wind. More movement up ahead. Reddish-brown streaks moved between tall stands of gray-green sagebrush. White heads with black bars bobbed and grazed. No lion.

The small herd of pronghorn spotted us. A dozen heads turned. Their black, stubby snouts tilted forward, catching our scent. Then they went back to grazing sage. They were probably a mile away.

The larger females walked at the front of the herd, their black horns shining. I knew that pronghorn were the fastest animals on land over a distance of two miles, able to maintain speeds of more than fifty miles an hour. Their pit bull chests held massive lungs, and their blood was thick as syrup with oxygen-carrying cells. They could outrun any truck on this irregular sagebrush plain. They were an American original, with no relation to any antelope from Africa. They'd actually descended from goats. When they ran, they didn't pop and leap with the coy prance of an African antelope. Instead, they ran more like their predators, with their heads low to the ground, their knife-thin legs flying up nearly to their eye level. When they ran, they meant business.

The Diné named them *jádí*. The Runners. Some say they were whittled to this speed by the ancestors of mountain lions, what biologists have described as a North American cheetah.

Utah Game and Fish had introduced the herd about six months ago, during the summer. They'd hauled the pronghorn up in horse trailers, put them out in the Escalante, and popped open the metal doors, and the pronghorn knew what to do from there. The locals did, too. Within a few weeks, two teenagers from Big Water, Utah, had shot and killed two of the pronghorn. Game and Fish tracked them down and arrested them. Most of my neighbors in Church Wells wanted those teens dragged out into the desert and shot like rogue coyotes.

"Think the lion ate one of them?" Clayton asked.

I shrugged. "Maybe," I said. "Let's go look."

We walked onto the plain. The sun had walked down west faster than I'd thought. It would be dark in less than three hours.

We walked another mile toward the pronghorn herd, following those softball prints in the sand.

"You think we'll catch up to the lion?" Clayton asked.

"I dunno," I said. "They say mountain lions can range thirty miles a day. With a cub following her, she might be moving a little slower. We might see her."

Since I was young I had read that mountain lions had more names than any other animal in the Americas. So many people had encountered them. They range farther than any mammal species in the Americas, living in Alaska and hunting, breeding, and dying all the way down into Patagonia, in the southernmost parts of South America. Where there are mountains, so there are lions.

The Diné say that *Náshdóítsoh* (Mountain Lion) appeared when the Emergence People had escaped the flood in the Fourth World and ascended into this world. *Náshdóítsoh* had always ranged in the Glittering World. He and *Mąʼii tsoh* (Wolf) had appeared and visited and took some of the Emergence People women as their wives. The Emergence People then wandered for many years, ranging from *Hajíínéí* (The Emergence Place) to places like *Tséligaiiʼííʼáhí* (White Standing Rock) and *Dził Náʼoodiłʼii* (Traveler's Circle Mountain).

In their ranging, *Náshdóítsoh* traveled with the *Bitʼahnii* (Within His Cover Clan), a people made by *Asdząą Nádleehé* (Changing Woman) when she cut a piece of her skin under her right breast in her great house in the expanse of waters in the West. *Náshdóítsoh* stayed with them in their ranging and protected them until they came to a tall rock standing like a black tower against the sky. There, they noticed that when the *biih* (deer) traveling with them would graze the grass, then other deer came and grazed. The men put on deer masks, stalked closer, shot the deer with their bows, and killed them. When they skinned them and butchered them, a lot of their hair blew into a pile at the base of the black tower. So they named the tower *Aghaalá* (Lots of Hair Blowing Around). Mountain Lion stayed behind and lived with the people who settled around *Aghaalá*. These people became the *Honágháahnii*. The People Who Walk Around.

We walked, and the pronghorn grazed, keeping a force field of distance from us marauding bipeds. To them, we were no better than lions.

After another mile, the sagebrush hissed as the colder air dropped, and the wind blew with the falling sun.

"Do you think we might see her?" Clayton asked again.

The trail. Softball prints as large as my palm. Then a thin trail in the sand revealed dainty little footprints not big enough to cover an apple seed, with a thin strip of a dragging tail. The three little stripes crossed one of

the mountain lion tracks, cut it in two, and continued into the sand to the east. They were kangaroo rat tracks.

"Ah, crap," I whispered.

"What?" Clayton asked.

"Those tracks," I said. "You see that kangaroo rat trail?"

"Yeah."

"Kangaroo rats really only move around at night," I said. "You hardly ever see them in the day. If they're crossing the mountain lion's trail, then there's at least one night that's gone past. These tracks we've been following are at least a day old."

"Dang," said Clayton. "And they're still here. Like the mountain lion was here just a few minutes ago."

"Yeah," I said. "But I don't think we're going to see them today. No way."

I could see my breath in the air.

Clayton clapped me on the back. "Hey, at least we found the trail. That was a miracle by itself!"

I nodded. "Yeah," I said. "We got lucky."

"I don't believe in luck. There's something more to it than that. It was meant to happen."

"Maybe," I said, "we were meant to be lucky."

We climbed back down the other side of the mesa, scooted on our butts down a sandy escarpment, and walked a long wash choked with sleeping brown tamarisk. We stopped for a water break and watched the sun dropping in flares of red and orange copper. The back-shine struck the gray mesas with purple and gold light.

"Oh, man," Clayton said. "God's glory right there."

"You bet," I said. "Something like that."

We found the truck, threw our packs in the pickup bed next to the spare tire, and drove back up the dirt road.

It was all there. The sunset. The thrill as real as the sweat against our ribs under our thick jackets. The tracks spoke it: this was now lion country.

The mountain lion and her cub walked in my mind: trotting, hunting, and sleeping under the stars. They had a life contained in something that made sense. I had college applications I needed to start filling out. I had to save money to pay bills for a degree I would have to earn so that I could *be* something. They had to worry about catching and killing a jackrabbit or a deer every few days.

I didn't know who had the better deal.

I talked with Lyle Parsons about these things.

"You didn't take a gun with you, did you?" Lyle asked.

"No. I didn't even take a camera."

"Would have been nice to get a photo of that golden eagle, though," he said.

"Yeah."

I told him about how and why the mountain lion would have come down out of the Kaibab.

He nodded. "True," he said. "But she also could have been feeling what humans are often feeling. It's a type of *wanderlust*."

I'd never heard that word. I asked about it.

"Wanderlust is that feeling people have that tells them to get themselves to that next horizon," Lyle said. "It's a deep sort of calling. You can't contain it. It'll make you lonely, but it's part of you."

Wanderlust. It sounded like a good word.

They said that mountain lions never really hunted together, that they lived mostly solitary lives. That they were always on the move. Maybe that made it easier for them to listen to those inner voices they heard vibrating up through their bones. Those voices telling them, *See that mesa? There may be good hunting there. Go to it. Go.*

Maybe those voices kept them fed, kept them alive. The lions who never heard those voices stayed in one place and starved.

After school that day, I picked up Yanabah and Glen from school. I thought about that new word: *wanderlust*.

The rainbow in the arroyo. Those two plastic soda bottles sitting empty in the back of my closet. *Nashdóítsoh* and the *Honágháahnii*. The People Who Walk Around near *Aghaalá* peak. They'd heard those voices. I was starting to understand those voices. But I was seventeen. I was an idiot.

It's a deep sort of calling. You can't contain it. It'll make you lonely, but it's part of you.

I remembered that day with Clayton. We had stepped out of the truck in Church Wells. I had invited him inside our trailer before he drove his van back into Page.

He stayed for five minutes. We filled up our water bottles.

Then we stepped out into the desert.

It was the first time any friend of mine from high school came into my family's trailer. It would be the last.

THE PROM NIGHT REJECTS

The sun walked down the edge of the mesas and sparkling waters of the Lake Powell. Prom Night. Senior year of high school.

If you would come to bask in its depths, gun your speedboat, or stand up in your water-skis, you must pay, my dear. Unless you go to The Chains, where you can fish or swim for free. You drive to a spot about two hundred yards from the long, floating chain that keeps boats from the rim of the 610-foot-tall Glen Canyon Dam.

The American government had staked the dam in the center of the canyon in 1956 and completed it in 1966. Once they started filling it with the Colorado River, it didn't reach its full pool until 1979. By then, the lake had more than 1,900 miles of shoreline and was one of the largest bodies of water in the West.

This lake had been a canyon once, carved by a river that had ranged all the way to the Gulf of California. The Anasazi and other older peoples had migrated through this green, watery slit for centuries. They'd camped in the shade of cottonwood trees, made love and birthed children in side canyons that opened into cathedrals of ribboned sandstone expertly potted by invisible hands of wind and water and gravity. They'd foraged for amaranth and purslane, snared rabbits, and chased down desert bighorn.

When Major John Wesley Powell traveled these canyons, he felt something he'd perhaps forgotten during the bloodbath of the Civil War, where his arm had been stripped away at the Battle of Shiloh. The small streams and their grasses and willows and alders popped green and alive against the red and brown sandstone. Powell had seen all this while boating down

the Colorado to help the American government find water in the isolated deserts of the West. And he'd found it here.

These slits of green life conjured words from his Scotch Irish ancestors, who'd used the word *glen* to talk about streams covered with green flowing through a sharp valley. So Powell named the place Glen Canyon.

Now there were no glens. There was no canyon. There were no petroglyphs. There were no woven baskets. No stone houses where people had migrated and lived for hundreds of years. Now there is the black silence of five hundred feet of water that the Americans had conjured with their concrete dam. Then they named it Lake Powell, after that restless man who had explored the running rivers. The writer Edward Abbey thought it a travesty. He called it "Lake Foul."

In high school, these things surfaced only in the memories handed down to us and in the books we read. But at least we read them.

And we, too, were restless. So we came here to The Chains to fish instead of attending our senior prom.

Clayton got out of his white van, and I hopped out of the passenger side. Caden Sanders and Danny Bigthumb stepped out of the back.

They grabbed the fishing rods. Clayton hefted his small cooler of frozen anchovies we'd bought at Stix Market in Page that afternoon. I grabbed the plastic bag with our Subway sandwiches, pretzels, beef jerky, and gummy worms.

Caden buttoned up his plaid flannel shirt and rubbed his red goatee.

Caden and his family lived in a well-kept ranch house on the western edge of the mesa. Their back door looked out on *Naatsiis'áan* (Navajo Mountain).

"That's everything, right?" Caden asked.

"I think so," Danny said, checking his hook and weights on his line. Danny had tall cheekbones, a thin, muscular build, and black hair in a flattop. He'd grown up wandering the canyons near Lechee and Kaibito, Arizona, just outside of Page. And so we had some good stories to swap about our Rez childhoods. He was also a hell of a joke-teller but could be a quiet, observant person whenever he wanted, just taking in the world from behind the gray lenses of his glasses.

Green water lapped the shore. The golden light of near-sunset dyed the sandstone bright blond fringed with orange. This is what photographers called "the golden hour," just before the sun tilted to dusk.

Our friends were manicuring the last details of their tuxedos, combing their hair into place, shaving their faces, and taking that corsage out of the

refrigerator so they could strap it to their date's wrist. Some checking their pockets to make sure they'd remembered their seventy-five-dollar tickets that would buy them a catered meal and a photograph next to a plastic Greek-esque column with white and blue balloons tied to the corner. They would drive to the parking lot of the Marriott next to the golf course in Page and walk into a room and dance to music written and performed by artists in the cities at the edges of America, far from this desert and these canyons. Many of these artists and musicians owned houseboats on Lake Powell and came to this desert to vacation. We lived here. We fished here. We were always on vacation.

We'd told our parents we were going fishing. Our friends gave us nothing but protest.

"How can you miss out on such a *special night*?" went the common refrain.

"It's a night when we learn to become mature," one of my friends said as we walked to his parked car at the middle school where we worked as peer counselors for kids in therapy after they'd been betrayed or abandoned by their parents. "It's a night where we learn to be *grown-up*."

"No," I said. "It's a night where people *pretend* to be mature and grown-up. Real maturity takes years. It takes practice. Like anything important. Like love."

"Love?" he said. "Are you shitting me?"

For my mother, it was all part of the Jim-Won't-Let-Me-Spend-Money-On-His-Graduation saga. I didn't let her buy graduation announcements. I didn't want any custom linen-paper business cards with my name emblazoned on the pitted surface in stylish silver ink. I didn't want any artifacts or trophies to say I had once walked the halls of Page High School. I wouldn't wear a tie for my senior portrait. Didn't get one.

"Just save the money for my college, Mom," I said. "This is all just one last chance for the high school kraken to take a bite out of my ass before I leave."

"Jimmy," Mom sighed, "if you don't get your picture taken, you won't even be in the yearbook with all your friends."

"Just save the money for my college, Mom."

"What the hell is a *kraken* anyway?" she asked. I explained.

I went to see Lyle Parsons to hear what he had to say.

"Hell, man," he said, "I didn't even show up to get my high school diploma. My mom had to drive down to the god-dang high school and pick it up for me. I refused to go to my graduation. It was a worthless piece of paper. I learned more from reading and living on my own."

"I was actually thinking of skipping graduation," I said. "But my grand-parents are flying in from North Carolina and Florida. I think they're demanding a worthy performance."

"Well, you better be out there walking," Lyle said. "I taught you for three years at this school, so I know dang well you got at least a good English education."

So Mom and I didn't have to fight about graduation. But the senior prom was a separate debate.

"I can't believe you're not going!" she yelled at the stove one night in the trailer, pulling back her mane of wavy blond hair before it fell into the chili simmering in the Dutch oven on our propane stove. Her silver bracelets clinked as she turned down the heat. "Look, Jimmy. You need to get out there. You need to date girls. You need to get a *life*. If you were a dork or some nerd, I would let you know. If you were ugly, I'd *tell* you."

I nodded and bit a tortilla chip. Mom didn't shy from her opinions.

"But you're *not*. You and Darren are both interesting, handsome boys. Lots of girls would like you if you just *opened up a little*."

She dropped the lid on the Dutch oven and killed the blue flame.

"What's the big deal!? You act like everything has to fit inside your per-fect little world! Just go to this dance. One night. I'll rent the tux. I'll pay for the corsage. Knowing you, you won't even drink or try any drugs, so I don't have to worry about the truck. Just take it. Have some fun! Dance! Mingle! Big F-D!"

Big F-D: my mom's abbreviation for Big Freaking Deal.

"College money, Mom," I said. "Not tux money. And it's not about the money. It's the principle of the thing. I don't *want* to go. So I'm not going to go."

"You're *going* to the prom," she said. "I'm finding you a date."

"In a perfect world, Mom," I said. "In a perfect world."

The best way we knew to fish for striped bass, or "striper," was to take a half-frozen anchovy, stitch your line through its body, cast out from the cliffs, and let the line sink down forty or fifty feet. You'd find the schools of striper resting up against the walls of the canyon. And they were always hungry.

We could catch as many as we wanted that night. The Bureau of Recla-mation and Arizona Game and Fish and the Park Service all wanted the striper gone from Lake Powell fast. They had introduced them to the lake to be a sport and trophy fish for the tourists. They thrived. Too much. They

soon decimated the trout, perch, and sunfish in the lake. They gobbled any fingerlings that Game and Fish tried to introduce. The department estimated the striper population had grown to more than three million. Some reached more than five feet in length and weighed nearly two hundred pounds. Pictures of these monsters were scotch-taped to the glass doors of Stix Market.

Other times, anglers would hit a "striper boil," where a massive school of shimmering, black-lined silver fish would go into a hurricane feeding frenzy around your boat.

Caden and his brothers had once hit a boil. They ripped out foot-long strippers without baiting their hooks. They caught forty-seven, took the fish home in plastic bags, and buried them in their garden as fertilizer. The corn was really great that summer. So was the squash.

The plight of the striper in Lake Powell was the first of many of our early lessons in the American psyche. Americans had introduced a fish that overpopulated, overconsumed, and overfed. They had done it to cater to the wealthy sport fishermen on their vacations. But the power-seeking beings in charge at the time had screwed up, and now they wanted the fish gone. The stripers were the undesirables. The rejects. The survivors. We understood that.

We jogged down the steep slopes of the cliffs to the lake. We balanced against the sandstone edges to keep from falling into the water. It was early May, and no one was swimming yet. It had been warm that day, but we all knew that the desert didn't hold any heat once the sun went down. We'd all brought our flannel shirts and our windbreakers for a reason.

"First cast of the night!" I said as Clayton balanced his rod out behind him. He cast, and I cast my line, and mine drifted down. We reeled in slowly. Clayton cast again. I cast my line. On my second cast, the open reel of my Zebco fishing rod fell apart. The line spooled in coils of near-invisible neon.

"Whoa! Shit, Jim!" Danny said, laughing as he reeled in his line. "You gotta take that thing back to Walmart and get a refund!"

I had fished with the pole only once before, and it had been fine. Let the teeth clench.

"Do you want to run down to Walmart and swap it out, man?" Clayton asked.

And the wind came. I lost my balance. Sand slapped my hair and eyes. Spray like bullets of ice water flew off the lake. Clayton backpedaling from the water. Randy covered his eyes against the sand and spray.

Whitecaps pulsed and slapped the cliffs.

A white blur shot past Caden. It was a plastic grocery bag that wind had probably blown loose from our camp. The bag drifted out over the water.

"I got it!" Caden yelled, sliding toward the edge of the sloped cliff.

I wanted to warn him.

"Got it!" he yelled, smiling.

Then a new gust of wind slammed into us and sent more freezing spray up from the lake. Caden lost his balance and fell into Lake Powell. The cliff was a steep drop-off, so he went under, head and all.

He came up paddling for shore, and we formed a human chain to get him. His teeth chattered. We all laughed.

"Well, at least the plastic bag is safe," Caden said, blinking away the freezing water running down his face.

"Did you bring extra clothes?" I asked.

"Spare pair of socks," Caden said.

Caden sat on a towel on Clayton's passenger seat, and away they went to get new clothes for Caden.

Danny and I shared some RC Cola by the water and told the dirtiest jokes we knew as the sunset cast Tower Butte and *Naats'iis'áán* (Navajo Mountain) in gold and purple. A long yellow line rimmed with a gloaming blue when Clayton's van's headlights appeared in the parking lot.

He and Caden came walking back to our small camp with flashlights and a bag of marshmallows.

"In case we make a fire," Clayton said. "I forgot them before."

"Do we *have* matches?" I asked.

"Umm . . .we're going to Walmart, right?" Clayton grinned.

I shook my head and smiled. "Badda-bing. You got it."

The Walmart trip was simple. They let me swap the rod. Back to The Chains.

It was windy dark. No moon. Sand swirled across the headlights. We had to yell to talk.

I jumped out into the dark, slid the van door open, yanked the replacement rod out, and slammed the sliding door shut.

Snap.

Even with the roaring wind and the darkness, I heard that sound.

The top quarter of my new fishing rod hadn't cleared the door when I slammed it. It had broken off at least six inches. I leaned back and laughed.

"Dude?" Clayton yelled. "What's the matter?"

He came around with his flashlight. "Oh, man! Are you *kidding* me?"

"I *know*, right?"

"Do you want to run back to Walmart and get a new rod?"

I shook my head, and the wind whipped my hair across my face. Nah. Screw it. Wasted enough time. Most of the rod still attached.

"You sure?"

"Yeah. Big F-D."

Great. Mom's words, right out of my mouth.

Clayton clicked his flashlight, and we Prom Night Rejects walked to the lake through the windy darkness.

When we got back to our camp near the sloped cliffs, all our stuff was gone. Everything.

"Maybe they moved it," Clayton said.

"Shit, man," I said. "The hits just keep on coming."

"Hey!" a voice called through the wind. "Guys! We're down here!"

It was Caden. A flashlight shined out of the black.

"Get any bites?" Clayton asked, sitting down next to Danny.

"A few," he said. "No catches yet."

I sat next to him. The sandstone froze my ass right through my jeans.

The dark was complete. Waves lapping cliffs. Distant parking lights glowed like earthbound stars. *Yikáísídáhí*—the stream of star-pollen Changing Woman had once scattered across the night's sky to remind people to lay pollen out before them when they prayed in the morning—spread out over us. Wind howled. This was what we wanted for prom night. This was our dance space.

I cast my line into the water.

"Dude, is your reel off?" Danny said, reaching for some sunflower seeds. "Your cast sounds all funny."

"No. My rod is busted."

"Your *rod*?" Danny said. "I thought it was your *reel*, bro?"

"Oh, we'll tell you later," Clayton said.

"Whoa! I got something!" Danny said, rising to his haunches. Caden whipped out a flashlight, and the yellow beam cut through the dark to Danny's line dancing taut at the surface of the water.

Something thrashed a cold spray of water. Danny's rod bowed with the strain of a fight. In another few minutes, Danny had pulled the fish to the smooth rock shore.

The fish's sides glistened with silver and emerald lines, like some dazzling alien armor. Its fins flexed. The mouth—lined with rows of sharp grabber

teeth for catching smaller fish and frogs—gaped for the liquid flow of oxygen, that breathing our ancestors gave up long ago, long before we emerged as *Nohokaa' Diné*—the Five-Fingered Earth Surface People. This *łóó* (fish) was still able to breathe this way. The large-mouthed bass still took in the sacredness of water, ate from it, lived in it.

"You guys can have him," Danny said. "I won't eat him."*

"All right," I said. "My brother and sister like eating fish every now and then."

The bass bucked and gaped as my pocketknife stabbed quickly just above the eye to kill him painlessly. His shimmering body went limp and dripped as we put him in a plastic bag in the cooler.

Thank you for your life, friend, I said to myself. *We'll waste none of you.*

"First of the night!" Clayton said, raising an RC Cola in salute. We all raised ours and cheered. I didn't enjoy it, though. My hands smelled like the bass, and I tasted his scales every time my hand brought the can to my face. A silent reminder.

We fished the small coves we could find near The Chains. The wind scuffed and hammered and threw spray up over the cliffs. We packed up only after our hands went numb.

We coasted over the Glen Canyon Dam bridge, vaulting its web of steel more than seven hundred feet above the Colorado River below, across a quarter mile of dark space. When erected in 1959, it was the highest steel arch bridge in the world. Others have been built higher since. The safety lights of the Glen Canyon Dam blazed their phosphorescent-white marks against that dark space. The concrete monolith arched across the ancient canyon like a grave marker for the ideas of the mid-twentieth century.

The ghosts of the men who had dreamed it up might as well have been speaking from each poured-concrete section.

We will own the water, they said.

We will own the water, and so we will own the land. And we will protect you. Water for your crops. We will save the rain in perpetuity. You will no

* Traditionally, many Diné people do not eat fish. Some say it's because in the *hajinee* (Emergence Story), a giant fish devoured people. Some say it's because of the memory of the water monster that flooded the Fourth World after Coyote stole its child. Some say it's because the fish live in the sacredness of water. But a lot of people on the Rez still don't eat it. There are many fast-food restaurants on the Rez. Long John Silver's (or, as some people on the Rez call it, Long John *Slivers*) isn't one of them.

longer survive on Father Sky's handouts. You will survive on our handouts. In this desert, you will grasp a thing called Abundance. Water coming out of your faucet to drink. Water bathing your children. Water for your hospitals. Water for your green lawns. For your hot tubs. For your fountains in your backyards. For your swimming pools. For your golf courses. Don't forget those. For your restaurants. For your hotels, where you can host senior proms in ballrooms and silently tell your young people that this way of life—this Abundance—can go on forever. Just like this concrete dam.

Thus spoke the ghosts of the concrete—poured a foot at a time, twenty-four hours a day for three years—enough to line a highway from San Pedro, California, to Fairport, New York. Behind yearned twenty-seven million acre-feet of water, summoning 40,000 pounds of pressure per square foot that the forces of the gravity had been guiding south to the ocean longer than humans had been able to read or write or build anything. What does the freedom song of a body of water sound like?

And the dam would somehow all go on forever. Like the prom memories.

These were the idiotic ramblings in my eighteen-year-old mind as we drove over the bridge, past the tall red butte near the visitor center's parking lot. Since I'd passed into legal adulthood, I'd had these stupid kinds of thoughts often.

Halfway to the other shore, Clayton pulled into the parking lot next to my pickup truck. He realized he didn't have his fishing license.

I reminded Clayton we'd already been fishing for three hours. No one was likely to care.

With my luck . . . It's better to be safe than sorry. I'll be right back."

"No problem. Just don't jam your fishing license in the door."

Clayton laughed and shook his head. "I'm never forgetting that!"

"Me, too," I said. "Hey, it's Prom Night. *It's about making memories.*"

I popped the tailgate on the truck, and Danny and Caden wrapped themselves in the wool blanket I'd thrown into the back. They shared some of the beef jerky while I gutted the bass under the parking lights in the wishing fountain in front of the Carl Hayden Visitor Center.

The building sat like a concrete pillbox against the edge of the canyon. Carl Hayden had been raised in the Saguaro Valley, near modern-day Tempe. He'd served as sheriff of Maricopa County and gotten himself elected to the Senate before the Depression swung in. Once it did, Hayden, a Democrat, supported FDR's New Deal and saw dam building as a way to employ skilled workers and to improve the lives of farmers in the Southwest. He

also designed and controlled the funds of the Federal Highway Project and several other road-building projects. Whenever my tires vibrated on the highway, I heard Hayden's ghost humming along. At one point, some of his supporters wanted to name the dam the Hayden. But Hayden shirked that kind of aggrandizement. He was happy with the visitor center raised in his name in 1969.

The wind rustled through the early leaves of the sycamore trees growing against the red sandstone dome.

"Dude," Danny said, "if the cops see us . . ."

"They're not coming down here." The gills dripped at the end of the knife.

So this is what water and gravity had sculpted and shaped over the eons, back when all the desert country where I lived had been covered in the Carmel Sea and the Western Interior Seaway, back before dinosaurs had ever dreamed that furry, milk-sucking vermin might someday forever change the face of their planet once they'd faded to dust or been corralled into the world's chicken coops. Back before we'd all emerged as *Nohokaa' Diné*—the Five-Fingered Earth Surface People.

"The cops won't come down here tonight," I said. "They're all at the prom making sure the good little boys and girls don't drink too much and die in a flaming car wreck in their little rented tuxedos and little lacy gowns."

"Jim," said Caden. "You're weird, man."

The wind roared over the darkness of the water-filled canyon that was now Lake Powell.

Demonstrators from the Sierra Club had shown up here to protest the Glen Canyon Dam and the lake a year earlier. Many of the protestors wore their long gray hair in ponytails. Many of them had driven down from Moab and other small towns near the Canyonlands, carrying as passengers their memories of Glen Canyon's beauty. Some of them had known Edward Abbey, and some had guided the Colorado River rapids below Lee's Ferry.

Many of them called Lake Powell a "dead lake." Some refused to even call it a "lake." They called it a "reservoir."

Some Page locals took offense to this.

"If the lake is a reservoir," said one of my friends, "hell, then I guess the Grand Canyon is just a drainage ditch."

The water slapped the cliffs in the dark. The parking lot lights buzzed overhead. And the cold wind blew strong.

The bass's scales shined bright silver and green. That line from one of my

favorite childhood books, *Jurassic Park* by Michael Crichton, ran through my mind: *Life finds a way.* Between growing up in a dead lake behind a concrete dam and surviving the striper invasion, this largemouth bass had found a way. Life found a way. When the Americans came into the Southwest, they often built dams in life's path. But life would find a way around them.

I held the shimmering purple stomach and pinched it open. A small frog leg fell out, shining as though carved from pearl.

"Oh, dude," Danny said.

"Well, now we know what he's made of," I whispered.

"Aren't you going to put those in the trash?" Caden asked, indicating the guts and gills.

"Why?" I said. "The ravens can get at them easier here."

I wrapped the bass's cleaned body and set it in the cooler. Its armored head went in a separate small bag. Clayton pulled up a few minutes later.

"So why did you keep the head?" Caden asked.

"For my dog to eat. Tilly likes fish heads," I said.

We set up camp on a strip of rocky beach haunted by stands of tamarisk, working by flashlight to bait our hooks and cast our lines. Slices of hot dogs and worms and PowerBait for this shore.

We talked about the future. I was going to college in Pennsylvania on a scholarship. I had gotten a job with Wilderness River Adventures, a company that ran white water trips down the Grand Canyon and float trips through Glen Canyon from the dam to Lee's Ferry in Marble Canyon. I would be the "shop monkey," someone to repair equipment, pack boats, and provision food and other supplies. I would take any way into that life that I could get. If you're willing to put me into a canyon where I get to see the largest rapids in the Western Hemisphere of the world, then I'm your monkey.

My line ran from the reel. I caught the broken rod before it ran into the water. A dull green catfish slathered in brown mud thrashed in the flashlight's glare. It was at least a foot long. The whiskers barbed out from its flat, smooth face, trying to make sense of the air and the strange beings who had pulled it from the dark waters.

Before midnight, Caden snagged a heavy bite on his line and landed a green-yellow carp. There is that fishing joke about the best way to cook and eat a carp: Get a long cedar board and tie the carp to it. Season it with garlic and red pepper flakes and salt and pepper. Roast over the fire. When

the carp is sizzling, take it off the flame. Untie the carp from the board. Then eat the board.

"Not keeping it, huh?" I said.

Caden shook his head.

The carp thrashed his way back into the cold darkness and vanished into his world, spared from our appetites.

We fished for another hour. Only Caden got any hits on his line.

Caden was my only friend who'd grown up as a Mormon and had actually questioned his religion. It had started with his dad, who had gone off and read books critiquing the Church of Jesus Christ of Latter-Day Saints—about how the Avenging Angels had actively committed murders in the name of Brigham Young so that Young could consolidate his power over the church in Utah, how Young had written prophecies about people who lived on the moon, how the church's founder, Joseph Smith, had written several times that he was a more important religious leader than Jesus of Nazareth.

Caden still remembered the morning when his dad had walked into the living room while everyone was cinching their belts and tying their shoes to go to Sunday service. He told them he wasn't going with them again. Ever.

Caden and his brothers burst into tears.

"It was like my dad told me he was dying of cancer," Caden said. "I knew I wasn't going to see him in heaven. We weren't going to be together after this life."

He talked with his dad about his rationale for leaving the church. And it began to make sense to his rebellious teenage mind. Eventually, he applauded his dad's decision. But he and his family didn't officially leave the church.

"I just couldn't do that," he said. The wind tossed his thin brown hair forward over his eyes. He brushed his hand thoughtfully over his adult-thick goatee. "My family would basically be shunned. I'd lose all my friends."

"Just like that?" I asked.

"Just like that."

"Well, if you decide to bug out, you can always count on me." I clapped his back. "Me and the other Prom Night Rejects."

Fish until you are numb. Then go inside the van and blast that heater and eat marshmallows and spoonfuls of peanut butter as we cruise down Lake Shore Drive toward the Lake Powell Resort at Wahweap Marina.

Wahweap was *the* premier marina on the lake. The *only* marina on the

lake for the locals coming in to rent powerboats for the day, for the upper-income Californians shooting in to water-ski over the weekend, and for the multimillionaires and Hollywood celebrities like Kevin Costner and Robert Redford cruising discretely out on the lake in four-story houseboats.

"So how are you spending the rest of Prom Night?" I asked Clayton as he dropped me off at my truck.

He and I decided to drive to the prom and bear witness to the horror ourselves.

And thus the Prom Night Rejects did arrive at their senior prom in May of 2000, the Year of the Millennium. They had ranged the dark, borne the wind, and thrown line to water black as the First World. A sacred world. Now they would return to their society, the world of corsages and rented tuxedos and illicit alcohol and sex and MTV and ESPN and college acceptance and military recruiters and Hale-Bopp Comet prophecies and presidential races for power over the whole American affair.

The American affair was a tradition handed over by the European conquerors and the Great Gatsbys. And Americans hadn't been shy in their abuse of other people. We wanted nothing of it. It had nothing to give us. What you wear to a prom sometimes looks like the clothes you get buried in.

We parked at the Courtyard by Marriott. Yellow and white lights and the DJ had just put on a Paula Cole song. I can still remember the lyrics: "I don't want to wait for our lives to be over. I want to know right now, what will it be?"

I'm sure there's a reason I remember this lyric.

The photo station—complete with plastic Greek-esque column with white and blue balloons—was still open.

I told Clayton I wanted to unwrap the bass's head and bring it inside with me as my date. I wanted to get my prom photo taken with it.

Clayton, like any wise friend, nixed the idea.

Instead, I found my brother and gave him some crap about not going fishing with us. I told him I'd found him a hot date, though, just waiting to make out with him in the back of the pickup truck. It had fins and whiskers and everything. He just rolled his eyes.

"Your hands smell like dead fish," his date said flatly.

Five dirty jokes waited to emerge. I simply explained that I'd gutted a fish.

"Gross," she huffed. She walked away. My brother—like a good boyfriend—followed.

Clayton and I walked out of the small ballroom—also festooned with strings of white lights and blue and gray paper—and back into the main lobby. On the wall, we noticed a framed Gary Ladd photograph. We had to. When you see it, you'll notice it, too. Ladd was a resident photographer who owned a gallery in Page. His masterful pictures of Lake Powell, Glen Canyon, Antelope Canyon, and the other sandstone wonders of the Glen Canyon area had sold around the world.

In frame, dawn broke over Lake Powell and lit the miles of misting water like a sheet of hammered gold. Small wisps of cloud steamed from the edges of domed mesas and towering buttes. In the bottom edge of the photo, the paved road we'd driven just a few hours ago was neatly clipped from the image. But we knew it was there.

"Wow. Is that even *real*?" Clayton asked.

A balding hotel manager sidled up behind us. "Oh, that's about three thousand dollars' worth of real."

"This thing costs three *grand*?" I asked.

He nodded. "And we got it on a good deal. It's an original."

The title was *Winter Sunrise*.

Three thousand dollars' worth of real.

I imagined Gary Ladd, having to haul his middle-aged ass up on some cold mesa, to hump his camera and his equipment on his back, to spend patient hour after patient hour waiting in the cold darkness for that right sunrise moment and that right angle of light. I respected him for it. You didn't take pictures like his without an intense work ethic and dedication to the craft.

But it also made me sad that someone would pay three thousand dollars for it.

To see that sunrise, a man or woman would have needed to rise early. To know the space. To walk to the top of a mesa. To navigate sagebrush and cactus in the dark. To wait with thermos of coffee or tea and to huddle in a thick jacket. To watch the arc of the sun as it broke over the western buttes of the lake. Perhaps some people had done this before.

People could have that experience without the three thousand dollars. They were willing to pay to have it simulated for them in a picture frame. It sounded crazy to me at the time. But I was also beginning to understand that people paid a high price for giving their life to a middle-class suburb, where they were dammed behind the concrete of Phoenix or Los Angeles.

27

They were willing to use a lot of that money to migrate to where I ranged without having to buy a plane ticket or rent a car. I only filled those two plastic soda bottles, and away I went.

Perhaps some people had grown up like I had. Maybe they had ranged like me. Maybe some ditched their senior proms to go fishing with their friends. Maybe they, too, were Prom Night Rejects. Maybe Gary Ladd's winter sunrise was a portal for them.

People will pay any price to get back what they once had.

RUNNING RED RIVER

I finished high school with my scholarship promising a journey to a college in the East, the land of my fathers, where my family had emigrated during the wars when Hitler had invaded Eastern Europe.

You need to make money. A lot of local kids worked on Lake Powell. Some booked tickets and ran boat tours, some cleaned houseboats, and some hauled luggage down to the docks. They were on the lake, in the sun, all day. And most of them loved it.

The restless kids worked on the other side of Glen Canyon Dam. They ranged out in the canyon, on the river.

I showed up at the company shop on the eastern edge of town on the other side of the mesa by six o'clock every morning in my crappiest jeans, beat-up sneakers, and torn T-shirt.

I learned to build a seven-day menu for a boat trip through the canyon. I made and pulled ice blocks that lined the massive coolers on the thirty-two-foot army-surplus flotation rafts that carried fifteen passengers through the guts of the Grand Canyon and over and through (and sometimes under) the largest rapids in the Western Hemisphere of the world. I loaded those rafts onto our long flatbed trailers with steel rollers and unloaded them at Lee's Ferry in Marble Canyon.

I learned that complaining was for fiends and malefactors. I learned that hard work was fun.

I packed wet bags and dry bags and folded sleeping bags properly and pressure-washed and painted rubber rafts. I repaired grommets and cut

webbing. I tied the bowline knot and the two-half-hitch and the sheepshank and the sailor's knot. I packed ammo cans and greased truck hitches. I cleaned port-o-shitters—the stainless-steel toilets that guides had to take down into the canyon as part of the park's pack-in, pack-out policy. The lids for the shitters sealed tight as jam jars, guaranteed not to spill if they went overboard in a rapid. There was never a shortage of shit to clean when the trips got back.

I also learned that river guides are some of the funniest and most alive people in the world.

By the end of the summer, the manager for the float-trip division saw my hustle and asked me if I would come work for him.

"What will that mean?" I asked.

"Well, your boss already told me he's promised you a spot for next year. But you'll maybe get a couple trips a year. If you work for me, you'll be in the canyon *every* day. And you'll sometimes be out there all day, if I need a turnaround guide."

"What's a turnaround?"

"You'd be doing two tours in a day. One in the morning and one for the afternoon."

I brushed my wavy hair out of my dirty face. "That sounds good to me, man."

So that next summer, after my freshman year of college, I ran the Colorado River as a floater.

My mom liked the idea. She wanted me home every night to take care of the horses and that floundering fruit orchard she kept trying to grow. She also wanted me to pick up or drop off my sister and brother, Yanabah and Glen, at their summer daycare at the local Lutheran church on Lake Powell Boulevard.

And after a few days of training and learning how to drive the Mercury engine behind the army-surplus pontoon rafts, I started to like it more, too.

There was something intimate in what remained of Glen Canyon. In those hours and river miles, I guided my passengers over water that flowed smooth and quiet, green and glassy, below six-hundred-foot walls of wind-polished Navajo sandstone. My sense of it: most of the people who took the path to the white water were the adventuring type. When I spoke to them, I was preaching to the choir. But the people who took the float down Glen Canyon maybe didn't have the time or the health or the nearly two thousand dollars to take the downriver plunge. When you talked with

them, you actually were saying some things they hadn't heard before. And they always had a great time.

I became the naturalist who sighted the blade-bodied rainbow trout, the blue-taloned osprey, and the harpoon-beaked blue heron. I became the historian who interpreted the ancient Puebloan petroglyphs carved into the canyon walls when Christ was only a toddler. I became the storyteller who recounted the journeys of Glen Canyon explorer John Wesley Powell and entrepreneur Charles H. Spencer.

But the day the Colorado River reminded me of its name, I had to be something else.

I was running a South Rim tour. Groups of tourists who'd paid to be part of a tour package had risen at dawn and climbed onto a tour bus with their morning coffees and their fleece blankets against the morning chill. During their two-hour bus ride north to Page, the guides packed their water jugs, first aid kits, cans of soda, and our ammo cans of sunscreen, photo guides, and any other survival gear into the Wilderness River vans.

We were taking down two vans that day. It was going to be a large tour group.

We said good morning to Chuck, our chain-smoking van driver, and climbed in with our packs and ammo cans. We applied our sunscreen, told dirty jokes, and spotted chuckwallas—those large lizards with black pebbled skin—sunning themselves on the rocks, praying and receiving the heat of the sun. The sunbaked shamans.

"They say if those lizards get in trouble, they climb down into the rocks and puff their bodies up," said Neil, a fellow guide. He smiled, and his blond goatee caught the morning light. His silver hoop earrings shimmered as he laughed. "I guess Nature looks out for those who know to ride it out."

"Yeah, but then you're just living like a lizard," said John Bigthumb, one of our local Navajo guides. He and I had played football together in high school. "You've got to live like a man."

"Then I guess you'll be dying like a man," Neil offered.

"Guess so," John said. "Long as I don't have to suck you off anymore. This $3.25 an hour wage is killing me."

"I always said I'd treat you right. I'll be throwing in a Snickers bar on every side hand job from now on. How's that?"

"Sh'yeah, right," John said. "I can get better pay working at Walmart."

"Yeah, but Walmart won't allow the hand jobs," I said. "Remember that. You've got to supplement the income. You're saving for college, son. And

you've got those six kids you had with those five other women. Think about it. That's all I'm saying."

The van passed through the chain-link and barbed-wire security gate to enter the tunnel that led to the bottom of the dam.

The Bureau of Reclamation (BOR) had to purchase five bulldozers and seven other earthmovers to clear more than thirty tons of river sediment, sand, and debris before laying the foundation of the Glen Canyon Dam. That meant carving a two-mile-long tunnel in the canyon wall. Though it was now closed to the public, Page designated it as an emergency fallout shelter.

The BOR had two guards posted at the top of the tunnel. The tall glass windows on the guard huts were shaded with pages from that day's edition of the *Arizona Republic* that dropped the inside temperature from 116 degrees to a tolerable 93. Coils of bright razor wire crowned the eight-foot sliding gate. All to check an ID.

But familiar faces grow familiar, and we stopped bothering with the ID badges by mid-July.

The Glen Canyon Dam ranks in the top five of high-probability terrorist targets by the US Army Corps of Engineers in 2002. The dams near a populated area and was the first of seven dams on the Colorado River. If someone decided to plow an Airbus through the top, where it was weakest, the escaping water would recarve Glen Canyon in less than five minutes and destroy every other dam downriver, including the Hoover Dam at Lake Mead. No more downriver agriculture, no more Imperial Valley, where more than a quarter of the nation's food crop grows. High-stakes stuff, as my boss, Monty, liked to say.

We passed through the open gate with a wave.

We dropped through the dark tunnel. Every few feet, the rock walls dripped with water that had pushed through the porous Navajo sandstone from the lake. Small streams of water seeped along the paved road. Any metal in the tunnel hosted colonies of algae that glowed green in the headlights and multiplied in any scarce sunlight that came in through the ten-foot-wide adit tunnels. Excavating crews had made those tunnels so they could push out the rock as they dug the main tunnel down to the base of the dam that a generation of Americans financed and built more than forty years ago to hold back the flow of water. The flow of life. But life had pioneered a way into this tunnel. There is much to be said for creatures who know how to keep their heads down and ride it out.

The sunlight at the end of the tunnel blazed a half mile in front of us. There had been rock falls in the tunnel before. Vans had been nearly crushed. Sometimes a splinter of panic worked into that inner part of my brain I'd inherited long ago from reptile ancestors not much different from the chuckwallas zoning out in the sun above us. In Mr. Muñoz's biology class, I'd learned that scientists called the nut-sized microbrain the amygdala (Latin for "almond"). Just sit tight, this almond chanted in that ancestral fight-or-flight song. Just ride it out. You'll see the sunlight soon. Be a Tough Noodle.

Into the sunlight we drove. The concrete tidal wave of the Glen Canyon Dam arched above from one canyon wall to the other like some inherited curse and blessing. From its hydroelectric underbelly churned forth the Colorado River, thick with the blue-green glimmer of *Cladophora* algae, moving with gravity at the speed of a brisk walk.

This was an illusion. When the Spanish encountered this river in the early 1600s, they had called it the Río Colorado—the Running Red River—because it ran red with silt and sand and whatever the hell else it wanted to take with it when it pulsed and drummed through its snaking channel from the snowpacks of the Rocky Mountains through the carved cathedral of the Grand Canyon to the marshes near the gulf of Baja. Men and women had learned its cycles and rhythms. A people we now call the Anasazi had captured its water and nutrients on terraces and floodplains. They sang planting songs and ripened the corn, squash, and beans.

The river would pulse in a flood at more than 85,000 cubic feet per second. It flowed a warm seventy degrees. That day, it pushed through the hydro-electric turbines of the Glen Canyon Dam at a controlled flow of 9,000 cubic feet per second, chilled to a near-constant forty-one degrees, flying off the bottom of Lake Powell. The water hadn't seen the light of the crystal shield of *Jóhonaa'éí* (the Sun) in six months. In this water, hypothermia comes in four minutes. People had drowned after their limbs went numb.

We waved to the guard in the tactical Kevlar vest. He lifted his hand from his AR-15 rifle and waved back.

We loaded the water jugs, ice bags, sodas, and other gear into the small trailer hitched to the ATV the morning crew had left for us. I drove the ATV down the metal gangplank bolted into the canyon wall. There was only an inch to spare between the steel rails and each side of the four-wheeler.

Hanging gardens of watercress and maiden-hair fern trickled crystalline water over the growl of the four-wheeler's motor. I tried to silence that

chuckwalla-almond brain that kept reminding me this was water seeping through more than a thousand feet of rock *around* the concrete barrier of the Glen Canyon Dam.

Life finds a way.

I focused the steel gangplank and hoped a bolt didn't give out. Seeping water sometimes eroded the sandstone around the bolts, and they'd fly out under the stress. It had happened before.

I reached the concrete dock against one of the dam's spillway tunnels and turned the cart to run the four-wheeler back up to the parking lot. By the time I unloaded half the gear, Neil and John had gotten down the walkway.

Neil carried carton of eggs and something wrapped in a long black towel.

"What's that for?" I lifted a case of soda into one of the large Rubbermaid storage bins against the edge of the dock.

"A surprise," Neil said.

A small fiberglass-hulled boat motored around the corner of the dock from the long row of rafts tied on the thick steel cable bolted to the canyon wall. It was our mechanic, Rob Whitehorse. He flicked his long ponytail and wagged his hips like a 1920s lady of the night.

"Hey, big boys! You come down to get your daily fix?"

"From you, Rob, I need it twice a day, baby," Neil said. "You're all I can think about anymore."

Rob laughed as he tied the boat off to the closest raft. "It's good to know that limp spaghetti noodle between your legs can still think of anything."

"Are you kidding? It's living to keep you happy." Neil laughed.

We took the metal stairs to the water and jumped into Rob's boat. He ferried us to the rafts, and we prepped the boats.

After hefting our gas cans, loading our coolers with ice and soda, carrying down our water coolers, counting our life vests, mopping our steel decks and pontoons, and checking our engines and propellers, we tied off our rafts, and Neil walked up to the dock with his black towel and his carton of eggs.

He unrolled the towel and took out a golf club. It was a number 3 driver. He opened the carton of eggs. It was full of white golf balls.

"Let's see how far we can hit them?" He laughed.

"Do you have a tee?" Rob asked, climbing the steel stairs.

"Oh, shoot," Neil said. "You mean you pawned that one I left down here? God, Rob, you're such a Navajo."

"Sh'yeah, right," Rob said. "I turned that thing into an arrowhead for

when I raid your house tonight and scalp you. Not that you have much hair, anyways."

Neil cackled into the sun.

"Here, just use this." I tore out one of the cardboard cups from the carton and set it down on the ground. It held the golf ball perfectly.

Neil went first. He wound up and let it fly. Rob laughed as he sliced the ball far to the right. It landed in the dark green river with a plop and vanished. The river kept flowing.

John went next. Neil offered me the club. I refused. I knew that some of the water flowing out of the concrete guts of the dam had once run from the sacred mountains in Colorado, down *Tooh Bika̜'í* (Male River), what the American government called the San Juan River. That river was a sacred place, where traditional Diné people said that the Hero Twins had once gone into the spirit world. It was still a place where warriors went to pray. I didn't like the idea of hitting golf balls into it.

"Why not?" Neil grinned behind his Oakley sunglasses.

"Because it's kind of fucking stupid," I smiled.

Neil and John and Rob took turns hitting again. They sliced to the side. One of John's hits flew straight up like a pop fly. Rob's ricocheted off the safety rail and would have hit me in the balls if I hadn't jumped up in a spread eagle to dodge it. Rob fell over laughing.

Neil handed me the club again for the last ball.

"Fine." I shook my head, wound up, and swung. The club whacked the ball square, and the ball sailed out over the half-mile-wide current and landed dead in the center. The river swallowed it.

Neil and John and Rob cheered. I felt like throwing the club into the river but just handed it back to Neil.

"What's that?" John pointed to where the ball had landed in the current. A flock of dark, thin birds flew across the surface of the water. They looked like they'd sailed into the canyon from a panel of petroglyphs. Even from the quarter-mile distance, I could see the curve of their reed-thin bills, like something blown from glass.

"Ibis," I said. "They get down here into the canyon this month. Then they follow the river down to the marshes near Baja."

The summer before, I had been at the dock and watched a peregrine falcon soar around the ibis. She herded them into a tight flock and then ran them back and forth across the water until she'd tired them out. Then

she flew down into the flock and pumped her wings a foot above the water. Just before the ibis banked to turn, she flipped her talons forward and tore one of them along its back. The thin, dark bird flopped into the river, and the flock sailed on. The falcon hooked the body and towed it to the gravel bar in front of the dam. Then she fed.

It reminded you of where you were: six hundred feet of concrete arched above on one side and cathedral walls of sandstone ran up from the river on the other. You were there, humming in the tension between the technologically absurd and the naturally divine. Where the flesh of the ibis became the flesh of the falcon.

The sun emerged from the edge of the canyon and cooked the steel frames and rubber pontoons. When the tour bus drivers radioed to let us know they were entering the tunnel, we dumped buckets of cold river water over the pontoons to cool them off. I dumped my towel in the river and draped it over my row of four gas cans to keep them from swelling in the 110-degree heat.

The passengers arrived in their hardhats, bearing purses, day packs, camera cases, fanny packs, and plastic grocery bags full of bottled water, granola bars, and sunscreen.

In my boat sat a pair of New York artists, a small family from New Jersey, and a large family from Georgia. We soaked up the heat, drank up our water and cold sodas, and floated casually down the first seven miles of what remained of Glen Canyon.

After stopping to see the petroglyph panel and using the solar composting outhouses installed by the Park Service, we slowly drifted through Horseshoe Bend, which most of my passengers had seen only on the covers of the LIFE magazine annual "America's Greatest Monuments" issues in their suburban grocery-store checkout lines. Now you see it on Instagram.

We ate and swam at lunch beach, then loaded up and drifted past the first thousand-foot cliff. The lower part of that cliff had its black sheen of desert varnish carved away by a flood in 1983, when the operators at the Glen Canyon Dam had to do a full release in order to save the dam from possibly collapsing. That year, the river flowed at more than 80,000 cubic feet per second—the level that had originally carved the canyon.

The water was glass when we turned the corner at what I called Merganser Cove, a large green eddy where those dark-headed, long-beaked ducks fished for small trout and minnows. We pulled into the shade and tied up with one of our veteran guides, Ken Smith. He took out a series of

metal rods and small chains of a beaver trap used by the first pioneers as they came through the Colorado River country. He unfolded the trap and draped it over his neck. Everyone started laughing when they realized it was actually a harmonica holder like they'd seen at Bob Dylan concerts.

He played a song he'd written about John Wesley Powell traveling through the Colorado. We untied, and Ken drove on while I talked about the new worlds of ecosystems that had begun in Glen Canyon since the creation of the dam. The new water. The new animals. The new history. How the ecosystem that we saw around us was a modified ecosystem. But it was a working ecosystem. And it would be a working ecosystem three hundred years from now, long after the silt buildup had destroyed or forced the renovation of the Glen Canyon Dam.

Until then, we floated through this world of tamarisks growing on the banks of glass-calm water.

But when we passed into Two-Mile Draw, I knew the day of glass-calm water was done.

Two-Mile is a steep-walled rifle-barrel corridor named for its length. We'd traveled halfway in when a black plume rose into the blue sky from the edge of the two-thousand-foot cliff ahead.

Smoke from a fire, perhaps. But as the rest of the dark clouds snaked over the canyon wall and fell into the empty space, I knew it was a summer monsoon storm.

When the storms' thunder shook the rubber rafts, the kids stopped laughing, and their parents looked to me. I smiled and pointed to where the peach and tan canyon walls now shined maroon and brown with oncoming rain.

My little almond-chuckwalla brain was chanting its fight-or-flight song clear as wind blowing onto the whorl at the top of my head: Water is coming your way. Just sit tight. Ride it out. You'll see the sunlight soon. Be a Tough Noodle.

I handed out plastic garbage bags for ponchos.

"Remember to put a hole in the top," I said. They laughed with me when the rain hit. They stopped laughing when the wind came.

The first gusts tore the buttons from my poncho and sent it sailing into the mist and rain screen as I guided the boat toward the safety of the bank. Visibility was two or three feet.

Everyone moved to the center of the steel-frame raft when hail came in thumb-sized stones that ricocheted off our heads.

We saw nothing and heard only the sound of rock falls as the storm roared through Two-Mile's dark throat.

Eventually the bank gave way, and mud exploded in a twenty-foot jet over the bow. I fired the 135-horsepower Mercury engine and backed away into the current before I used a towel to wipe mud from a screaming teen-ager's hair.

The soft current guided us through the darkness of the flinty storm. The kids cried, and the artists quaked in their ponchos. I laughed and said I'd seen much worse. No one believed my lie.

Pounding water and breaking rock pulsed through the mist, the chaotic rhythms of creation and destruction rolling against the canyon walls; we were travelers beneath the dark skin of the storm and audience to the violence of water and gravity.

When the sun finally spoked through the clouds, we had drifted to the bottom of Two-Mile. As the mist cleared, we saw a different canyon.

Looking up Two-Mile, we counted no less than thirty waterfalls pouring a thousand feet into the sides of the corridor. The falls broke in colors of flinty sand and oxidized-copper green, flashing and spraying as they slit the sandstone and darkened the desert varnish.

Cameras clicked and smiles returned before the passengers unloaded at Lee's Ferry for the half-hour bus ride back to Page.

I took no photographs. There was no point. What could you really photo-graph of that moment?

That day, the river ran red.

Our full-throttle return upstream to the dam took an extra hour as the rafts struggled against the swift current and propellers broke against drifting tamarisk trunks. Beaches were drowned, and beaver and heron clung to gravel bars and boulders to escape the roiling waters beneath thousand-foot waterfalls.

Some of those waterfalls left *nááts'íílid* (rainbows) in the blue air.

Guides who'd moved through the Glen and Grand Canyon for decades said they'd never seen this.

The Río Colorado—the Running Red River—returned that afternoon. We were fortunate witnesses to its copper current sprinting south into Marble Canyon, where it would swell and strengthen the white fury of the Grand Canyon rapids. We floaters had taken the first shock; we wished our downriver buddies good luck.

I tried telling this story to Lyle Parsons, my former English teacher, later

when I stopped by his double-wide trailer about a half hour before sunset. He lived near the Page airport with his wife and his two sons. He slurred when he asked me questions about what I'd seen. I could tell he'd been drinking. Probably all day. What else do you do on a summer day when you don't have a lawn to mow?

He moved the garden hose watering the tall pine tree next to his concrete patio to a small peach tree.

I was trying to explain the moment to him. Lyle Parsons had traveled more miles than I could dream. He'd ranged through every western state for more than twenty years in a van with his country-western band, Medicine Wheel. He could play every Johnny Cash and Willie Nelson song in his sleep. He'd had different girlfriends in every town he stopped in, and he dated them only if they cooked a good meal for him, because he got tired of eating restaurant and bar food.

But that was a life I would never see. It was a life Lyle would never see again, either. He had spent the day watering his trees and drinking cans from a twenty-four pack he'd probably bought at Fred's Liquor Store. Each moment a can drunk. He would probably spend the next day apologizing for it.

I knew there was a sadness at the root of it. But sometimes sadness is what comes of giving a shit. Sometimes storms have to come. But storms bring rain. And rain brings rainbows.

His wife brought him a bowl of salad while we talked. She set it down like a truck stop waitress and moved back into the house. Lyle added ranch dressing to the lettuce until his bowl was like a soup of white vomit.

"So you saw some waterfalls," he slurred.

"Yeah. There was a rainbow in every one of them."

"A sky of rainbows," he mused. He stirred at the salad dressing.

"Yeah," I said. "Something like that. And the river ran red. Just like it used to. It ran red the whole day."

"The whole day?" He grinned. "Far out, man."

JIM DANGER

Jim Danger.

I got that stupid name at the concrete dock under the dam on the day Neil dropped his Oakley sunglasses into the water. They were worth more than a hundred dollars, and he offered the other guides ten bucks if they would go get them.

The water at the dock was about thirty-five feet deep. The water was forty-one degrees. The other guides just shook their heads.

"I'll get them," I said, unzipping my life vest. I sucked air for a couple of seconds, then did a headfirst dive toward the bottom.

I had gone after sunglasses in the river before. Once a lady had dropped her Ray-Bans off the dock at Lee's Ferry. I dove for them. Just as I went under, another guide parked their boat and bumped my raft so that it drifted directly over where I'd gone under. When I turned from the muddy bottom to come up, a spinning propeller churned the water into shreds of silver just inches from my face.

Well, I thought. *This is it.*

But that almond-chuckwalla brain—that blessed ancestor from the First World living inside my skull—whispered. I spun my feet up and planted them against the steel frame. I crawled upside down along the frame until I could kick off and surface away from the spinning propeller.

After I grabbed Neil's Oakleys off the concrete bottom, I sat and watched the green water turn and twist around the white sun. It would be easy to stay down here, in the First World of water and ancestry. I understood why people sometimes just gave in and let themselves drown.

I kicked back up toward the sun. I gave Neil back his glasses and shook his hand. He gave me my ten bucks.

"Nice going, Jim Danger." Neil laughed.

That same day, someone stuck a "Danger" sign on my ammo can beneath my name. The name stuck, too.

Later, I gave one of Neil's passengers the ten dollars and told them to use it to tip him at the end of the trip.

People yelled it at me when this Croatian tourist lost his watch that his young wife had gotten him for their engagement. I dove for it off the beach at the petroglyph panel. The current took me underwater. I swam about ten feet before I found the watch shining on the sand in the green water.

I came up and found myself in the middle of the river. The current had carried me down about a quarter mile before I got to a small sandbar in the first curves of Horseshoe Bend.

A great blue heron, *Táłtł'ááh álééh* (One Who Walks on the Bottom of the Stream), that great ancestor from the First World, watched me emerge stumbling and shaking from the river. He cocked his head, and his yellow eyes wondered. I stood shivering in the 105-degree heat. He had a point.

"Ahee'he Táłtł'ááh álééh," I called. The heron turned his gray body and flew to a gravel bar on the other side of the bend.

On the way back to the boats, we were swarmed by *wóóneeshch'įįdii* (cicadas), those restless travelers.

"Hey, Jim Danger!" Johnson Redhorse yelled from behind me. "Brunch is here!"

Diné grandmothers would roast *wóóneeshch'įįdii* on large pans like peanuts. Johnson and I caught several buzzing through the air. We thanked them for their lives, popped off their heads and mandibles, and ate them whole. Most of the passengers got sick.

"What?" Johnson smiled. "They taste like peanut butter!"

I agreed. There are many tastes waiting us in this Glittering World if we say *yes* to them.

On the river, I would learn what saying *yes* really meant.

I walked into the shop of Wilderness River Adventures, unclipped my sunglasses as I passed under the loading door, and stepped around one of the downriver rafts that had been pulled in for repairs the previous night.

"Yo, Jimbo Danger! Any money today?"

It was Lindsay. Her bright scarlet hair fell from her yellow WRA baseball.

On her first day, we asked her if she dyed it; she said she was a natural red-head. We asked if she dyed it anyway. She laughed.

Lindsay was a physics major from St. Louis who'd left behind a laboratory internship at the prestigious University of Chicago to guide river trips on the Colorado River that summer.

I checked in with the boss. He said I was running lunch beach with Ken. In the kitchen, I found Ken cutting onions. The fluorescent lights reflected nicely off a single bald patch in the middle of his hoary head, just above his ponytail.

"Old man with a knife," I said and began to shake my head. "Beginnings of a bad idea."

Ken Stout lifted his deep-set blue eyes. He took a latex glove off his dark, tanned hand. "Just means I've had more time to practice throwing the bastard," he said, motioning with the knife before he grinned and went back to cutting.

I knew that when Ken ran lunch beach, he always sprang for extra items out of his own pocket. Guacamole and fresh watermelon were delicacies his guests needed in the canyon. It was all about having fun.

When we drove the van out, we stopped in the parking lot of Big Lake Trading Post. An old Navajo man rested in a white plastic deck chair in front of a tray of watermelons.

"Yá'át'ééh," Ken said. The old man nodded. I walked up and picked up a melon. "Three'll do."

Ken took up one of the watermelons from the crate and ran his calloused fingers along the rind. He was feeling for pale spots the size of pimples, where the fruit's sugar seeped out, caught the air, and showed the melon to be ripe and sweet. Mormons called them "bee marks" when they began growing watermelon just up the road in Utah more than 110 years ago; the bees from their hives would fly into the melon patches and settle down on the sweetest melons that leaked their sugar. The early Mormons saw the pale pimples and thought the bees were drilling through the rind with their stingers.

Ken was a third-generation Utah Mormon. His family had raised horses in Johnson Canyon, forty miles to the north, where the mountain creeks fed alfalfa fields during their downhill run to meet the Paria River. Ken had left the ranch during the years Lyndon B. Johnson sent Ken's friends to die in the rice paddies of Southeast Asia; he took his guitar and played in the streets of Salt Lake City, Sacramento, and San Francisco. He drifted

from job to job: busboy, mechanic's apprentice, short-order cook, fishing guide in Montana. He enrolled himself in a tech school in Prescott and then migrated up to Page, Arizona, when he'd heard that the Salt River Project was looking for workers for its new Navajo Generating Station.

The Navajo Generating Station went online in the mid-1970s. It is the largest coal-burning power plant in the country. The fiery maw eats coal from *Dziłíjiin*, an eight-thousand-foot-high mesa where Anasazi, Hopi, and Diné people have lived for more than seven thousand years (that we know of). That coal is taken off the mountain in two ways. For a time, it traveled through a chute that took coal chunks floating in a slurry of groundwater. This slurry chute sucked more than three million gallons of groundwater per day from Black Mesa in order to deliver its coal to a power plant on the Colorado River in Laughlin, Nevada. That plant is now closed. But do the math, and that comes out to more than a billion gallons of groundwater per year stolen from the springs and shrines and ponds of Black Mesa. That water is never going back into the ground.

The other line of coal comes off the mesa via a railroad built directly to the Navajo Generating Station. This plant is slated to close by 2020.

My stepdad's family was relocated during the Navajo-Hopi land dispute. This dispute was incited by attorney John Boyden in order to gain control of the mineral rights to the coal on Black Mesa. Boyden would eventually collect more than two million dollars of taxpayer money to arrange for the government sale of the mineral rights. They and many other families had to leave their old grazing grounds behind. Today, those grazing grounds have been stripped by shovels the size of four-story buildings.[*] The root line of Ken Stout's livelihood led back to those four-story shovels and my stepdad's family's eviction. So did my mom's. She was an occupational

[*] Many Hopis disagreed with Boyden's tactics and felt ashamed to be represented by people who would try to evict Diné and sell the land. Caleb Johnson, a Hopi student at Princeton Theological Seminary, wrote to the Senate on behalf of traditional Hopi priests. He noted that the boundary issues on Black Mesa had been *created* by the corrupt Hopi leadership. Real leadership had a religious component in the Hopi way of life. The man whom Boyden had installed as Hopi chairman was not a real leader. He was not respected by his neighbors and was in fact a federally convicted felon. Caleb Johnson had gone to school in my hometown, Ganado, Arizona, and had graduated from Ganado Mission in 1958. (See Judith Nies, "The Black Mesa Syndrome: Indian Lands, Black Gold," *Orion Magazine*, summer 1998.)

health nurse at the power plant. Sixty percent of the people who lived in Page were employed at the power plant. Everyone was in-league. It was hard for anyone to be truly evil in the arrangement.

Ken Stout worked up through its ranks. He and his people controlled coal furnaces that could incinerate an armored car, and he had flexible hours that let him run the river with dumb college kids like us.

The boats hit lunch beach. Roast beef and pastrami under sheaves of lettuce and rosy disks of tomatoes shined from the table. They smiled, and the guides smiled. Fitz had pulled in first. He stood beside the ten-foot stalk of a desiccated century plant in the shade of a tamarisk, picking at a bough, talking to Papa Don.

"Hey, Jim Danger," Fitz called. "Just admiring your century plant here. Nice one, young man." I had pulled the plant from a cliff edge the week before, loaded it into my boat, and left it to be admired on lunch beach.

Fitz towered over Papa Don. Tall, with a triathlete's build, Fitz had a sharp, deep-lined face and a strong nose that had been broken in two places. He was an angry second-generation-Irish Minnesota-backwoods reprobate when he'd joined the Green Berets in 1959. The army sent him to Vietnam as a weapons specialist before the major conflict broke out. He returned to the States, moved to Las Vegas, married, and worked as a firefighter and fire captain for thirty-three years. Fitz spoke with a stutter, though he hid it well—except when he cursed. Many of the new river guides caught Fitz's stutter on their first day: "Watch where the f-f-fuck you're g-g-going" or "K-k-iss this old m-man's ass pucker" were common punctuations in the daily conversation of Tom Fitzgerald. He laughed as much as the rest of us, though, and he was a good man. He'd divorced his wife after twenty years but remarried her six years later when she was diagnosed with intestinal cancer, so that his firefighter's insurance could pay for her treatments.

"Papa" Don Trujillo was a Page regular. He and his wife had moved to the town in the 1970s, when Don found work at the Navajo Generating Station. Don was built for their type of labor; short, stocky, and bold to the task. His thick brows and a white beard down to his collarbones made him look like a happy Hispaño Santa Claus. Everyone loved Don. He had been a guide for a long time but knew when to break the rules. He encouraged recklessness, shared what he had, and laughed at himself. That was Papa Don.

Papa Don was leading the trip that day, and so when he came up to me while I was restocking the roast beef, I thought he was going to ask when I'd like his boat to leave the beach so I could begin stowing the food.

"Jimmy, how's it been?" Don said. He was soaked after diving into the river and throwing the passengers' kids into the water so their parents to snap a photo or two.

"We need to have a meeting," he said. Papa Don informed me that one of the guides was puking behind the trees because he'd done too much drinking the night before. This happened with a lot of river guides when they got too involved with the American affair. Not everybody could have their senior prom every night, and not all of us were the Great Gatsby.

At least he had the sense not to vomit in the river. Puke floats, and the passengers don't like to see it.

Don wanted me to step in and finish the trip for him. I was glad to replace this malefactor.

I grabbed my pack from beneath the Navajo willow at the corner of the beach. I loaded the boat and did the trip from the top of Two-Mile Draw down to Echo Peak. The echoes come off the canyon wall toward the two-thousand-foot-high sandstone peak as loud as cannon fire. We reached the final stretch, at Lee's Ferry, where Mormon settlers led by John Doyle Lee settled along the Colorado and built a ferry for the wagon trains moving in from southern Utah. It was the only spot where the canyon walls dipped low enough to allow the wagons to cross the river before the walls rose again and spanned into what would eventually become the Grand Canyon, sixty miles downriver.

We parked our boats afterward in the willows near the dock. Papa Don called up to the shop and let them know we were coming back upriver to the dock at the base of the dam.

A group of three boats pulled ahead by a half mile. Papa Don, Shari, Donny, and I took up the rear, since my boat was the slowest. Echo Peak sprawled to the sky, its sand dune spanning featureless along its flank.

At the bend at the end of the corridor, strands of the dune on Echo Peak dissolved in the wind. Sand scattered in helixes out into nothing. Weird.

Feathery explosions erupted along the water toward Papa Don and Shari's boats. Don's raft reared back, lifted straight up, and flew backward fifty feet. Papa Don vanished beneath the water and faded into the blown spray. His boat cartwheeled and landed right side up. The wind pushed it ashore faster than the boat would have gone if he'd gunned the engine.

Static popped through the radio clipped to the helm: someone was trying to call for help. The static broke out again, then a voice.

"Don's in the water! Don's in the water!"

The static swarmed over the transmission, then a return: "Say again?"

"The boat flipped! Papa Don's in the water!"

Static. Wind. Rain flying like bullets.

I pushed the throttle halfway. And there he was.

Papa Don's life jacket was an orange flare in the gray haze. The other two guides saw him, but the wind held them by their pontoons.

At the bend where the tamarisks grew high and thick along the bank, the trees were still against the blue sky. No wind. You could have walked over and laid out a picnic blanket.

The wind that had thrown Papa Don's boat was a microburst. This murderous wind comes when a change in the atmospheric air above causes sudden violent bursts to knife down into a small area. Microbursts are famous for downing multimillion dollar aircraft and pancaking trailer parks. Now I was in the path of the knife, and a guide was in the water.

My boat reared, and two of the seventy-pound seat cushions slid off the frame back toward the motor well. I turned the wheel slightly to the right and moved along the skim of the gust. It put me at an angle, but I could still drive forward. The boat reared up two more feet, and I cut the throttle down and steered to the left, then right, left, right, zigzagging up the corridor where Don and his life jacket drifted in the current.

I called on the radio to warn the guides farther ahead not to come back here. One of the yellow lengths of safety line stretched into the current from the raft on the right. Someone had thrown it but it had missed Papa Don, who was now drifting midchannel. He clung to the pale plank of a seat cushion.

Papa Don had less than four minutes before the water numbed him.

Shari gunned her Merc full throttle, but she drifted backward as though her motor were reversed. Donny, the other guide, was pulling close to Don. He reached for the life ring that hung at his right. The wind came again and folded the tamarisk trees along the bank. Donny flung the pale hoop. The wind blew it behind him and it bounced onto the shore.

Might as well throw a kite in this.

Each boat had a throw bag the size of a water jug, filled with fifty yards of red-and-yellow coiled rope. I'd checked mine before my trip and knew that when I threw it out, a small hole at the base of the bag would trail the rope behind it. Papa Don would be able to grab it, and I'd tow him to the back of the well and yank him out. That was the plan. My glasses clotted over with rainwater. Then my bucket blew past me and landed in

the motor well. Its rope handle dropped down and caught in the propeller. My engine died.

Shari yelled to Donny. Donny had missed Papa Don and was also being pushed downriver by the microburst. He was cupping his hands around his mouth, yelling, "Swim, Don! Swim for shore, Papa Don!"

"He can't swim," I said under my breath. "He's sixty fucking years old."

This could be very stupid. I jumped into the river. The water was cold, but the knife was sharp. I had the rope away from the prop in two dives and eight cuts. I started the engine. The rain lashed like copper wires.

Papa Don had drifted to the middle of the current; he wasn't moving.

No funeral for Don, please, I said to myself. *We are not going to be in the goddamn newspaper.*

I jerked the shift lever down, popped the Merc in reverse, and gunned the engine. The boat whined toward Don while I maneuvered the bow away from the wind.

I threw the safety line out from my right hand. Papa Don reached his arm feebly, slowly, and his fist clenched around the rope. He lost his grip twice, and I had to rethrow it.

I pulled him to the boat in three long-reaching tugs and lifted his two hundred and fifty pounds from the water. His limbs were totally numb. It was like hauling a dead walrus.

He came up breathing like he was having a heart attack. I turned him over. His skin was cold as the rubber pontoons.

"Don! You all right?"

He looked up and smiled. "Hey, Jimmy. It's windy as shit out here."

"Fuckin'-A right it is!"

Then we both laughed deep, and the wind blew hard against us.

Ten minutes later, the wind vanished and the blue sky shined. The desert often has merciful amnesia.

Papa Don sat on the pontoons of my boat, putting on dry socks. I found Don's ammo can floating near the sandbar in fine shape. I'd loaned him my towel to dry himself. His feet were dark as mahogany, and one heel was peeling. Cold water and intense heat did that. Every river guide had a peeling heel.

He got the second sock on and breathed deep.

"Well, shit, Jimmy." Papa Don laughed. "Thanks for saving my life."

He looked from the water to the bronze light of the sun broken by the peak above us, gleaming like white shell on every wave of the river.

I never told this story to anyone. But I told it to Lyle Parsons about two weeks later. He sat in his recliner in the soft air of the swamp-cooled living room, bouncing his son on his knee while we discussed whether Patrick Stewart or Derek Jacobi played the better Claudius in *Hamlet*.

He let the boy down to run and grab a picture book from the sun-room. We walked outside and sat in the shade to water the spruce tree at the edge of the fence. We talked about how we are often set upon by our environment, but how there is something in us called a "spirit" that can react to save us. Then I told him this story.

I had no one else to tell. He was the clearest voice in my life.

"Well, Jim," he said, "you're responsible for another person's life now. That's what it means to be a man."

"I don't know about that."

"I do." He grinned.

The wind sighed through the spruce tree. The Diné collected these spruce branches and their needles to make *ch'ó yiilbáá'* (spruce collars) to wear whenever they danced to summon the *Diyin Diné* (Holy People).

Through spruce trees, the wind spoke with a clear voice.

"Move," it said. "Range. Emerge."

WATER IS LIFE

Tó aglaan'ii. Water.

Water is life. Drive into any Reservation community today, and you'll see that phrase artfully spray-painted onto an abandoned shed or windmill water tank.

Tó éí 'iiná até. Water is life.

I understood how Ganado's water flowed into the community after speaking with the man in charge of giving it out.

That summer, I had come back to Ganado to research and record oral histories. I funded the trip with work for *Arizona Highways* and the Navajo tribe's weekly newspaper, the *Navajo Times.*

I drove to Ganado alone, back to the wash where I'd built dams, outrun witches, and tracked animals. This is where I met the ditch rider.

Aaron Peshlakai and John Curtis guided me along the wash next to Hubbell Trading Post that morning to show me a river restoration method the Park Service had adopted nearly a decade before. I wanted to interview the local ditch rider who regulated the dam at Ganado Lake so I could understand the irrigation system of the valley.

But the ditch rider had other things to teach.

"That's Stuart over there," J. R. said, pointing with his lips.

A short, solidly built man wearing a bright-white baseball cap walked in a crisp gait. It was Stuart Claw, the ditch rider.

"This guy's a bit weird," Aaron said.

Claw strode around a cactus patch and stepped over a silvery saltbush before shaking my hand. His white hair grew to his ears, and his dark leather

skin creased along his eyes and mouth, yet he seemed no older than fifty. As we shook hands, I could tell he'd lived off the Rez long enough to forget the traditional Navajo handshake and to grip firm. The traditional handshake is softer, almost a caress, meant to acknowledge and not intimidate.

Claw wore dark blue jeans, a red-and-white cotton button-up shirt, and a thick leather belt. The toes of his boots looked like they'd been through a sandblaster.

Aaron and John walked back to their duties at the trading post. I shifted my notepad and asked Claw if it would be okay to take the tour.

Claw looked to the northern horizon, as though spotting for deer. "In other desert climates, such as Egypt and Spain, ditch riders are military officers." His baritone voice was crisp at the edges, like his walk. There was no Rez accent. "They wear uniforms as good as any army lieutenant's. In Navajo, we are called *Tó'nelozi*. In Mexico, we are called *zoñero*. In New Mexico, we are called *mayordomo*."

Claw led me to his blue Ford F-150 pickup and handed me his last business card from the dashboard. His e-mail address was "Cobra 52." I asked what that came from.

"Army Special Forces," he said. "I was Special Forces advisor during Vietnam. Fought alongside some of the French Foreign Legionnaires in the jungles there. Drunk dregs of humanity. Needlessly abused by the chain of command."

And the truck was moving. Claw said he was going to show me a bit of everything. We sped west on Highway 264.

Claw was born in a "male-style" forked-stick *hoghan* in Ganado, then moved to California, then came back and graduated from Ganado High School. Then he joined the army. Now he was a government man. In his spare time, he was an artist.

"I'm a painter. It's a curse. That's why I don't do it very much," he said. "It just sort of comes out of my fingertips. I can't avoid it. It just happens."

We drove past red mesas topped with pink sand, jagged with skeletons of sun-strangled juniper.

After high school, Claw studied at the Institute of American Indian Arts, then Northern Arizona University for a year.

"I was starving, like most artists." He grinned and drank from one of three water bottles at his feet. A small plastic trash can full of empty bottles sat on the floor between us. "You're a writer?"

"I'm trying to be," I said. "Always trying."

"I wanted to be a writer. I wrote a novel in the summer of 1958. Wrecked my uncle's typewriter getting that thing down. But it was no good. I burned the manuscript."

He turned off the road and pointed to what looked like a small rail bridge on concrete pillars that spanned the distance of a football field over a nearby wash. I had seen the small bridge every morning on my bus ride to Ganado High School more than eight years ago. He explained it was a flume built in the summer of 1941, designed to carry water across the arroyo as part of a government project to develop farming plots along the wash.

"It's a beautiful structure," he said. "And it was never used."

"Why not?"

"December 7th. World War II took the money. And it was never finished."

We drove the southern back road. Claw said there were 400 Navajo veterans from Ganado. About 150 of them were still alive.

We exited the truck and walked to a distant block of concrete on the flat plain. The sand crunched beneath our feet like old paper, seared flat and smooth by the dry heat. Claw explained that the concrete block was a drop structure with a flashboard door designed to block and pool the moving water, then release it to a farm plot. At the second drop structure, Claw picked up a thick cedar board that had been used as a platform over it.

"That's a nice board," he noted. "I'm taking it with me."

We walked to the truck and drove back into town.

Claw said he was in the army between 1968 and 1977, where he served with the Green Berets.

"It was natural. It was very easy." He turned onto a northern back road at the town outskirts and to a ruined stone house, its roof scattered in the sagebrush and cheatgrass.

"A Navajo nurse used to live in that stone house," he said. "She served in World War II, where she was captured by the Japanese in the Philippines. I've heard she spent the war in an internment camp."

Claw tapped my shoulder and pointed to a sharp point at the top of a distant mesa, its pale and reddish colors marbled like a cut of mutton. He said that point was where Navajos had once stationed a signal fire to warn others in the valley below when American troops rode up from Hopi lands at Oraibi to burn crops and kill sheep grazing along the wash.

The Americans had trouble fighting the Navajo. The Diné knew the land, knew their horses better, were constantly escaping ambushes and patrols by slipping into the juniper groves and slot canyons like coyotes. The American

solution was total war: burned Navajo crops and dead livestock guaranteed weak, starving Navajos too tired to run. I pondered this history as I pondered the drop structures gathering heat on the sandy plain.

As we rounded a turn, he slowed the truck and pointed ahead to a tall hill rising from the edge of a mesa. The lone hill was almost magically symmetrical, its sand smoothed by rainfall into a dome as perfect as any in Byzantium. "That's *Na'ashash'íí.*"

"Round Top Hill," I said.

"Uh-huh," he said. "That's a holy place. They say White Shell Woman stopped here on her way to the sea in the west."

Claw told of a band of Navajos that took refuge there and fought off a war party of Apaches by shooting their bows from a prone position at the top of the hill. My mind saw them: fighting under the desert sun with a juniper bow and flint knife, skin leaking sweat, sand scraping knees and belly, just screaming and shooting.

I told Claw the story of an Anglo man I knew who once tried galloping his horse straight up Round Top Hill.

"What happened?" Claw asked.

"He only got a third of the way." I pointed with my lips to the base of the hill. "A rattlesnake snapped at the horse. He got thrown from the saddle and separated his shoulder."

Claw laughed and offered me a sip from his water bottle. I had learned long ago of the blessings of water. It is no surprise that most modern Rez towns still carry the names of springs. And anything rare in the desert is something worth fighting over. In my Rez perception, war was never far from water. Stuart Claw was slowly proving me right.

He accelerated the Ford up a hill, and *Na'ashash'íí* moved out of sight.

"When you have a battle," Claw said, "your senses are alive like they never are. If you ever hit a target with a rock, you are determining the weight, the shape, the angle, all with your hand. You don't worry. You shoot. You hit. You move on. It was easy in the Green Berets. But that's because I was Navajo. We're the hardest, meanest, toughest people on the planet. But we don't know it anymore."

My friend Ferlin's parents used to drag him out of the house the morning after a snowfall and roll him around on the ground, rubbing snow against his naked chest and back, to make him tough. If he screamed from the shock, they just crammed snow into his mouth. My friends and I did the

same on snowy days, whether our parents forced us or not; it was a fun way of proving you were Diné, a Tough Noodle.

Claw pointed out spots in the adjacent mesas where he'd found Anasazi ruins and pottery. He claimed there were three thousand Navajo and Anasazi campsites in the Ganado Valley and he'd seen most of them during his weekly hikes.

"I like to imagine being here a thousand years ago," Claw said. "Just being on top of a mountain and looking down at the valley at night, seeing the cooking fires burning below. Like stars or something."

We drove past *Da'saanibitó* (Porcupine Pond) and headed toward Ganado Lake, the beginning of the Ganado irrigation system that had been built by Juan Lorenzo Hubbell and the sons of Ganado Mucho.

Hubbell's irrigation ditches were the standard of the time: as wide as two cows and three feet deep, they carried a steady, sandy current to an evaporation pond at the south end of Hubbell's homestead, then to a gravity-fed system of small irrigation ditches. Other Navajo farmers used the ditches also. The system was sinfully inefficient. Claw said for every five buckets of water, they lost three to evaporation.

He pointed to where the Bureau of Reclamation had recently filled in the old irrigation ditches and put in a system of steel pipes four feet under the sand and maroon clay.

When we reached the base of the earth and stone dam at Ganado Lake, Claw indicated the beginning of the system at the inlet pond, a small pool thick with cattails planted to catch debris leaving the lake. As a ditch rider, Claw was paid to be as fair as the rain clouds and to give each farmer their entitled use of the water.

We walked to the top of the dam, and Ganado Lake reflected the sky in drifting mirrors of blue, white, and red. The most powerful clan of the area took its name from this natural lake, *Tó'tsonii*, the Big Water Clan. Ganado Mucho, the local chieftain, had been named for this water. To the Mexicans and the Americans, he was Ganado Mucho—Many Cattle—but to the Navajo he'd been *Tó'tsonii Hastiin* (Big Water Man).

Not bad for a man who wouldn't qualify as a "full-blooded Navajo" by today's standards. The father of *Tó'tsonii Hastiin* was a Hopi slave who'd bought his own freedom and married into the *Tó'tsonii* clan. Ganado Mucho had proved early on that he could lead. In war, his shrewd negotiating skills earned him the name *Bitsoyeyeithi* (He Who Speaks With His Tongue). His

persuasive abilities and calm, assertive disposition helped him rise in the stock business, and he gathered many cattle, sheep, and horses as he rose to the head of his clan. But when there was a war, Ganado Mucho planned and led the attacks.

This brazen posture came with a price in his later years, when the head-man developed piles and ulcers on his skin (which stories attribute to witchcraft). For six years, the lingering sickness ate at him, until he died in the winter of 1893. I'd met many Ganado residents that summer—including a former president of the Navajo Nation—who claimed to know where he'd been buried.

I'd always felt the chieftain's spirit whenever I'd traveled to what remained of the "Big Water" of Ganado Lake.

Claw led me to the yellow steel gatehouse, where someone had spray-painted, "Get Down Bitch" and "Ride BMX Bitch" on the front door. Claw sighed and looked down into the lake.

"That's great," he said. "The water came up three or four inches."

The average rainfall in Ganado is about eleven to twelve inches a year, most falling in August, September, and October. That's about a third of what Pennsylvania would get in a summer. But every night since my return to Ganado, dark clouds cantered in from the east and south, drumming and thick with rain. Thunder announced their arrival. It rained every night. A rare blessing.

As Claw unlocked the gatehouse, a dragonfly landed on a loop of razor wire and stretched its wings. *Tániil'áí.* The blue of his head and thorax glinted like glass. Also a blessing.

As we entered the gatehouse, Claw produced his crank handle, a steel tool that resembled the propeller wrenches I'd used as a river guide. He attached the handle to a large nut on valve 2, explaining how one full crank raised the gate below a half-inch. Fifty cranks opened it completely.

The average Ganado farm was around ten acres. Claw recited the require-ments: it took one acre-foot—one acre of water one foot deep—to grow a cornfield, about three acre-feet for alfalfa. Ganado Lake holds twenty-seven thousand acre-feet of water at peak pool. The water was down six feet that summer.

After locking the gatehouse, Claw and I leaned over the rails of the con-crete bridge. Largemouth bass fanned their tails in the green waters. Claw pointed along the dam to the familiar Rez trash: white plastic shopping

bags from Bashas' and Safeway grocery stores in Gallup, broken bottles of Garden Deluxe and Zima, rusted tuna tins punctured from rifle practice, and green plastic Skoal tobacco cans.

Claw flicked sweat from his brow and adjusted his baseball cap.

"I try to clean up the trash here once a month. I had some posters up about the trash, but people got angry and tore them down. They say Indians never pollute. Or that if you pollute in front of an Indian, he's going to cry a long, shiny tear. But that's bullshit. They say Indians don't beat their wives. That's bullshit, too. We have a lot of myths to get rid of."

Claw likes to fish. He subscribes to *Field & Stream* and *Outdoor Life*. He likes the precision of it. You have to know the temperature, season, size of hook. You've got to be able to read it and then go for it.

We picked up trash on our walk to the truck. As we drove back to Ganado, Claw pointed out a back-road where my friends and I had competed in footraces in elementary school.

They shut down the road because people went there to dump their garbage in the wash and then drove away before anybody could spot them.

"There was too much dumping going on. The government isn't doing its job. That's why it exists. Council delegates don't know how to do anything. They're not skilled at anything. They're just bottom-feeders. Scum of the earth."

We stopped along the other entrance to the closed road to Ganado Lake, where two Navajo Tribal Utility Authority (NTUA) men had come to investigate a suspected leak in the irrigation pipes. Claw nodded, asked several questions to see if they'd actually checked, then walked over to some rabbitbrush to piss. I joined him. Looking out over the sandy plain to the green trail of cottonwoods and willows growing in the curves of the wash beyond, Claw said the leak could be an artesian well. He said fault lines cause artesian wells to leak or swell, then push the water to the surface. He shook and zipped his pants closed.

"Why that theory?" I asked.

"Scientific-ass guessing," he grinned.

On the other side of the road, Louise Tsosie's driveway led to her gray, stuccoed *hoghan* under a far grove of cottonwood trees, surrounded by old, rusted cars and a small pack of skinny sheepdogs.

"Do you know who lives in there?" Claw asked.

"Yes." Louise gave us injured lambs in the winter. We kept them in a large

cardboard box next to the radiator in our bathroom, bottle-fed them until they could stand on their own, and kept them until the spring. Then Darren and I would herd them back to Louise.

Claw nodded. "I'm related to her. I used to live down here. When I was seven years old, I went to that *hoghan* to borrow some salt. I had to cross a small bridge over the irrigation canal to get there. But a big, mean rooster jumped out from behind the sagebrush and attacked my chest. I ran away, afraid, slipped and fell into one of the canals. I almost drowned before I pulled myself out. So that was my introduction to the irrigation system."

We got out and walked to the cornfield, where long, wavy green leaves curved from their stalks like hair taken out of braids. To check the moisture, Claw relied on the Navajo hand test. Pick up a handful of the sandy clay, squeeze your fist tight, then flatten your hand. If the dirt lay in his palm in the shape of a small hand grenade, then no water was needed. If the soil was too dry, it simply ran out of his hand. The Navajo hand test. Scientific-ass guessing.

"We're only missing one farming plot. Plot number 13. Nobody wants that one," he said. I smiled. The sway of superstition still endured on the Rez.

On the drive back to the trading post, Claw pointed out some small mesas in the distance. "That place out there is called *Nineelnééh, dina' dziłghá'í adajiihi'* (Where the Apaches Came Down). It was there the Apaches came," he said. "They attacked a pregnant woman, cut out her fetus, threw it on an anthill. Then they went west, down toward Burnside. The Navajos from Ganado got together, followed them, and stopped them. Then the Apaches fled to the north. The Navajos got there faster and stopped them. Then they waited for them at Burnside. After what happened, you could still see the Apaches' bones there for years. The Navajos waited there, facing the Apaches. They waited for their horses to go mad with thirst. The horses ran off, abandoning the Apaches. Then the Navajos sent in the young men, twelve-year-olds, with clubs. They brained them and bloodied them. But they left one Apache alive to send back to the others, to tell them never to come back here. The rest, they left for the crows. That was the end of forty people."

I went to the high school down on the grassy plains at Burnside. Claw smiled when I mentioned school.

"The only reading material for us back then was the Sears and Roebuck catalogue. And with one of those you had toilet paper for a year." He laughed, remembering how he taught himself to read from children's books.

His grandmother came to the school at Ganado Mission. They sat there with cookies and milk. They sang "Frère Jacques." She never went back though. Later in life, she would cry because she never learned to read and write.

"Later, when I had learned to read and write, I developed a system of symbols for her, so she could write down her Navajo," he said. "We worked on it together, so it worked. People don't work as well together anymore."

I asked her name.

"Yanabah Winker," he said. "*Yanabah* means 'She Fought Her Way Back.'"

Another story: Navajo men from Ganado found coral beads from a cut necklace. Then two pigeons raced overhead, then down. This was a sign that enemies had come. Comanches. They killed a mother and were going to strangle her baby but didn't. They found a Navajo man underneath a juniper tree putting piñon pitch on a sore, and they put so many arrows into him that he looked like a porcupine. Then the Comanches left east, toward New Mexico.

"Towards Gallup, a Navajo warrior party followed them," he said. "On the second night, a Navajo man crawled up to two of the captive women and asked them which of the Comanches was the commander. The women pointed to a large man sleeping by the fire. Other Navajo men crawled into the camp, and they launched their attack from within. In the panic, the Comanches shot each other. At a birdcall, the Navajos withdrew. That was the way to defeat the Comanche raiders. You have to kill their leaders. That is the Comanches' name in Navajo, *Naałání*, Many Enemies. But some escaped and took the women to a Mexican household."

Despite the 1863 Emancipation Proclamation and subsequent constitutional amendments forbidding slavery for Southern blacks, Indian slavery wasn't declared illegal in New Mexico Territory until 1872. Claw nodded. He said it probably went on longer than that.[*]

[*] Most large haciendas in Albuquerque and Santa Fe kept Indian slaves: Apaches, Puebloans, Navajos, Hopis. John Lorenzo Hubbell got his middle name from his great-grandfather, don Lorenzo Gutiérrez, who had joined three hundred New Mexican troops in 1805 for a two-hundred-mile raid into Navajo country that ended at Massacre Cave. Some of those slaves taken during that raid had descendants who were serving the Gutierrez family when John Lorenzo Hubbell was born.

Many say the Diné got their revenge thirty years later, when a government-sponsored expedition of nearly one thousand New Mexican volunteers and

Claw sipped water. "The Navajo men wanted to get one of the women back. So they went to the north to *Dibé Ntsaa*. There they got medicine from *Bijooshí*. The Third Cavalry was sent to put him down in 1840, after he beat up a missionary. He made his medicine up in the mountains near Shiprock, New Mexico. He put a basket over the boys' moccasins, struck the basket four times, and sent four horses to search for the woman. The woman, years after they'd found her and brought her back, would always say that she felt something strike her heart four times. One of the horsemen found her in a red dress, wearing a gray sombrero, living amid farmland. The Navajo men rode up there during a big fiesta. They gave party gifts of sheep and took her home. My grandmother remembers that woman didn't want to leave. She remembers her crying and singing Spanish songs."

We coasted down the road, tires bumping over sandy ruts as we passed Hubbell's holding pond. Claw pointed the lip of the dry pond. A *téél halchí'í* (robin) landed there and twitched its wings.

Claw recounted his family's warrior heritage. His uncle, Leo Claw, was MIA on April 24, 1945, during a battle on Okinawa. George Claw was a sergeant major in the Marine Corps. Virgil Claw also served during World War II and was captured in New Guinea.

"That's the way a lot of people have to get out of here," Claw said, nodding

(*continued*) Pueblo allies left Santa Fe to punish the Navajos for their raiding and to capture Diné women and children for slaves. As the expedition approached the Chuska Mountains, the Navajos, led by the chieftain Narbona, ambushed the New Mexicans in a mountain pass named *Béésh Lichii'í Bigiizh* (Flint Rock or Copper Pass). The two hundred Navajos waited until the New Mexicans were strung out in a long line through the narrow pass—Narbona compared them to a long branch that could be quickly cut into firewood—then they attacked with arrows and clubs and decimated the weary New Mexicans and Puebloans. This was the battle where Manuelito earned his war name *Hashkéh Naabaah* (Angry Warrior). They say he scalped one of the New Mexicans and—in Navajo warrior fashion—chewed on the scalp like it was a piece of beef jerky before his rage found its bottom.

While the Mexicans often raided for Navajo slaves (some chieftains claimed that half of the tribe was enslaved by the late 1860s), the Diné also took slaves of their own (as did the Hopis, Apaches, Utes, and Comanches). However, captives were usually adopted into the Navajo families and treated as clan relatives. Juana, the famed wife of the chieftain Manuelito, was originally a Mexican captive; she and many other Navajo captives opted to stay with the Diné rather than be returned to their families after the Americans arrived in *Diné Bikéyah*.

to Hubbell's ancient barn, stockyard, and stone trading post. He looked ahead into the valley. "There's no jobs here. You have to break out of what you are when you get here."

As we coasted downhill, Claw recalled his Spartan childhood, how his parents tried breaking him out of himself. "In upbringing, you are taught, 'Americans are the Enemy.' You are Navajo when the Americans come. And there will always be Navajo. You can't sleep on your backs. You can't sit on your backs. You have to be ready at all times. Be able to shoot from your belly as you wake. Punishments were severe. Whipping. And I was the oldest son, so it was toughest for me. They'd keep me out in the snowstorm in only a T-shirt. That's why Special Forces training was a walk in the sun. And we were always taught growing up: *Bił na'ahxidíí'diiltóhii niniyo ninalwo.* 'The one you will trade arrows with someday is out there running in the morning.' So you better be ready for him when he comes for you."

Claw gently took my notepad and pen, balancing the steering wheel with his knees while he wrote the phrase in all capital letters.

"And there's another phrase we were taught," he said. "It means, 'We want to see you, in our mind's eye, among the enemy, your war club swinging, your shield tight against your body, with your tail wagging out behind you.'" He smiled as he turned into the trading post driveway, his dark skin pinching along deep lines at his eyes and mouth.

"Your *tail*?" I asked. "What does that mean? A tail?"

"Back in the far days, Navajos would use lion hide for their arrow quivers," he said.

"Ah. *Náshdóítsoh.* Mountain lion?"

"*Aoo'.*" He nodded. "And it was considered good form to leave the tail of the lion attached to the skin when you made the quiver. So when you fought, the tail swung out behind you in battle. When you saw combat. When you saw your friends killed. That's the sort of thing they had to deal with in those days."

Claw parked under a shady elm near the trading post and wished me good luck in collecting stories. He said he liked talking about Ganado for his own mental treatment, but that his stories would probably be no good on tape. I wasn't surprised; most Navajo people I've met look on tape recorders like they were loaded guns. I nodded, thanked him again, and wished him luck with the growing season.

"Ah, the water belongs to everyone," he said. "We'll just try to keep it fair. I got to go. It's hard for me to keep still when I know the sun is walking."

YELLOW EVENING TWILIGHT

People seek mountains. This should not surprise us.

Diné medicine singers—the *hataałi*—ranged from mountain to mountain to gather herbs, to look for visions, to seek their chants to heal their people.

Some of them would range straight through the lands of their enemies—the Utes, the Puebloans—to reach these mountains. If they were caught, they were tortured, taken as slaves, or killed.

But still they ranged out.

Mountains are places of *hasbídí* (doves), *dólii* (bluebirds), *tsídiiltsoí* (yellow warblers), and *ch'agii* (blackbirds). They are places where the *Diyin Diné* (Great Ones) drove their power into the earth with knives of white shell, turquoise, and obsidian and blessed them with abalone shells. They are home to bears and to elk. Medicines grow there. Water flows there.

And water is life. *Tó éí 'iiná até.*

The Navajo word for "strength" is *dził.*

The Navajo word for "mountain" is *dził.*

Bits'áádóó nihidzil dooleeł. Every day you can grow stronger. Every day you can be on the mountain.

But first you must go to the mountain. You must accept the mountain. You have to say *yes* to the mountain.

Today I have come to the mountain the *bilagáanas* call San Francisco Peaks. They named all its peaks separately. The tallest one they named Mount Humphreys. This name comes from a Civil War general who butchered Southern soldiers for perhaps something his people called glory, then

helped promote the levees system along the Mississippi that doomed the delta to ecological turmoil.

I call it *Dookʼoʼoosłiid*. Shining Clouds on Top.

I am going up this mountain with two of my brothers.

I am with Leo Sabol, and it has been two years since I have returned west. I have known Leo since I entered the land of my fathers, the coal hills of Pennsylvania, where I attended Grove City College. He was one of the first people I ever heard read John Keats and understand what he was talking about. We were friends for years. Then we stopped talking because of a woman. And now we are talking again. We are talking as we travel across the country together. We are talking while we walk the streets of Mark Twain's hometown and talk with some teenagers walking barefoot toward the 7-Eleven across from the cabin where Benson Blankenship once lived with his father; he had discovered a runaway slave living on Sny Island across the river and snuck food to him instead of turning him in for a reward that would have kept his roughneck father in whiskey for at least a summer.

But that's what stupid kids do sometimes. They push against their parents. Samuel Clemens knew plenty about that. Benson Blankenship was his best friend when they were kids. When he grew to be an old man and named himself Mark Twain, he put Benson in a novel and renamed him Huckleberry Finn and put him on a raft and made him range down a river and range beyond himself.

Clemens and Blankenship were like brothers.

Leo and I are still talking as we drive through Dodge City and through the smell of cattle shit and slaughterhouses and hear the trains screaming out something about the America that built this town and had to hire Wyatt Earp to keep the peace but now hires local sheriff's deputies to keep the Mexican migrant workers in line and on time to the Tyson chicken slaughterhouse and the beef feedlots.

We are talking as the low grasslands of Colorado rise into buttes and mesas and we are talking when the gray shadows of the Rocky Mountains appear for the first time and we are talking when I pull over to give prayers to *Sisnaajini*, the white-shell mountain of the East, outside of Alamosa.

Then we are talking about where to pull over and sleep in a hotel after we've eaten too much at the Mexican buffet in town but we are driving and it's dark and I can go a little farther and I promise to pull over but I don't. Instead I am driving and seeing the green eyeshine of pronghorn and coyote and elk. We drive through a thunderstorm and Leo falls asleep and I drive

another 150 miles and pull into the parking lot of a Holiday Inn in Durango, Colorado. Leo asks if I want to get a room but I sleep in the parking lot.

We wake up and keep driving until we are through Moab and hike back into Arches National Park. We are talking only when we have to because we deem the silence profound. It is rare in the city of Pittsburgh where Leo lives. I had heard that silence when Clayton and I went after the footsteps of a lion on that mesa in the Grand Staircase.

We are talking on the road west and we are passing through Green River when we learn that the small float in the gas tank of my 1999 Honda Civic has swelled with the heat and is now stuck like a piece of steak in a child's throat and choking off the gasoline from falling into the tank and feeding the engine. The local mechanic says that he can't get the part for two more days. We can only fill up a gallon at a time. We decide to risk driving the 120 miles from Green River to Richfield, Utah. We are talking while Leo rents us a Toyota from the airport in St. George while the Honda awaits a $250 surgery on its fuel tank. We drive south and east and we pass through Church Wells and Page, Arizona, and I am at Lyle Parsons's front door.

Lyle is a friend and mentor. He is thin and his hair is long as that of a prophet wandered down from the mountaintop and his eyes are grayer and bluer than I remember them because he looks at his wife with a new kind of love, for she has been out wandering in the wilderness and that wilderness is called Cancer. His sons have been his responsibility for the past year and he reads to them every night. He has stopped drinking his usual four beers and three shots of tequila in the small shed after he fell in the middle of the night and broke his rib and had to stay in the hospital and couldn't buy any more alcohol. He had to actually think about how he had spent the years with his liver and gallbladder and pancreas in a choke-hold of beer and whiskey and tequila and pot. His wife had to have both of the breasts that nursed her sons cut from her to survive the wilderness of Cancer.

And when he gets out of the hospital he starts taking all the money he would have spent on alcohol and putting it into a bank account and he uses that money to buy a drum set for him and his oldest son. He put that drum set in his office next to his bookshelves weighted with the ghosts of Shakespeare, Jung, Sagan, Merton, Mann, Lao Tse, Pirsig, Sun Tzu, Castaneda, Chaucer, Homer, Chomsky, Thoreau, Asimov, Abbey, Zappa, Bowden, and Singer. Lyle Parsons and I have used years of hours to talk our way through the ideas in these books. Also filling the bookshelves in his office are statues and pictures and paintings of *mą'ii tsoh* (wolves), and Lyle Parsons has loved

wolves since he was younger than his son. He had packed a Volkswagen van full of homesteading tools, oatmeal, axes, and rifles and refused to pick up his high school diploma when he graduated from high school in Tucson, and his mother had to get it for him. He wanted to go and live where he could hear wolves howling at night, and he has said that when he dies he wants Julia to take his body up onto the tundra and lay it out as a feast for wolves, and every one of those wolves' eyes on the shelf is yellow.

Leo and I are talking with Julia about her walk through Cancer, and Leo is sharing his walk and how he was in his first year of law school in Ohio and he found a bulge on his testicle while scrubbing in the shower. His doctor said it was cancer and asked him if he would ejaculate his sperm into a plastic cup so they could put it in cold storage in case his testicles would need to come off. He would need to poison himself if he wanted to live, and he told him names of drugs that would put any possible tumors into a chemical chokehold until they died. Leo never drank four beers and three tequila shots or smoked pot in a small shed, but the wilderness of Cancer grew up outside his door. He walked through it and lived with his parents for five years and gained eighty pounds and hated himself. He lost the weight, moved into an apartment, fell in love with a woman, and then she moved out.

Leo never went back to law school. But he regained muscle and became strong. He lifted weights, read *Men's Health*. We swapped exercise tips and laughed out loud when I lifted myself on the Iron Gym chin-up bar in his study and the molding broke and I fell flat on my back but didn't hurt myself. We slept at Leo's house that night. The next morning, we were driving while the stars were still out, and we were talking.

We continue talking with Lyle Parsons and his wife about how her female parts had to be taken so she could survive in this Glittering World as *Nohokaa' Diné*, and Leo is talking about how some of his male parts had to be taken so he could survive in this Glittering World as *Nohokaa' Diné*.

When Leo has to speak and he is impatient, he rubs his wrist where he wears a yellow rubber bracelet created by a cyclist who has also walked the wilderness of Cancer, where the ground leads you to a mountaintop and either you walk up that mountain and back down and live, or you stay on that mountain and you die and you leave this world. But all roads in the wilderness of Cancer lead to that mountaintop, and Leo touches that rubber hoop when he thinks about it and remembers the walk, and his fingertips feel the writing molded into that yellow rubber, LIVE STRONG around

the yellow hoop on his wrist. I have seen the same yellow hoop around the black pupils of *Táłtł'ááh áłééh*, Great Blue Heron, that ancestor from the First World.

That yellow hoop watches me when *Táłtł'ááh áłééh* flies over my boat while I am driving upriver in the canyon. The water is skimming the pontoons, and the heron's gray and blue feathers are moving in the wind, and I can reach up to touch them if I want. He looks down at me. I pull back my hand, and the river is running red, and Papa Don is in the water. I have thrown him a line, and the rope is yellow, and Leo's bracelet is yellow, and the wolves' eyes are yellow.

The Diné call that color *łeetso*, and that is the color of *tádídíín*, the sacred corn pollen that I have put to my forehead and into my mouth during the Blessing Way, the pollen that comes out of the tassels in the morning and promises the harmony and balance that lead to long life, *są'ah naagháí bike'hózhǫ*, the color of autumn, the color of the corn, the color of abalone, the color of *'e'e'aah* (the West) and Evening Twilight and the sacred mountain of the West. The Diné call that mountain *Dook'o'oosłiid*, where the snow is like Shining Clouds on Top. That sacred mountain teaches *iiná* (action), and it is the mountain where I am walking with my two brothers, and one of them is Leo.

Leo and I are ranging up the mountain, and we are walking through *azeediilch'ílii* (blue-flowering lupine) and tall grass and then *chéch'il bika'í* (scrub oak) and *t'iisbái* (aspens) and *ch'ó deenínii* (fir trees) and *ch'ósh gai* (white spruce), and the plants change like we are emerging into new worlds with every dozen switchbacks up the mountain. The mountain forces us to bend forward and humble ourselves as we walk up the slope and the air grows thinner.

We stop and breathe and drink water on a boulder pile, and we visit with the enemy—two doctors from Pakistan who drove up from Tucson, who had fled their homeland when tribal warlords and Muslim clerics and corrupt bureaucrats armed by the American government started kidnapping doctors. They share oranges and apples, fruits cultivated by their Middle Eastern ancestors in the Euphrates River Valley thousands and thousands of years ago. They say the beauty of the mountains in *Diné Bikéyah* reminds them of their mountains. They are funny, and we all laugh. The brave are often funny. I hug them as we leave and tell them I hope they see their mountains again.

Leo and I are walking, and Leo and I are talking. He is asking me about

mountains. And he is asking me how many mountains I have gone up. And I tell him the first was Mount Pisgah in the Great Smoky Mountains in North Carolina. I went up wearing a coonskin cap like those worn by my grandfather's ancestors who colonized the ridges of the Appalachians. But I'm really thinking about a mountain ridge called Pretty Place in the Blue Ridge Mountains and how the Scotch Irish ancestors of my grandfather had migrated down the ridges of Pennsylvania and colonized those mountains. They built a chapel there and built a descending stone amphitheater toward a cross big enough to crucify two prophets at once. The whole chapel looked out over a river valley thick with hemlock, waterfalls, deer thickets, trout streams, raccoon dens, and hawk nests, and this is where people came to LIVE STRONG and grow their crops and grow their families.

I'd gone to Pretty Place on a small bus in the dark on a small road. I'm telling Leo about going with my grandfather and his wife to a sunrise service named for the fertility goddess Eostra and now renamed Easter for the Nazarene prophet who some claim took on a second life after being tortured to death on a small mountain. That mountain was named Golgotha, and it was a place of skulls.

But now I am at Pretty Place. I imagine I will walk into this stone amphitheater and look out on this river valley draped with blue dew and the gray brushstrokes of sunrise and understand the quiet holiness of awaiting day.

But I might also be in the wilderness of Cancer now when I see the Baptist church has hauled in drapes and halogen lights and costumes and stage sets and foam boulders and microphones and a synthesizer. Everything is plugged into something, and feedback is buzzing, and you can't see the cross that could crucify two prophets at the same time, and actors with bad wigs ramble through their lines.

They are showing me a story I've read more than once about how the Supreme Creator of my grandfather's universe fed his own son to the lions. Still, I chanced to see the silver gleam of a spider's web strung between two branches of a dogwood tree just outside the yellow-orange glare of a stage-light and see something of *Na'ashjé'ii Asdzáá* (Spider Woman) and a ghost of the Diyin Diné while I waited for the theater production to end and the lights to go off.

The crew wraps the 220-volt cables and packs the microphone stands, and I'm hearing the oil-draped waves licking the rocks black on Prudhoe Bay, where my grandfather once said oil still sat in the sand and nothing could live there. These halogen lights and microphones have all been running on

that black blood, and we can't get it out because it's now part of our body, and the body will die and we are doomed.

Now we are leaving the wilderness of Cancer and coming back to the wilderness of the mountain, and my grandfather's wife is complaining that she needs to go back to the house to put on makeup before she goes to the service in the church in Hendersonville.

Leo and I are talking, and he is shaking his head as I am telling him this story, just as I have shaken my head when I lived it.

This is how *bilagáanas* use their mountains.

Of course, how the *bilagáanas* use their mountains has nothing to do with cancer or wars in Pakistan or the Cherokee who were cleared out of the Blue Ridge Mountains so a ridge could be renamed Pretty Place or how *Dook'o'oosłiid* is now called Mount Humphreys after a Pennsylvanian general in the Civil War who never saw the mountain or how sons are still fed to lions or how prophets still seek mountains even though they are sometimes tortured to death on them.

Of course, none of that.

Leo and I are walking, and I am carrying our water in a day pack. We are walking up into the sky. The trees are growing thin, and the air is growing thin. Our lungs are growing tired, and our legs are growing old. When we reach the first summit, we have become fifty-year-old men. We may as well be balding prophets bent by the slope and gravity of the mountain.

The trees are gone now. A *bilagáana* scientist from Harvard University named Clinton Hart Merriam walked out here in 1889, a year after he helped found the National Geographic Society. Merriam traveled from the bottom of *Tsékooh Hatsoh* (Grand Canyon) to the top of *Dook'o'oosłiid*. He described six worlds of plants that lived at different altitudes and how certain plants lived in certain bands of life between the earth and the rain and the sun.

Leo and I pass through the subalpine conifer forest and emerge into the alpine tundra world. We might as well be walking in Alaska. Our feet slip in the cinders and pumice and basalt of the ancient volcano. If I had walked this ridge a million years ago, I would have stepped toward the stratosphere to reach the top of the cone of the fire-venting mountain. Of course, the heat and fumes from lava would have incinerated my skin and lungs, and my ashes would have mixed with the other ashes that blew into the air when the mountain cried out into the sky. The chant of ash and nitrogen and phosphorous and calcium and iron wafted over a thousand miles of desert basin and blessed the skin of *Nahasdzáán* (Mother Earth) with black death and mulched the soil.

The Anasazi came and pushed their digging sticks down into the earth and planted their three sisters of corn and beans and squash. They built up villages on the plains around Walnut Canyon and Wupatki. They had children, and their children had children. They moved south when the fertility in the ground gave out and the rains traveled away. Their children fought the Spanish and were taken into slavery. In the bravery of their ignorance, they never knew they might be doomed. And neither do we.

We approach the top. We are seeing into the distance. I am using my binoculars, and I am naming the cars in the parking lot of the coal-burning power plant in Joseph City. It would probably take us four days to walk there.

A warbler flies past, and its feathers are yellow, and Leo's bracelet is yellow, and we are trying to LIVE STRONG.

The warbler lands on a black basalt boulder. Growing around the boulder and growing in the pumice rubble are small herbs with thick green and purple stems cobwebbed with white fuzz. This is a type of groundsel. I know its *bilagáana* name is *Packera franciscana*, and it grows between the largest peaks of Shining Clouds on Top. It grows nowhere else in this Glittering World.

The Diné call it *azee'háátdzid*. It is a medicine plant that you boil, and it brings a strong voice when one sings and chants to the Great Ones. Its flowers are blooming in every space between the dark rocks of the peaks of the sacred mountain of the West. And those flowers are yellow.

Leo and I are talking less, and there is no more mountain. There is only blue sky and white clouds. And I am walking with my brother Glen, and we are on the mountain, and we are talking. I am telling him the story of when I buried three cedar poles in front of our house in Church Wells ten years ago. This was a week after Papa Don was in the water. I strung old hay twine between two of the poles and planted grapes. The vines sprung up from being watered every morning before the sun walked up from the east and broke over *Naats'iis'áán*. Glen climbed the third, untied pole with his bare feet and hands.

Glen is not even as tall as my hip, and his hair is dark and long to the bottom of his red-and-gray-striped Winnie the Pooh polo shirt. He is squeezing his lips together and squeaking, like I have taught him. I have told him that is the sound bats make, and he has loved bats since he could speak. Nolan, my stepdad, taught him the word for "bat," *jaa'abaní*, and it is sunset, *'e'e'aah*, Yellow Evening Twilight. Two bats fly out of the purpling sky and chirp past Glen on the pole and two more and two more. Now eight are flying around him, and my mom is laughing. Glen is still squeaking.

I walk out to him and touch his thin shoulder. And the *jaa'abaní* fly past, and I feel their wings tap my neck and flick my hair. Glen and I are standing by the pole, and I understand why bats have their name, because their wings are so soft and in English *jaa'abaní* means "The Ones with Ears as Soft as Buckskin."

Glen and I are talking. And we are ranging up the mountain. He doesn't wear a yellow bracelet, but I know everything in him tells him to LIVE STRONG. His body speaks *iiná* (life) and he is clinging to that pole and the bats are flicking his dark hair and he's not going to let go and he's not going to fall.

And Glen and I are talking and we are walking up *Dook'o'oosłiid* and clouds are shining overhead. *Jóhonaa'éí* stands at the center and his crystal shield makes the Glittering World shimmer. Glen and I are ranging up through the different plant worlds, traveling more than two miles into the sky and walking into the alpine tundra.

The *tsídiiltsooí* (yellow warblers) dart across the dark rocks. The yellow flowers of *azee'háátdzid* (groundsel) tell us the wind is blowing west. Glen and I are talking about the forest fire that scorched the north side of the mountain and the Supreme Court battle between Native tribes hoping to keep this sacred mountain from being defiled for profit and the ski resort profiteers who want to blanket parts of the mountain with artificial snow made from reclaimed wastewater, the brew that government standards won't allow Glen or Leo or Lyle Parsons or me to drink.

But they are asking us to drink it. And we will drink it. And so we are doomed.

Glen and I are talking and Leo and I are talking. We are approaching the summit. There is blue sky and shining clouds on top. I chant my running song to myself, and I run to the summit with Leo. And I run to the summit with Glen, and I am singing as I always sing when I run:

Biih tsékooh yii'déé' ch'íníjéégi ateego k'e deeshwod.
Jádí halgai yii'déé' ch'íníjéégi ateego k'e deeshwod.
Náshdóítsoh dah 'azká góyaa yiidéé' ch'íníjéégi ateego k'e deeshwod.
Mai'tsoh ndíshchíítah yiidéé' ch'íníjéégi ateego k'e deeshwod.
Shash dzil bilahtah'déé góyaa yiidéé' ch'íníjéégi ateego k'e deeshwod.
Hózhǫ́ nahasdlįį.
Hózhǫ́ nahasdlįį.
Hózhǫ́ nahasdlįį.
Hózhǫ́ nahasdlįį.

Even the groundsel has abandoned the soil. We can live only in certain bands of harmonious places. Leo and Glen are behind me and then in front of me. We can live only in certain bands of harmonious people. There are some places we shouldn't walk unless we've prepared ourselves.

Leo and I are talking and we are at a cairn of pumice and basalt. We are on a peak where there is no more mountain. A pine bench gleams with lacquer on the black stone. Some *bilagáana* asshole has carried it up with him and put the bench on this sacred place.

I swear about this and Leo hears me. I say that if a *bilagáana* wanted to try and claim this peak then he should just piss on the rocks like the ski resort profiteers in the valley below. At least the rains and the snows could come and wash it off. I read a name burned into the backrest of the bench: "Aldo Leopold." When Glen sees the bench, he also swears. I no longer swear.

I explain to him that Aldo Leopold was one of the first forest rangers. He came to New Mexico to shoot wolves for ranchers and sheepherders. But he soon rebelled against his superiors. He wrote that *ma'ii tsoh* had a sacred place on the land. The wolf had a sacred green fire in its eyes.

Leopold wrote a book that was published a year after he died called *A Sand County Almanac*. He wrote that a "thing is right when it tends to preserve the integrity, stability, and beauty of the biotic community. It is wrong when it tends otherwise." And those words to me are the color of *tádídíín* (corn pollen) and guide toward *są'ah naagháí bike'hózhǫ́* and it is the color of wolves' eyes. He wrote that killing a wolf changes the land more seriously than killing a man. That essay is called "Thinking Like a Mountain."

Leo, Glen, and I are on the mountain and we cannot help thinking like the mountain. We now have the eyes of birds and see distances of hundreds of miles. We sit and eat apples, carrots, peanuts, and oats and drink water. We look out over *Diné Bikéyah*, seeing out past *Tsézhin Dilkǫǫh* (Smooth Lava Rock) and *Baa'oogeedí* (Where It Was Dug Into). We look toward the mesas of the Hopi and the land bending into the Little Colorado River. The sandstone lightning streak of *Tsékooh Hatsoh* (Grand Canyon) runs East and West. The Colorado Plateau steps up north and east into the dark shoulders of the Defiance Summit, toward Ganado, *Lók'aahnteel* (The Place of Wide Reeds).

To the North, a dark shape faded by blue air is only as tall as the edge of my thumbnail. But its power and shape stand real as obsidian under the sun. It is *Naats'iis'áán*, the Head of the Woman Strong as Pollen. Or it is the head of the war god. Now I am on the mountain, and now I am also in Coyote Canyon and I might as well be sixteen and I'm under *nááts'íílid*, the

rainbow. I am walking through the rainbow, and the *Diyin Diné* are flying through the sky. Leo and Glen and I are in the sky. We are in the same space but we are not in the same time.

I know that when I am standing here with Glen that *Jóhonaa'éí* has walked across the sky more than 730 times since I last stood here with Leo, just as I know that as I stand here with Glen that Leo is also with me. Mountains bend time just as they bend gravity. Time on the mountain is not the same as time in the doctor's waiting room or in the shopping mall. Leo and Glen and I are together. We are looking out over *Diné Bikéyah* as though we've stepped onto that *diyin atiin'* of the rainbow-road.

I turn to Glen. "This is your inheritance." My hand passes across the land in front of us.

"Huh?" he says.

"This is the land of your people. *Diné Bikéyah.* You are tied to this place. You have rainbows at your elbows and your arms and your center. You have a feather at the whorl at the top of your head. That's where the Holy People, the Great Ones, blew your spirit, your life. You are at the border of that place right now."

Glen tells me I'm weird.

I tell him to get used to living on borders.

We are coming down the mountain. We are running through the pumice and the basalt and the cinders. The groundsel is yellow around us and Leo's bracelet is dangling from his wrist and telling him to LIVE STRONG. Glen is behind me. This is a kid who can run at walls and backflip off of them. He can handspring into backflips. He is on the cedar pole and the bats are flying around us and tapping my white skin and his brown skin with their buckskin-soft wings. This skin was made by the same womb.

We are letting the slope and the gravity of the mountain pull us back to the earth like a rope around our waists.

The sun is dropping into the West, and the light is turning yellow. Now I am in my memory. I am on the phone and Lyle Parsons is telling me that his skin is turning yellow. The white in his eyes has turned yellow. He is explaining to me that his gallbladder has become blocked. His bilirubin that travels from his liver through his intestines with the gravity of his body has become blocked by *'ats'íís naałdzid.* That is the Diné word for cancer. It means "The Sore That Does Not Heal."

It is in Lyle Parsons's pancreas. That is the organ that creates the insulin that keeps in balance and harmony the glucose—the sugar of life—that

makes us move, that makes us have *iiná*, that makes us LIVE STRONG. The color of that organ is yellow.

And now Lyle is walking the wilderness of Cancer. His children have seen their mother walk it. They had to see her cut away her female parts to survive. And now Lyle will have to walk that wilderness, and his children will have to watch. His wife will have to watch, and there is nothing of the pancreas that can be cut away so that Lyle can continue to walk in this Glittering World as *Nohokaa' Diné* and teach his son to play drums and guitar in that office with the drum set that he bought with the money he saved when he quit flooding beer and tequila and pot into his liver and his pancreas every night.

The wolves are watching from Lyle's bookshelf, and their eyes are rimmed with yellow.

Before we hang up, Lyle Parsons says he is reading a book with his oldest son and his son loves this book. It is about a boy ranging through a river and ranging through himself. It is titled *Adventures of Huckleberry Finn*.

But all of this is memory. Glen and I are walking through *ch'ó deenínii* (fir trees) and *ch'ósh gai* (white spruce) and then *t'iisbái* (aspens) and *chéch'il bika'í* (scrub oak). I am whispering my running song again as we walk through the ferns at the bottom of the mountain. I am walking with Leo and I am walking with Glen and I am trying to walk in Beauty. I am thinking of Lyle Parsons. I am singing:

As the deer runs out of the canyon, my feet are running.
As the pronghorn runs on the grasses, my feet are running.
As the mountain lion runs off the mesa, my feet are running.
As the wolf runs out of the pines, my feet are running.
As the bear runs down the mountain, my feet are running.
It is finished in Beauty.
It is finished in Beauty.
It is finished in Beauty.
It is finished in Beauty.

I am walking through the field with Glen and the grass touches our legs as softly as bat wings and *Jóhonaa'éi* is walking to the West.

Photographers call this time of day "the golden hour." It is a one-hour window between late afternoon and sunset, a thin band of time and light when canyons seem deeper and mountains seem taller. The wilderness

seems wilder, and bats fly around poles. It is Evening Twilight, when the sky is yellow.

Mountains are places of *hasbídí* (doves), *dólii* (bluebirds), *tsídiiltsooí* (yellow warblers), and *chagii* (blackbirds). They are places where the *Diyin Diné* (Great Ones) drove their power into the earth with knives of white shell, turquoise, and obsidian and blessed them with abalone shells. They are homes to bear and to elk. Medicines grow there. Water flows there.

And water is life. *Tó éí 'iiná até.*

The Navajo word for strength is *dził.*

The Navajo word for mountain is *dził.*

Bits'áádóó nihidzil dooleel. Every day you can grow stronger. Every day you can be on the mountain.

But first you must go to the mountain. You must accept the mountain. You have to say *yes* to the mountain.

And if you see me sitting in a chair somewhere, and my eyes look distant, and you call my name, and I don't answer, you know where I am.

WE KNOW HOW TO STAY BLOOD

Anyone from the Rez who's seen the Disney apology movie *Pocahontas* knows the song lyric that repeats this old wisdom: You can't step in the same river twice.

I once sat in a writers' coffeehouse session. During a break, an Anglo man introduced himself as a poet and philosopher. He claimed to be descended from the Mohawk tribes in the Northeast. We started talking about how the Mohawk had navigated the rivers in the region. Our conversation turned to the Delaware River in Bucks County, Pennsylvania, where I was living at the time.

"What is the river?" he asked.

"The river?" I said. "Which one?"

"Well, when I say 'river,' you think of one thing, and I think of another."

"Yeah, because we're different people and we have different stories."

"But what is *the river*?"

"I guess there is no 'the river,'" I said, "in the way that there is no 'the human being.'"

He crossed his arms and sat back and shook his head. He was expecting a different answer.

What do I tell a guy like this? The river is where *Nahasdzáán* (Mother Earth) moves her body so that the water given by *Yah Dilhil* (Father Sky) and *Tó Neinilí* (Water Sprinkler) can meander and twist. And *Nahasdzáán* slows the water and pushes it beneath her skin and into the soil, and it feeds the plants, and the plants feed the animals, and the animals sometimes

feed us. The river is a place where *tabaah ma'ii* puts his five-fingered tracks down at night and searches for crawdads. The river is a place where *tsétah dibé* drinks before climbing back into the ridges of the canyon. It's a place where *táłtł'ááh álééh* hunts for *ch'al* (Frog) and *łóó* (Fish), as he did in the First World, and where sacred life is remembered.

The old Anglo man shook his head. "So. What is *the river*?"

"I'm sure you've got your answer."

"It's not *my* answer," he said. "It's *the* answer."

"So what is *the river*?" I asked.

"When you say 'river' and I say 'river,' we are in two different places," he said. "*The river* is our stories. It's how we understand the river. The river is *language*."

"Do you mean that we're *creating* the river when we talk about it?"

"Exactly," he said, unfolding his arms as though relieved. He caressed the manicured silver shrub of his goatee.

"So if I'm not at *the river* and the heron is, then the river ceases to flow?" I asked.

"It flows for the heron, and the river to him is something different from you and I," he said.

"I agree. But you're saying that the river is my stories of the river?"

"The spirit is our stories. We *make* the spirit."

Bullshit, I thought. The world does not start and end with us. It was made by the shadows of our forgotten ancestors long ago. The Great Ones make the spirit. Even if you don't believe that we were once *Niłch'i Diné*, modern science still understands that life in the oceans created the oxygen we breathe now and that we are the inheritors of a blue sky and flowing water given to us by the blue-green algae that grew up from the waters along the edges of the land, that First World of long ago. And our ancestors didn't want to stay there. They wanted to emerge. They were restless. Some might call this 'evolving.'

"That's interesting," I said.

I asked him about his writing. He told me he was a poet. Then he gave me a business card that said he was. I don't remember the business card making it home with me.

The old man was right about stories. They are a present reality. This encounter with the old man happened nearly two years ago, but as I wrote this and as you read it, it happened in this moment.

Stories do create our reality. But many things in this Glittering World

keep on shining with or without our eyes to see them. And those things often give our stories to us. We are—once again—inheritors. And we are inheritors—oh, thank the *Diyin Diné*—of rivers.

Rivers refuse time. They reveal time when they carve into ancient layers of earth. They create our perspective of time. I grew up seeing those ancient layers in the Grand Staircase. In the Grand Canyon. In Glen Canyon. And I go back to those places. If I were an animal, a biologist would say I *migrate* to them.

We are in the river today, this summer that I have returned to Navajo country. Leo, Glen, and Yanabah are with me, all in the same space and time.

Leo and I had traveled back to *Diné Bikéyah* together. We drove north in my same green Honda Civic, and we celebrated the car's 200,000-mile birthday as we drove toward the Black Hills of South Dakota. We stopped at a "Sioux Indian village" the National Park Service had set up at the base of the trailhead to Mount Rushmore. A ranger stumbled and mumbled through a speech on how the Sioux had used all the different parts of the buffalo. The rangers had set up a tipi. They had turtle shell rattles on display. The kids picked up buffalo skulls and held them up for their parents to take pictures.

And then everybody walked up the trail to see the sixty-foot sculpted faces of American presidents in a granite mountain the Sioux called the Six Grandfathers in their sacred Black Hills, *Pahá Sápa*. The local elected officials named the five-thousand-foot mountain after a New York attorney, Charles Rushmore, who came out to bind up their legal borders, fence lines, and deeds and would often walk out to the mountain to shoot the animals who lived there. They named the mountain for him "just for the hell of it."

The name for the ridge before Rushmore came out to hunt there was Slaughterhouse Rock because it was a place where the locals could go out and shoot as many bighorn sheep and elk as they wanted. These people believed they were creating a better world for their children.

When you walk into the Mount Rushmore monument, there's something you should know: You will walk up the stairs from the parking garages carved into the mountain. You will pass hollyhocks and sphinx moths and hummingbirds, and you will notice the land is beautiful. The worn granite and the ponderosa pines seem to dance together. These pines gave the Black Hills their name: when you see them from a distance on the grass plains below, the hills are thick and dark with trees.

You will then walk up a colonnade with all the state flags and their dates

of admission to the Union carved in relief into the granite columns. These columns will focus your attention directly on the faces of the United States presidents. The many American tourists and foreign visitors to the monument seem happy with this arrangement. Some might call it "patriotism." Some might call it "propaganda." Take your pick.

But I hope—as you are driving up to the monument—that you noticed the faces of those presidents from a distance. Here. Hold your forearm out in front of you. The distance from your elbow to your wrist is the ridgeline running to Mount Rushmore. And then look at your thumb. Then at the nail of your thumb. That is the size of the carved president's faces in comparison to that ridge of the Six Grandfathers.

America's history is small indeed when written on *Pahá Sápa*, the place where the Mountains Emerge into the Sky. It is a creation place. An emergence place, where Inktomi, the spider, led the first man, Tokahe, and the first people out of the Earth Mother to hunt buffalo and to raise their children on the grass and under the sky.

This information is inlaid in no granite plaque in the monument that I could find. But I told the story to Leo as we followed the slope of gravity out of *Pahá Sápa* and down toward Edgemont, South Dakota, where the green cottonwoods shimmered over the Cheyenne River. We coasted south on the highways through Wyoming and on to Page, Arizona.

I had returned to Arizona that summer to take up an eight-week assignment with the National Park Service. Because I was a teacher from autumn to spring, I would be working with the middle school in Ganado to create lessons that would teach students about their local history, the stories of the Hubbell Trading Post, of Ganado Mission, and of *Lók'aahnteel*—The Place of the Wide Reeds.

But first, Yanabah and Glen and Leo and I were going to the river.

Yanabah and Glen borrowed my mom's Dodge Ram to haul the two rented kayaks and the aluminum Grumman canoe. We took Highway 89 south, where Echo Peak reached its eighteen-hundred-foot slope into the cloudless blue sky as we passed through The Cut, a massive man-dug breach through a sloped mesa of Navajo sandstone, and drove down the 8-percent-grade hill along the mesa toward the turnoff at Bitter Springs that took us into Marble Canyon.

We pulled into the launch ramp and unloaded the kayaks and then the canoe, letting them half float in the river. I'd made sure we'd gotten to Lee's Ferry with a half hour to kill before the rafts from the morning tours arrived

at the dock. One of them would haul us upriver and leave us at the small eddied beach at Monk Rock.

As I was strapping down the cooler and tying the water jug to the rear of the canoe to chill in the cold water while we floated with the current, I noticed the paddle.

Crap. I could hear the long-ago voice of Dr. Charles Gorman, my old scoutmaster, saying, "Be Prepared."

The woman who rented us the kayaks was supposed to give us these paddles that would snap together in the middle with a female and male end. Turned out she gave us two females, and they no-snappy.

Glen noticed my body language from shore. "What's wrong?"

I held up the two paddles and tapped their ends. Glen started laughing. "Oh, crap! What do we do now?"

"Just go break off a bunch of thick tamarisk branches. Make them as thick as your fingers at least."

So we packed the hollow shafts of the paddles with tamarisk branches. Then I grabbed some duct tape from my rucksack and bound the shafts together. *Badda-bing.* A Rez-rigged paddle. It would work the rest of the day.

A husky twenty-something guide pulled up to the dock, unloaded his peeps, and waved us aboard. Leo and I hauled the canoe over one raft. Yanabah and Glen lifted their kayaks up to the other. I threw my rucksack in the canoe, and Yanabah and Glen tossed their gear into the center of the raft.

I gave the guide the thumbs-up. "Good to go when you are, boss."

"Wow," he said. "You guys pack fast."

"And light." I smiled.

We motored out of the wakeless zone and throttled upriver into the corridor toward Echo Peak and Falls Canyon. I remembered that corridor well. I could see Papa Don's boat flying back, spinning like a coin on its edge, and then slamming into the water.

We motored past Falls Canyon, then Waterholes Canyon. Then into the bend before Two-Mile. Then up Two-Mile.

"How many years is this for you, guiding down here?" I yelled to the guide over the wind and the Honda engine.

"First," he said. "There's nothing like it. Nothing! I'm supposed to go back to college at Southern Utah University this fall, but I might just stay here and work through the winter. Try and get in with the downriver guys, then try and do float and downriver next season."

"Nice," I said. "Gotta love what you do. Life is short for a reason."

I pointed up to the edge of the canyon once we were halfway into Two-Mile. A streak of desert varnish shone against the wall, iridescent as a crow feather. "Beautiful waterfall path! *Tsédahiilínígíí ayóó' nizhon'íí!*"

"Yeah, a lot of the other guys tell me they once saw that waterfall dropping more than a thousand feet! They said this whole stretch in Two-Mile Draw here was just full of waterfalls after this crazy summer monsoon blew through here. And the whole river ran red that day. Damn, I wish I could have seen that!"

"The whole day?" I grinned. "Far out, man."

On the Honda engine hummed. Merganser Cove. Lunch beach. Horseshoe Bend. Up to Ferry Swale camping beach, upriver to the miners' steps next to the gravel bar that had claimed many a propeller, and we drew into the soft-sand eddy of Monk Rock.

"Hey," Glen said, pointing up to the formation of Monk Rock, which really looks like a hooded monk bent over and walking to the south. "It's the Jedi."

I laughed and tipped the guide and wished him safe travels.

We got into the boats and moved with the current. I told Yanabah and Glen how to find the channel, and they paddled forward.

"On a small, narrow channel in the river, you're going to see me put the canoe onto the shore," I said. "I'll slap the water with my paddle before I do. Then pull into the shore with me."

We moved down the current, and Leo asked about the massive arches he saw in the canyon walls that almost seemed chiseled into the sides.

"Those are spalling arches," I said.

"Spalling?"

"Yeah, water gets into the rocks from rain, or it seeps in through the rock. Then, when the winter comes, the water freezes. The ice expands. It cracks the rock. Some of those arches are more than thirty feet deep. The water had its way with the rock, and gravity took care of the rest. Water and gravity, man. It's moving the rock, and it's moving our blood. Veins in the rock and veins in our arms. *Tó éí 'iiná até.* Water is life. Massive changes from small moves. The way of the world."

Leo shook his head as the current took us south and the thousand-foot sandstone wall, exposed by water and gravity, towered past us. "Amazing."

About a half hour later, I slapped the water, and we pulled the boats to the side of the canyon. We hauled them out of the current and tied off to some tamarisks. We checked the straps on our sandals. I threw some water and food into my rucksack, and Yanabah and Glen did the same. It would

be a six-mile walk toward the smooth sandstone of the canyon wall to see the petroglyph panel.

The panel that I'd interpreted in Glen Canyon at least five hundred times is sometimes called the Descending Sheep Panel. It bears rock art dating from a thousand years ago. The panel depicts stairs leading out of the canyon, probably passing on knowledge to the other Anasazi hunters and farmers of how to leave the place. A hunter stands before a herd of three desert bighorn, clearly marked as a ram, a ewe, and a kid. Many guides interpret this as a hunting lesson, teaching to take only the older rams when hunting so that the young ewes will keep the herds healthy. A line of five descending sheep moves across the panel below what is probably a clan symbol of two bighorn sheepheads spinning around a central circle. Across its bottom edge, seven pronghorn move along the sand in a straight march so precise that you can imagine the artists snapping a line to mark where the pronghorns' backs would line up.

In the upper-right-hand corner of the panel is a symbol that looks like a *W* from our alphabet. This symbol is a mystery. I would sometimes speculate that this might be an ancient star constellation the terrace farmers marked while they were living in the canyon, since when you are in that terrace in the summer, you are facing perfectly south and looking up at the wide *W* of Cassiopeia in the night sky. The Diné name for this symbol today is *Náhookos Biʼáadii* (Whirling Woman, who spins around the central home fire of the North Star with Whirling Man on the opposite side of her).

If I wanted to figure out what kind of peeps I had for the day, I would tell them that the *W* was a symbol of ancient Anasazi prophecy foretelling the coming of President George W. Bush, the greatest leader this country had seen since George Washington.

Some peeps grew looks of disgust. I tended to talk with them the rest of the day.

The National Park Service marks petroglyph sites as class 1, class 2, and class 3. Class 1 sites are in areas where they are safe from erosion and easy to walk to. The Park Service feels that the public should be able to see these petroglyphs at any time, and the rangers use them to educate the public about the Anasazi civilization. Class 2 sites have more eroded petroglyphs that face into the wind and are harder to walk to. Park rangers generally keep these a secret from people, but they will let certain hikers and casual campers know about them if they seem trustworthy. Class 3 sites are exposed to erosion weather and face possible destruction over time.

Rangers are explicitly ordered not to tell anyone about these petroglyphs, for their protection.

The Descending Sheep Panel is a class 1 site. It is good to have these sites open to the peeps of the world. But there are costs.*

The petroglyph panel where I was taking Yanabah and Glen and Leo was a class 3 site.

We wandered through a tight arroyo and past rocks cobwebbed with black widow nests. *Ch'óhojilyééh* (sacred datura bushes) threw their dark leaves to the sun and opened their white flowers to the sky. They say eating small pieces of the datura leaf is like taking peyote. And the stuff grows everywhere, immune to the grazing cattle of the *bilagáana* colonizers. In the older days, people would use it in ceremonies for visions that would help them find stolen objects or locate thieves. My mom told me stories of people who had eaten it coming into the emergency room in Ganado and Chinle. The old Diné saying about *ch'óhojilyééh* (which means "One That Makes You Crazy" in English) is that you eat a little and then you sleep a little; if you eat a lot, you never wake up. In the ER, they would have to pump people's stomachs to keep them from dying.

We walked past stunted box elders in a bend of the arroyo. A buzz of flies and the smell of death told me something was ahead. A gray fox lay on his side against a rock, half of his body eaten. His teeth stretched in a rictus laugh at the cosmic mystery of death. During his life, he had hunted prairie dogs, rabbits, and mice along the canyon. He would even have chased ground squirrels into trees and climbed nimbly to eat them.

Now something had hunted him and had been fed. Fair trade.

I scattered sand over his head in an improvised burial. We walked to the canyon wall. At the end of the three miles, we found the petroglyph panel.

Massive torsos of *yei* gods exposed their chests to the Colorado River

* In 2010, an Anglo fisherman from North Carolina named Trent Ganey carved his name into this petroglyph panel. One of the river guides noticed and radioed the Park Service. The rangers sped down the river in their chase boat and asked different fishing parties if they knew anybody named Trent. After they found him, Trent Ganey said he'd carved his name into the wall because he didn't think there was anything wrong with doing it. And he thought it would be "cool." Once he was told of the history of the panel and the magnitude of what he had done, he apologized immediately and pleaded guilty. Trent was fined $10,000. It cost more than $9,000 to fix the damage. (See Cyndy Cole, "What's in a Name? Vandal Learns the Hard Way," *Arizona Daily Sun*, 26 January 2011.)

below. Their striped bodies and horned heads seemed positioned to defy any intruders to the canyons. But between these deities, I could see why this was a class 3 site. The sheering winds had scooped sand and small pebbles up against the rock face and left bullet-sized pockmarks against the gods' faces and arms. Carefully chipped bighorn sheep stood poised on stiff legs, thin horns curving back into their rectangular bodies striped with the same patterns I'd seen at the Descending Sheep Panel miles upriver.

On that panel, a clan symbol of the two bighorn heads whirls in a cycle that would never end. Prey and hunter. Sheep and Anasazi. Birth and death. Day and night. Water and gravity.

Despite the opinions of the self-proclaimed poets in the coffeehouses of the world, none of these forces needed me to tell stories about them in order for them to *be*. They didn't need my story. I was *their* story. They were creating it, and I was able to participate in it. It is all quiet and certain. The wind scrapes away the traces of the petroglyphs and blows me the air that fills my lungs and gives me life.

"Wow," Glen said. "Those *tsétah dibé* are as big as us."

"They might be bigger," I said. "And they've been walking these canyons just as long as the Anasazi who came in here probably eight hundred years ago. And those descendants of the Anasazi drove out the Spanish in 1680. When the Spanish came back, some of those Puebloan descendants ran into the mountains. That's when they met your ancestors—the Diné. And they didn't enslave each other. They didn't fight each other. They learned from each other. They made a harmony. They taught each other. The Diné learned to weave. They learned about sheep. They learned about corn. They married each other. Made children with each other. You probably come from one of those children. Who knows how far back the source of the river really goes. But those *tsétah dibé* were sacred animals. They fed your ancestors. You remember them at the sacred mountain of the North, *Dibé Ntsaa*. That's a place of winter, of obsidian stone, of bighorn sheep, that teaches *Sihasin* (reverence). They say that is also a place of the *Hajíínái*, the Emergence Hole that the First People used when they came into this Glittering World."

"Uh, Jim," Glen said. "You're weird."

We laughed, and the canyon walls echoed down to the turquoise snake of the Colorado River.

Then Yanabah stopped laughing and turned to her left. "Oh, wow," she whispered. "Look."

We turned from the bighorn sheep petroglyphs and saw them.

A herd of nine *tsétah dibé* clustered together on a slope of the canyon wall. Four ewes grazed the wisps of summer grass, while two young rams moved along the edges of the rocks. Two skinny kids played and ran back and forth with each other up and down the slopes. A tall ram with crescent horns curving back over his head craned his dark brown neck toward us and picked up our scent.

The ewes raised their necks and watched us. Their eyes were the color of yellow evening twilight. Their flat pupils shined dark as obsidian.

"That's a family," I said quietly.

The bighorn sheep stood in lines of carved stone and shining black desert varnish. The herd walked together against a far canyon wall. The kids chased each other up the slope and jumped between the rocks.

I wondered if that herd's ancestors were etched into this petroglyph. They were still here. Their ancestors had learned the river's story long ago, and they chanted along with it, season after season, to survive in a beautiful harmony. Tough Noodles.

I touched Yanabah and Glen's shoulders. "They're still here," I said. "Love kept them here."

"Jim . . . once again . . . *weird*," Yanabah said and laughed.

"You know what I mean." I smiled and stalked forward quietly to see how close the ram would let us get to the herd. The ram allowed us within twenty feet, then huffed, and the herd turned their white butts to us and sprang a couple yards away to graze.

When we got back to the shore, we snapped into some apples, ate some granola bars, and drank water until our bellies felt heavy. Then we pissed into the sand.

"Check your streams," I said. "Make sure you pee clear."

"You're *weird*, Jim!" Yanabah yelled, squatting behind a willow.

We climbed back into the boats. We paddled into the current. We passed through sun and shade. We stopped at lunch beach. We stood next to the century plant. We paddled under the thousand-foot cliffs and watched the yellow evening twilight burn the black desert varnish into sheens of green and blue. We stopped to hike into Waterholes Canyon. We rowed hard into the final corridor at Echo Peak, and the wind roared and threw forty-degree spray into our faces that stung like cold metal. Yanabah and Glen paced through the wind in their kayaks. But the wind turned the aluminum Grumman canoe like it was a rudder. Leo and I wore out our shoulders just keeping the canoe straight and moving. We stayed in shallow water as

we pulled the canoe through the wind. The memory of Papa Don flashed with each paddle stroke.

"Shit, Jimmy," he'd said, laughing. "Thanks for saving my life."

I had to laugh too as the freezing spray stung my chest, face, and neck. My teeth chattered in the hundred-degree heat. I didn't know how to tell a story like this. The river was telling it for me, with no problems of translation.

Once we cleared the corridor, Yanabah and Glen paddled ahead. The river took on a wavy calm. *Jóhonaa'éí* walked down out of the clouds and threw light across the water. Yanabah and Glen paddled ahead in silhouette. The yellow evening light flooded the world around them. The water under them sparkled like crystal.

They're moving ahead of me, I thought, paddling with Leo.

I realized that if the world held enough merciful coincidences, this would always happen. Yanabah and Glen would move ahead of me into a world I would never see. They would outlive me and emerge into a world I would never know. And I wanted it that way.

But the river would know. The river would carve it. The flow of water had already carved so much for me and Yanabah and Glen. We had all emerged from the same water. The same darkness of the same womb. We have no story of our time in that water, that First World. We had no choice of that water. But it gave us the start of our story, our emergence. It was real, whether we knew it or not.

The dock at Lee's Ferry came into view.

"Almost there," Leo huffed, shaking the water out of his hair.

Every river tells us a story. It teaches us that even water and gravity are restless.

We are all being pulled along.

THE HOMECOMING

Leo and I drove out of Page, Arizona, crossed the Black Mesa country, past *Tsiiłchin Bii' Tó* (Oak Springs), Rough Rock, Many Farms, *Tséta', Tséyi'*, and *So' Silá*, to Ganado. *Lók'aahnteel.* The Place of the Wide Reeds.

Home.

The maroon mesas appeared. The tears came with the smell of the sagebrush opening its scent to a gentle *níłtsá bi'ááad* (female rain). There were reasons for this.

"You all right, man?" Leo asked. He touched my shoulder. The yellow bracelet shifted on his arm. LIVE STRONG.

"Yeah," I said, wiping at my face. "Salt from my sweat. In my eyes."

Leo nodded. The gray sagebrush sped along the window. "I hear ya."

I had come back to Ganado that summer of 2012 to work at Hubbell Trading Post as a park ranger. I would also be working with an eighth-grade English class at Ganado Middle School. The local teacher who had partnered with me was the granddaughter of Howard Gorman, the former vice chairman of the Tribal Council and one of the founding forces behind Ganado Mission. If there had been such things as local *naat'áanii* after the Diné moved onto the Reservation and into the twentieth century, Howard Gorman was definitely one of them.

In the two days before my service at the trading post began, I took Leo out to Canyon de Chelly, where my friend Levi Bigwater ran Tó'tson'íí Ranch, a horse-guiding business he started with his dad and his brother, Nathan. Since pulling his truck out of the mud outside Warren Brown's auntie's house after our last Halloween, Levi had graduated from high school and

joined the Marine Corps. While I was in college to become an attorney or a teacher, Levi was learning how to shoot an M-4 and how to throw hand grenades. He had run operations as a staff sergeant on a Marine base off the Horn of Africa.

Not bad for a Tough Noodle from Ganado.

After I'd pulled my Honda down the bumpy dirt road to the ranch and shaken Levi's strong hand, he introduced me to his cousin, Quentin. I hadn't seen Quentin since we were throwing each other to the ground during our pickup football games on the Ganado hospital campus lawns.

We saddled up two mustang geldings Levi had picked up at auction. I rode Chase, a rough pale Appaloosa with a blond mane, and Leo rode Solado, a roan gelding with a white star.

Levi asked if we wanted to wear helmets. I tapped my scuffed straw cowboy hat. Nah. Leo went with the helmet.

We rode out for Three Turkey Canyon. Two black Rez mutts ran ahead.

"Nice dogs," I said to Quentin as we trotted out.

"Yeah, that's Minnie and Diesel," he said. "They're our back-up food supply. If we get stranded out there, we'll just eat them." He smiled and tapped the 9mm pistol holstered at his side.

We rode down the rocky slopes of the canyon, through scrub oak thickets and pools of water green with reeds. Cottonwoods shimmered and rattled like rain falling on rock until we found it: Three Turkey House. Straight-edge masonry rose in half-moon granaries supported by cottonwood vigas, and a two-story house emerged from the slope of the cliff. Along the back wall of the south-facing alcove stood three turkeys as tall as Leo, painted in bright red and white ochre.

Three Turkey was a beautiful structure. But I knew it was an artifact of fear and retreat. The Anasazi who'd colonized these canyons had built their homes high in the air and farmed their corn and beans and squash in a time when the rains had become rare and their priests at Chaco—tripping on niacin-depriving corn gruel and the shimmer of the turquoise that people brought to them in their kivas—had failed them. Community preyed community. If the crops failed, clans would raid each other down the watersheds. They built higher and higher into the canyon walls. They probably built their last structures seven hundred years ago.

After that, they expanded up along the Río Grande until the arrival of the Spanish forever changed their movement. The people called the Hopi innovated their deep-rooted seeds on their mesas.

The Hopis today call them *Hisatsinom*. The people of Taos Pueblo call them *hwee'die*. The Ancestors.

The Diné call them *Anasazi*—the Ancestors of our Enemies.

When I was a kid, I would walk around the washes and canyons of Ganado and find pottery shards from Anasazi groups every time. And I never took them with me. All my elders said those things held *ch'iindii*. *Eeyaa. Dooda.* Don't do that.

They say when the first Diné moved through the country and found those old houses, they saw bones lying on the stone floors and in the kivas. Something about living this way had killed these people. The Diné backed away from the ruins.

Some things carry ghosts.

This is why Diné people bury their dead far away from anyone. They make the ones who do the burying stay away from everyone else for four days. They do not mark the grave. And this is why the grave of even a great man like Ganado Mucho is so hard to find.

When my friends who worked at the trading post invited me to see the grave of Ganado Mucho, I asked what time they were leaving.

We went after our shifts and followed southern dirt roads in a Jeep. We climbed to the top of the hill above Cornfields and pulled to the side. We parked on a flat piece of ground fenced by sagebrush and cactus blooming in pink and yellow.

There it was. The grave.

A granite stone larger than my torso stood on a mortared stone foundation. One face of the stone had been cut and polished like any you might see in a cemetery in Missouri or any other state in the American affair. Two sets of names were etched by a mason's chisel. They described the same man. One read "Totsonii Hastiin" and the other, "Ganado Mucho." These had been etched by a man named Brown, a direct descendant of Ganado Mucho. Behind the marker stood an old wooden shelter that might have once been a *hoghan* or a sweat lodge. This location is believed by many locals to be the final resting place of the chieftain.

The Ganado Lions Club dedicated the marker in October 1972. Charles Griggs, the Lions Club president, was an Anglo man who had married Charlotte Adele Slivers, a Ganado native and the first surgical nursing graduate of the Sage Memorial Hospital School of Nursing in 1930. They had met during the war, while Charlie had been a combat pilot over Europe and Slivers had watched over him in a field hospital. Slivers's father had

been a cook for Juan Lorenzo Hubbell at his trading post, and his family had given over the land where the Presbyterians had built their hospital.

During the dedication of the gravestone, Griggs said that Ganado Mucho was "one of the great men of the Navajo tribe who worked for peace and who worked for fair treatment of his people."

There were no dates of birth and death. I appreciated this. The life of a man like *Tó'tsonii Hastiin*—the Big Water Man (Ganado Mucho)—cannot be buried between any dates.

I walked to the grave and touched the stone. Cold. Nothing there. The Pueblo Colorado Wash snaked to the north in dreams of pale green Russian olives and cottonwoods. That wash eventually found the Little Colorado and then the Grand Canyon. This was the meandering path Ganado Mucho used to save his life and the lives of his people.

During the war with that Rope Thrower, Colonel Christopher "Kit" Carson, and the Americans, Ganado Mucho is one of the last surrendering Navajo headmen. He does not travel with the first 1,443 people who surrender at Fort Wingate in the late winter of 1864. Nor is he with the 3,200 who leave Fort Defiance by the end of March. By July 8th, 5,900 people are confined at Bosque Redondo, next to Fort Sumner. Another 1,000 live in the depot at Fort Defiance. Ganado Mucho is not one of them.

Instead, he walks his band into the valley's sandy wash and follows it all the way south, through Hopi country, to where it drains into the Little Colorado River and then disappears into the rocky labyrinth of the Grand Canyon. He knows the way. He is half Hopi himself.

That year, the crops at Fort Sumner fail. The winter is brutal. The water is alkaline and nearly undrinkable. They start to call the place *Hweeldí*. The word means "Place of Suffering."

Ganado Mucho hears these stories. His slow and rational mind begins to sprint. Winter is coming. A small storm has drifted over the canyons, spinning snowfakes that fall like chips of ice into the secure labyrinth where he and his people have lived for the past two years. Nobody has ever found them. But his sons have surrendered. Friends have taken the long march to Fort Sumner, and so have their families. His large herd of sheep and goats are enough to feed thousands while the Americans decide what to do next. He can save lives, though it might cost his own.

That fall of 1865, he leaves his secret stronghold and surrenders himself and his relatives and his herds at Fort Wingate. Through an interpreter, he requests military escort for the women and children of his band. The

men follow behind with the lifesaving herd of livestock. The American commander agrees.

During the trip to the fort, Ganado Mucho has not yet reached the army's camp near Albuquerque when New Mexicans attack and kidnap his two youngest daughters. American soldiers—some of whom had tried to rape one of his older daughters just days before—search for the lost children. They give up and say they have been sold into slavery in Mexico.

After arriving at Fort Sumner, Ganado Mucho finds his son, Ganado Blanco, and other starving clan members. They are thankful for the sheep and goats, whose meat soon sizzles over their small fires and runs hot into their stomachs. They make it through the winter. The wound of his grief for his lost daughters begins to heal. Then it is torn open that summer when Comanche raiders sweep through Bosque Redondo, steal two hundred horses, and kill his youngest son while he is herding the remaining sheep brought from their homeland. The army is supposed to protect them from Comanches. The army is not there. Ganado Mucho and other men are not allowed to have guns. They fight off the Comanches with bows and arrows and shovels.

That summer, when Superintendent of Indian Affairs A. B. Norton arrives to inspect the Bosque Redondo, Ganado Mucho sits with Norton and explains he has serious promises for the American.

"I have lost one of my sons and I am nearly crazy," he says through the army interpreter. "I feel very bad. How can we protect ourselves when our enemies are much better armed than we are? We want to go back to our own country . . . we want to go back there the same as we are here. The land here will never be as good as our own country. The government does not supply us with wood here, and we had plenty there. If the government would put us on a reservation in our own country and keep us the same as here within boundaries, the government would see how we work. We think we were born to live in our old country . . . we think we were not born to live here."*

Ganado Mucho and his people are allowed to return. He keeps his promises. His people work. But his old country is not included in the new

* This information about Ganado Mucho's life at Bosque Redondo is largely pulled from Raymond Friday Locke's *The Book of the Navajo* (Los Angeles: Mankind Publishing, 1992). It is an enjoyable read that examines both the historical and mythic biography of the Diné people.

88

reservation boundaries. He returns there anyway. The United States government does not bat an eye. They appoint him one of the "head-chiefs" of the Navajos.

Ten years after the Diné have returned from Fort Sumner, the San Juan country in the north becomes safer when Manuelito's Navajo police force begins patrolling its river crossings against Navajo and Ute raiders. But Navajo young men—dishonored by being forced to depend on the American goods of lard and salt beef—still ride against the New Mexicans and their neighbors in the east.

They are not the only angry ones. *Haatałi* (medicine singers) and the younger warriors angry, ambitious, or adventurous enough to strike out at the New Mexicans and Americans set up spy networks all across the country between *Lók'aahnteel* and the Tunicha Mountains in the northeast. This confederacy of scouts and spies casts spells on different families—usually the rich ones—by stealing their victim's hair, spit, manure from a favorite horse, dirt from the victim's shadow, even their feces, and then burying them in a freshly dug pit. In this type of witchcraft, the sorcerer puts the victim into the grave.

Over the next few years, livestock die off. People grow sick with swelling and bleeding sores all over their bodies. American settlers have their livestock stolen. Many settlers are killed. Talk at Fort Wingate and Fort Defiance is of another war between the Navajos and the Americans. Amid these threats and rumors, Ganado Mucho—still considered the head chief of the Navajos—takes action.

The bloodshed starts at Juan Lorenzo Hubbell's doorstep.

Hubbell is gone that day, trading in Navajo City. It is a calm May morning out on *Be'ek'id Halchíí*, the large lake in the area that gives name to the local clan, *Tó'tsonii* (Big Water People). Hubbell's younger brother, Charlie runs the store up at the lake. The season is turning toward full summer. The flocks of Canada geese have returned to the *Be'ek'id Halchíí* and the corn in the trading post's garden has grown high to the elbow when a dozen riders trot over the sagebrush in a long line. Charlie spots the sun reflecting off the riders' polished lance heads and buzzard-feather arrow fletchings. Some of them carry clubs. A couple of Navajo workers at the trading post shift nervously.

The horses scream and show their teeth as the riders run them back and forth in front of the adobe trading post.

Charlie—a small man with wide ears and a thin mustache—probably

doesn't intimidate the riders. He notices how one of the workers, a young man named Hastiin Dejolie, licks his lips and eyes the lead rider as he canters forward. The rider is tall and wears a warrior's cap made with the scalp of a mountain lion. Everyone at the post knows him. He is one of Ganado Mucho's sons—*Hashkehyilnaya*. Charlie knows his name in English: Walks Down in Anger.

The riders yell and point at the adobe building. Charlie can only make out a bit of their broken Spanish as they point at the men who have gathered to the side of the store, where many locals visit and swap gossip.

"Hastiin Dejolie!" they yelled.

A small cabin stands near the trading post. It was built by a former soldier at Fort Sumner named Hardenson, who had taken a Navajo wife and moved onto the reservation to work as a trader. Most people know that Hardenson keeps a rifle.

Dejolie runs straight for Hardenson's cabin.

Half of the riders break off and chase him. Some kick off their horses, pick up rocks, and throw them at the running man. Dejolie raises his arms to defend, but it does little against the men who have now dismounted and fired their bows. He falls bleeding against the front door of the cabin, with at least four arrows in his abdomen.

One of the riders dismounts, winds up his war club, and hits Dejolie in the head so hard that blood sprays up onto the door.

The other riders dismount and pull down two other men. One of them, *Ashkii Dilghili* (Black Boy), they kill with arrows. The other, a young man named Haloishjahn, the riders haul down to the lake's edge. Walks Down in Anger forces his head underwater, demanding to know where he and his conspirators have buried the objects they've been using to curse people.

The geese on the lake flap and honk into the sky while Haloishjahn thrashes in the shallow water.

Once Haloishjahn tells the location of the grave, Walks Down in Anger lifts his war club and stoves his head in.

The riders gather their horses and gallop west. Charlie Hubbell watches them until he sees only their dust rising over the piñon trees.

He later learns the riders are rejoining another hundred warriors under Ganado Mucho, gathered from Klagetoh and Greasewood. They had interrogated a woman near Wood Springs who revealed the names of other witches and their leader, a powerful medicine singer from the canyon country of *Tséyi'* named *Hastiin Biwosi* (Man Shoulders).

The riders string out of *Lók'aahnteel* to the south toward *K'ii'tsoitah* (Where the Rabbit Brush Grows)—modern-day Cornfields. At the middle of the long line rides Ganado Mucho with his sons Walks Down in Anger, *Beshligai'iiłinii* (Silversmith), *Hastiin Yazhi Bibaghaa* (Little Man with Bushy Beard), and *Biłįį Lani* (Many Horses), his most beloved son.

When the riders arrive at *K'ii'tsoitah*, they find a crowd gathered around an *ałchį' adeez'á* (forked-stick hogan). Man Shoulders is inside, about to conduct an Apache Way ceremony. The riders dismount, and Many Horses steps to the front. They call Man Shoulders to come out.

Someone responds from inside the *hoghan*. They ask what the riders want.

Many Horses calls out the names of Hastiin Dejolie and others they've executed for being witches and cursing their neighbors. Now the riders have come for the life of Man Shoulders.

One of Man Shoulders' followers taunts the riders. If they want him, they have to come in and get him. Stepping inside a *hoghan* during a ceremony is something like sacrilege; killing the man conducting the ceremony creates many problems.

The horses stamp their hooves, impatient after the eight-mile run. Their forelegs are still flecked with the maroon mud of the Ganado Valley. In the yellow light of the late day, it looks like dried blood.

A horse blows hard as its rider dismounts. He is Walks Down in Anger. He walks straight for the forked-stick *hoghan*.

"If he will not come out, then I will drag him out!" he says.

Ganado Mucho dismounts. He calls for his son to wait. The seventy-year-old man strides ahead of his son, turns, and stands facing them from the log doorway. He places his hands on either side of the doorposts. His back is at the mercy of the men inside.

The old *naat'áanii* knows most of the men gathered in front of the *hoghan*. He grew up with Man Shoulders, who is still inside. They fought in wars against the Hopis, the New Mexicans, and the Americans. Man Shoulders' relatives hid out with Ganado Mucho near the Grand Canyon. Some traveled on the Long Walk with him. Man Shoulders and Ganado Mucho signed the 1868 treaty that allowed their return to their home country.

Ganado Mucho says they cannot kill Man Shoulders. "He's my relative. My older brother."

Walks Down in Anger backs off and launches into a long speech. It is hard to say what is happening. Perhaps Ganado Mucho actually wants to halt the riders' vengeance out of pity. Perhaps he is performing a piece of

his own political theater—playing the merciful peacemaker in front of his kinsmen so as not to invite their vengeance later.

After his son has finished, Ganado Mucho drops his arms from the doorposts and holds out his hands, as though pleading.

"Go ahead," he says. "Do now what you want with him."

The riders whoop as Many Horses leads them in a gallop around the *hoghan*. He twirls his rawhide lasso. He and the other riders rope the support poles of the *hoghan* and back up their horses, and the building topples. Ashes and smoke wheeze from the collapsed mouth of the doorway like a dying breath. Men crawl their way out of the rubble.

One of the riders recognizes Man Shoulders, draws a bead with his rifle, and shoots him through the leg. Walks Down in Anger wades in among the gasping bodies, grabs Man Shoulders by the hair, and drags him into the clear.

The riders take sandstone rocks from the ground and stone the medicine man until his broken, bloody, unrecognizable body lies hidden under the cairn.

Charlie doesn't see Ganado Mucho until later that day, when the old man and some of his riders appear at the store to warn Hubbell that a war party rides toward the valley from Canyon de Chelly to take revenge for the killing of Man Shoulders and his followers.

Hubbell rides out to meet Man Shoulders' relatives as they enter the valley.

Ganado Mucho is pleased to see Hubbell in the saddle. He has seen the younger man speak like a wise elder when the moment has called for clear words. Navajo custom demands a blood-price of livestock and goods, like the one Hubbell had negotiated with Ganado Mucho at Tuba City just four years before. Hubbell, a reader of Keats and Shakespeare, works the deal while the brown water of the wash trickles between their horses' hooves, slowly washing the maroon mud from their forelegs.

Man Shoulders' relatives turn their horses and ride back to Canyon de Chelly. Some camp along the wash to lead the horses that Ganado Mucho has promised them.

One death has been paid for. But the hunt is still on for the other witches in Man Shoulders' cabal. The killing begins. It gets so bad that word spreads to the army, and the cavalry from Fort Wingate and Fort Defiance shows up three days later.

Lt. Colonel P. T. Swaine, the commanding officer at Fort Wingate, dispatches Lieutenants Mitchell and McGuinnigle with some enlisted men

to protect the American settlers and their property in the region of the Pueblo Colorado Valley. The soldiers, however, are ordered to avoid any active part in the "difficulties" between the Navajos. The current Indian agent, a "solid churchman" from Montana named John Pyle, travels with the soldiers (much against his will) by buckboard wagon.

The cavalry meets briefly around a campfire in the wash with a local *naat'áanii*. While the coffeepot boils on hot rocks laid over the coals, Pyle calls the chieftains foolish for believing the nonsense of witchcraft. Pyle—who believes "the superstitions" of the Navajo are the "great drawback and obstacle of their civilization"—stays the night, but he is home with his interpreter by the afternoon of the next day before clearing out for Santa Fe the following morning. What has started as a suspected clan feud has now become a witch-hunt stretching over a hundred miles. And Pyle—perhaps remembering Indian Agent Miller, who had been shot to death with arrows just five years before—is not sticking around.

But the "superstitions" Pyle refuses to believe are powerful enough to frighten the Navajo war chief, Manuelito. Manuelito—with the trusted interpreter Hubbell translating his words to English—writes to Lt. Colonel Swaine about six men the conspirators have captured north of Fort Defiance, in the area called *Tsé Binááyolí* (Wind Blows Around the Rock). The army calls it the Tunisha Mountains. One of Manuelito's own cousins had been suspected of being one of Man Shoulders' spies. He is now dead. The medicine men who hold the six captives threaten to kill Manuelito later that summer if he interferes with their ceremonies of death. He believes they've already shot a stone into his head that has caused a lump to expand in his throat. If he rides against them, the stone will grow until it chokes him to death.

Manuelito—the warrior chieftain who won fame in his wars against the Hopi, who slipped through American ambushes, who attacked and killed Mexican slavers at will—is bowing out of the fight. The Navajo police riders from his clan won't take to the saddle, either.

So when Lieutenant Mitchell arrives a day later in the Pueblo Colorado Valley from Fort Defiance, he must ask for volunteers to travel into the Tunisha country to free the six captives.

Hubbell saddles up, as do Many Horses and some of Ganado Mucho's band. They ride the sagebrush plains and rabbitbrush flats until they ascend the red-and-white-marbled foothills of the *Ch'ósh'gai* (White Spruce) mountains. When they stamp through the tall ponderosa and juniper into that

northern part of the *Chʼóshʼgai* called *Tó Ntsaa* (Big Water), the horses wet their legs in the cool streams and graze on the green grass after the hot days of riding.

The party soon finds three men against a rock ledge, tied up with rawhide rope. Pines dot the red sand country below. The long-winged *jeeshoh* (vultures) circle in the lazy heat.

Hubbell speaks a spatter of Spanish and Navajo with the men's captors. They say the three men are witches who have been "shooting stones" into people—a practice of *ánt'įįh* (witchcraft) they have learned at Fort Sumner, probably from Apaches. Lieutenant Mitchell is under orders not to get the Americans involved, but now he will break his orders. He doesn't want any more bloodshed, and so he asks that the captives be freed. Hubbell interprets his words, and the Navajo captors refuse.

When Mitchell asks why they are so upset, Hubbell says that if the captors let these witches go, they will just go back to their killing. The next day, Ganado Mucho's scouts bring in more witches they have caught. That same day, Ganado Mucho—who Lieutenant Mitchell commends as the only "great chief" to have the courage to confront the witches—rides into the camp with his hundred horsemen just as the western light turns the pines a glistening gold.

Mitchell watches the riders come up against the ledge. When he hears their sumac and willow arrows clattering inside their buckskin and lionskin quivers and notices the dark red stains on some of their greasewood war clubs, he decides to disobey his orders again.

He fears Ganado Mucho's men have come to execute all the captives. He tells Hubbell to tell Ganado Mucho and his men that if the Navajo continue to kill "like a lot of dogs," the American army will split the tribe like a wedge hammered into a juniper log; then the Utes will come and steal the survivors' horses, cows, and sheep. The Navajo will be "penniless and finally annihilated and the Tribe would become extinct."

Ganado Mucho nods to Hubbell. He agrees to Mitchell's warning.

He likes Lieutenant Mitchell's words so much that when more men arrive the next day, Ganado Mucho asks the lieutenant and Hubbell to deliver the speech again. The aged *naat'áanii* knows these are not hollow threats. And he can use them to stop the killing from erupting into a clan-on-clan civil war.

The next day, he offers guides to lead Lieutenant Mitchell back to Fort Defiance. The following day, when three thousand Navajos show up at Fort

Defiance for rations of meat and corn, Ganado Mucho and his sons request that Mitchell speak his same warning.

Hubbell talks to them in Navajo, and the gathered crowd travels home with full rations. They seem to understand the finality of the thing. Historians will later call the event a "witch-hunt," perhaps remembering the Salem witch trials and similar persecutions in Europe. In Salem, nineteen people were put to the noose. In Navajo country, the killing puts more than forty people under the ground. But then it stops. Settlers stop dying. Fear passes away. Peace is bought and paid in blood.

Ganado Mucho's clan relatives allow Hubbell to trade in a new location, downriver from the lake. He played his part to restore *hózhǫ́*—harmony—to the Pueblo Colorado Valley. Hubbell is allowed to stay. It's partially why people like me are allowed to come here now.[*]

These were stories I had told to Lyle Parsons. And so my friends and I were here at the grave that did not feel like a grave. The rest of my friends idled around the gravestone. Some scanned the sand for signs of the actual traditional grave. Nobody found anything. One of the workers—a nineteen-year-old father who had a work assignment at the trading post—brushed sand from his new Arizona State Sun Devils T-shirt. He was a high school baseball player and said he might be able to get into Prescott's community college to play baseball on a partial scholarship. From there, he could play for Arizona State, get an MLB contract, and find his position in the American affair to provide for his newborn son. He also mentioned that he was descended from Ganado Mucho.

The wind blew warm from the valley of Cornfields. Another American dream.

Stuart Claw's words spoke in my ear. "We are Diné. Navajo. We're the hardest, meanest, toughest people on the planet. But we don't know it anymore."

We climbed back into the Jeep and left Ganado Mucho's grave. I wished I could have stood there with Lyle Parsons. What would he have said? I stared into the patterns in my jeans while the Jeep bumped down the dirt road. People didn't ask me what was wrong. They knew I was quiet for a

[*] This information about Ganado Mucho's role in the witch-hunt comes from Martha Blue, *The Witch Purge of 1878* (Tsaile, AZ: Navajo Community College Press, 1988). It is largely composed of oral histories taken from the Ganado area and archived at the Hubbell Trading Post National Historic Site.

reason. I knew Ganado Mucho had long left his grave. I wondered where he'd gone.

Thunder drummed in the East. The storms followed paths of wind from the Defiance Plateau. They promised rain. That was when I saw it from the Jeep window. In the East, clouds ascended in two great peaks in the sky. The soft angles broke in ridges rough and inevitable to form a white mountain of cloud that spanned most of the eastern sky. It was probably four miles high. It reminded me of where Ganado Mucho might be.

During one of our late-night drives, my stepdad once told me what happened for Diné people when they died. When your body and its muscles are put under the ground, your spirit is all that is left. You must guide your spirit forward with only your will. You will see before you an expanse of desolation. It will shimmer with heat, waterless. It grows no soft plants for *biih* (deer) or long grasses for *jádí* (antelope). But in the distance will stand a tall mountain, black with trees and springs, reaching to the top of the sky.

A meandering path leads to the mountain. You will face many temptations to keep you in the place of desolation. You must will yourself across the expanse. You must not stop. You will be tested to see if you are a coward or if you are brave. You will travel very far.

You will find a way to the forests of the mountain. You follow the meandering path through *azeediilch'ílii* (blue-flowering lupine) and tall grass and then through *chéch'il bika'í* (scrub oak) and *t'iisbái* (aspens) and *ch'ó deenínii* (fir trees) and *ch'ósh gai* (white spruce), and the plants change as though you are emerging into new worlds. Then you will meet your relatives who have gone before you. They will lead you to a camp. Here, they will begin to tell you your story. Of how you arrived at where you are.

To hear more of the story, you must walk up to meet more of your relatives. You keep walking up. Eventually, you will meet relatives who no longer speak your language. You must learn new speaking to hear the story. You keep walking up. You learn more. You hunt. You drink. You take it all in. You understand why you are here.

There are other parts of the story, ones we cannot imagine here. But Ganado Mucho is on the mountain learning them. And he is also teaching them to his relatives who have come after.

This mountain made of clouds reminded me of where the dead walk up to hear their story and live again.

Lightning lit its ridges. Thunder drummed from inside the dark edges.

The sound was a homecoming.

WEARING YOUR ADOBES

I picked up the boy in Kayenta. He would be spending the next four days with me while I was a ranger in Ganado. We drove out to Ganado just as the sun dropping a purple horizon across the black tower of *'Aghaałá* peak.

We crossed the grassy plains between sandstone buttes along the edges of *Dził́íjiin* (Black Mesa) and rolled over the waves of highway between Chinle and Ganado. Lightning flashed overhead. Thunder boomed. Rain spattered the windshield.

"This is a good sign," I said to the boy.

"Whoa! Look!" he said.

The green eyeshine of two mule deer flashed in my headlights. I slowed the Honda and drifted into the other lane to give the *biih* room if they decided to run into the road. I already had a dent in my car from when I had hit a yearling across from the Graeme Park farm in Bucks County at five o'clock in the morning on the way to the high school where I taught.

I had seen the yearling and the doe against the snow, grazing on a small hill. I let my car drift away from them. They dropped their necks and went back to eating. Then a silver BMW came roaring past, going at least eighty miles an hour on the country road. The deer shot their heads up in the BMW's fluorescent blue headlights. They bolted into the road as the BMW sped past.

I angled the car enough to miss the doe. But the yearling hit its head square into my left front fender. I might as well have hit her with a half-ton metal baseball bat.

I pulled to the side of the road. The yearling lay kicking on the icy pave-

ment. Her obsidian eyes drifted in her head, looking for moonlight, feeling for grass, scenting for her mother. Her legs ran through cold air. She was being chased. Death was coming.

I grabbed her ankles and pulled her to the side of the road. I sat in the snow and put her head in my lap and petted her soft ears, soft as the body of any bat flying around any cedar pole in the Yellow Evening Twilight. I had my buck knife in my pocket in case I had to kill her to end her suffering.

The breath on her wet nose grew colder. In five more breaths, her legs stopped moving. She was gone.

I didn't have the time to butcher her. To take her 'ach'iidííl (large intestine) and throw it back toward my suburban apartment so that it would become a deer again. I didn't have time to take the medicine in her unwounded skin. I didn't have time to take her head and put it under a juniper tree and sprinkle tádídíín (corn pollen) over it and thank the deer for her spirit and for her flesh that would feed the people. I didn't have time because I was living in a place without juniper trees or sacred mountains or corn pollen or the Great Ones who walked outside of hoghans during the chants. I didn't have time because I had to go to work at my job. I didn't have time because I didn't make time. I didn't have time because I believed in Time.

I made prayers and left the yearling in the snow. I got in the Honda and drove to my high school, where I would train young people to work and look for jobs and believe in Time as measured by clocks and participate in the culture of savages who left their deer kills to rot in the snow alongside their paved roads.

It was my birthday. I'd been walking the earth for thirty winters. What had those winters taught me? I never had the fender fixed.

Some things carry ghosts. Some things should.

"Those deer are probably going up to graze on Ganado Mesa," I said to the boy. "They'll have a good summer there." And we drove to Ganado.

The boy followed me to the trading post the next morning. We toured Hubbell's barn and house and blacksmithy and wagon depot and warehouse. We walked to the Ganado flea market and brought some Navajo tacos back to my cabin. After lunch, I asked the boy if he wanted to go to the wash. He said yes, and so we went.

We walked the paths I had walked when I was his age. But the geography of the wash had changed completely since I had walked this ground as a teenager. My friends Aaron Peshlakai and John Curtis had helped to change it.

The thick groves of water-chugging tamarisk, an invading species that had alkalized the soil and caused deep gullying in the wash, were now dead and gone. Aaron and John and six other local guys on the Civilian Conservation Corps crew had worked upstream with chainsaws and axes and sledgehammers and decapitated every tamarisk and burned them. An erosion consultant from New Mexico taught them how to build structures from the severed trunks and limbs that would help the water recarve its meandering course and become a healthy stream. With the help of National Park Service experts from Arches National Park, they also figured out a way to safely poison the tamarisks and Russian olive trees to keep them from regrowing.

Aaron and John told me stories of Russian olive branches with thorns so strong and so sharp they would stab through the workers' hats and work gloves. One guy had to go to the emergency room at Sage Memorial Hospital to get a thorn taken out of his scalp.

When they built structures out of Russian olive branches, they had to bury the branches upside down. If they took a limb of a Russian olive and buried it right side up, the limb sprouted roots and grew green shoots out the top.

Some things carry ghosts.

The boy and I followed the curving banks of the Pueblo Colorado Wash. I walked him out to a tall *t'iis* (cottonwood tree) and showed him a great horned owl's nest so wide I couldn't carry it in my arms. The nest sat perfectly concealed in a dome of shimmering green leaves. They say the *né'éshjaa'* (owl) was made when *Naayéé' neizghání* (Monster Slayer) threw the babies of the Monster Eagles from the cliffs of *Tsé bit'a'í* (The Rock with Wings, Shiprock).

Monster Slayer said that the owl would provide prophecies for the Earth Surface People who wanted to believe in fate. Sometimes the owl would speak the truth. Sometimes it would lie. It would be for the people to decide what was true and what was false. This would be the owl teaching people how to tell the difference between wisdom and foolishness.

"Weird," said the boy. "But I could see how that could be true."

"There are a lot of true things in the world," I said.

We walked past the log-and-rock structures that were helping the wash recarve its course. Where tamarisks had choked the current and dropped the water table, pools formed at the bends of the wash. Grass had taken root on the banks. Reeds grew in muddy water. Wide reeds. Cottonwoods

bent their rippling gray branches. Their leaves clacked in the breeze and mimicked rain falling on rock. A bird cried in the leaves. Its feathers burned red, blue, and yellow. A kestrel.

We followed a coyote trail along the bank until we got to the tallest cottonwood in the wash. The tree had grown straight to the sky in its youth, but now slanted out over the current after the stream had sprung forward in a red rush of spring runoff and early thunderstorm and had eroded out the bank at its roots. The tree toppled forward and rested over the water and has been living there ever since.

The boy asked how I knew this. I told him I saw it happen.

"You ran out here in a thunderstorm?"

"Where else would I have been?" I said. "What else was there to look at?"

We walked under its dead gray boughs. One branch as long as my forearm still grew green leaves.

Some things carry ghosts.

The water rippled a few inches deep and glittered like crystal on the waves of the wash's sandy bed. We followed those crystals along the same paths my friend Ferlin and I had used to track coyotes and chipmunks. Summer storms had reshaped sandbars and bends along the bank. It was here that I'd adopted the many important Diné patterns in my life, where I had been reshaped.

We moved upstream, toward Louise Tsosie's land. A *tsiyaalzhahí* (Cooper's hawk) *kek-kek-kek*ed among the Chinese elms and cottonwoods. The injured lambs we had helped raise for Louise during the winters were almost always strong by spring and ready to graze that summer.

We removed our shoes, tied together the laces, threw them over our shoulders, and walked upstream through the current. Grasshoppers ticked and flew along the bank. A robin sang in the cottonwoods. A ropy flash of light and scale slipped over the grass on the bank. The shape whipped and slid across the mud. I softly plucked the *tótł'iish* (water snake) from the current. The snake sunned himself in the soft pink branches of my fingers, rested his head over my thumb, and stared forward. His dark tongue flicked out toward the boy.

"Whoa," the boy said. "He's not even moving."

"Neither are we." Many of my Diné friends wouldn't do this. But I have been a snake catcher since I was six years old and nearly bit off a piece of my tongue while diving along a pond's edge to grab a water snake. I tasted blood in my mouth, and the water snake flicked its tongue like it knew.

Tł'iish (snakes) are powerful animals who know holy mysteries. They bring rain. They bring lightning. You don't touch them. You don't hurt them. You don't kill them.

I slipped *tótł'iish* back in the water.

The boy waved to the snake as it swam away to the other bank. "Bye."

The channel lay smooth with slick brown mud that shined like snake scales.

I walked into the mud and boy followed. Our feet sank to the ankles, and the warmth of the *hashtł'ish* filled the spaces between our toes. We walked fifty yards upstream through the curves of *hashtł'ish*. Mud is a curse and a blessing on the Rez. It ruins roads. It cancels school days. It causes flash floods that kill sheep. It also creates the frogs and the fish. It was used in the rain ceremonies that have now been forgotten. It is sacred, the *hashtł'ish*. In the desert, any wet earth is a blessing.

We stepped out of the stream toward the *t'iis łigai* (white poplars) growing at the bottom of the hill where the donkey had dragged me by the hand and had given me my scar.

The *hashtł'ish* caked around our feet. It wrapped over our toes.

Tumbleweeds and goat-head stickers covered the banks. The stickers and thorns poked into the mud on our feet. We couldn't feel it. The *hashtł'ish* had formed around our feet like pottery ready for the kiln.

"Hey, it's like we're wearing shoes," the boy said. "Like the ground is making shoes for our feet."

"I guess, instead of wearing Nikes, we're wearing Adobes," I joked.

The boy laughed and threw his head back so that his brown hair shone in the sun. "Yeah! We're wearing our Adobes!"

And something in that laughter cracked the center of my body as sure as a handful of ice will break and spall a two-ton boulder. It was hard to stay in the wash. My mind walks to other places I didn't want to go. But who can say what directs any current anywhere? Some things carry ghosts.

I know I am in the wash in Ganado. But I am also in the rainbow, moving through time. I am in a rental car. I am driving south to Tucson, where I've been invited to the Tucson Festival of Books, one of the largest book festivals in the country. One of my literary heroes, T. Coraghessan Boyle, is going to be there. Two friends are also getting married in Tucson later that day.

I am part of a panel called "Writing Arizona: Memoir and Its Sense of Place." I am going to be sitting at the same table with the poet Richard Shelton, whose work I had read in *The New Yorker* magazine, and with the poet

Alberto Ríos, who I had read in my Norton anthology while in college. The panel is run by the author Ken Lamberton, who won the John Burroughs Medal for *Wilderness and Razor Wire*, a collection of nature essays that he wrote while in prison.

Writers dream of these moments.

I am in the wash in Ganado. I am also in that day in Tucson. I had never been to the University of Arizona campus. Lyle Parsons would tell me about it all the time, and he'd always wished I'd attended.

Lyle and I had been talking on the phone for at least an hour every Sunday for the past six years. Since he'd gotten his pancreatic cancer diagnosis, we'd given two to three hours to our conversation instead. I had flown to Arizona that September to teach at a boarding school on the Reservation, where the students had read *Navajos Wear Nikes* in their English class. Lyle told me that he was worried about his four-year-old son forgetting who he was and never knowing his father's stories coming from his father's voice.

We sat down once a week, flicked on Lyle's recording equipment in his small studio, and talked over the phone with the microphone picking up everything, like any of the other oral histories I'd recorded. We talked about his childhood in the rural country of Louisiana, where he'd played with the black kids and the Cajun kids and they'd walked the swamps together and caught snakes. He moved to the Southwest, to Tucson, where he learned to love the Sonoran Desert, where he killed his first rabbit with a bow and arrow, sold the weapons, and used the money to buy his first guitar.

His stories are restless. The teenager with wavy black hair refuses to pick up his diploma at his high school graduation. He's a thin young man with a Frank Zappa mustache, living through his first marriage that withered, through the love for his daughter from that marriage (which did not wither), earning his dual degrees in psychology and British literature from the University of Arizona, working for a suicide prevention hotline. He holds a .357 Magnum revolver to his head and thinks of ending it all. He doesn't and decides to homestead in Alaska. Then he pursues a new dream as a tanned, dark-eyed journeyman guitar player over the next twenty years, his travels across the country and into Canada, where he and the rest of the band nearly froze to death when their van broke down on a back road during a fierce blizzard in Alberta. He gets a few gray hairs.

Lyle Parsons is traveling to Page, Arizona, where one of his bandmates had lived, and playing in a local bar. He works as a welder at the Navajo Generating Station and joins the league of conspiracy of burning coal from

the sacred *Dziłíjiin* (Black Mesa). More gray hairs, mostly at the temples, and his skinny hips have started to bulge with a belly. But his stance is still strong, and his hands are leathered and hard from work on the guitar neck and work under cars in mechanics' shops and work in smokestacks at the Navajo Generating Station that belches forth the soils of *Dziłíjiin* like some new concrete *Yé'iitsoh*.

His strength of youth slips, and so he finds a substitute-teaching job at the local high school. He gets certified as a teacher. He meets his wife. He takes care of his first daughter's daughter. He and his wife have a son, then another boy. He breaks the chokehold of alcohol and drugs. He cares for his wife during her breast cancer chemotherapy, then notices his skin is jaundiced because a tumor in his pancreas has swelled and blocked the flow of bile from his gallbladder. Between his surgeries, his treatments, the slow chemical poisoning meant to drive the tumors out of his body, he reads *Adventures of Huckleberry Finn* to his oldest son.

This all happens after our discussions of love and family duty and what the good life is and whether Shakespeare really wrote his plays and why *Othello* is the most succinct demonstration of his artistry toward understanding human psychology and why the Chevy Camaro is a superior car to the Ford Mustang, and us laughing about the time I drove my Dodge Dakota truck to work and the radiator hose exploded. Lyle had shown up in his blue truck with a pair of pliers and a utility knife. He showed me how to remove the rotted radiator hose, then ran me down to the local auto parts store. I bought a new hose, and he drove me back to my truck. We talked about the mysteries of women and whether they know they're more beautiful than men while we fitted the hose and clamped it down. Then we went back to his place to water his trees and continue the conversation.

That day, we talked about the upcoming presidential elections.

"I don't like all these presidential debates," he said. "They distract us too much. They keep us from getting to the real substance of the candidates. Namely, their lies."

I raised my can of root beer to that.

This all happens after he has told me he loves me as a son. This all happens after I tell him I love him as a father.

I send care packages every two weeks filled with high-energy protein bars that he can stomach while having to undergo his radiation treatments. I send graphic novels that I know he can read, even when his energy levels drop and make it hard to stay aware enough to read raw text. I send him

my copy of Carl Sagan's *Shadows of Forgotten Ancestors*. We talk of that book for two hours over the phone one Sunday, in between discussions of Noam Chomsky's perspective on the so-called War on Terror, the wealth disparities between rich and poor gullying ever deeper after the 2008 real estate speculating, the criminal actions of the Bush administration that had yet to be prosecuted, the lyrics of the Byrds' *Sweetheart of the Rodeo* album, the philosophies of Thomas Merton in his book *The Seven Storey Mountain*, and whether Jesus and the Buddha were the same person in different skins.

We believe in the same people living in different skins.

We speak on Wednesday night. I ask if he will be able to get down to see me at the book festival in Tucson.

"I'm trying to keep myself in good health to spend as much time with Julia and the boys as I can. I don't think I'm up for traveling, Jim. So I probably won't be able to see you in Arizona this time. But we'll talk when you get back. You can tell me all about it. Let me know what you think of the campus. It's beautiful."

"I will," I said. "Talk to you soon."

And I'm thinking this while attending a panel with the writer R. L. Stine, whose *Goosebumps* paperbacks I could devour in thirty minutes as a kid. Stine enchants all the kids in this massive lecture room, where he sits in a black turtleneck and sips from a small glass of water. He ends his talk with a story of how he might have seen a real ghost in a haunted house in his neighborhood in his small town in Ohio.

A boy asks him if he really believes in ghosts.

"As long as we believe in the past, we have to believe in ghosts," Stine says. "Some things really are haunted. Some things carry ghosts."

I am standing in the wash in my Adobes, and I'm also standing in the hallway outside a lecture hall in one of the classroom buildings. My panel starts in about five minutes. I'm in the hallway with my brother Darren. I've spoken to Ken Lamberton about when he wants me to enter the room.

I know I'm standing in my Adobes in the wash with the boy, but I'm also standing in that hallway when a woman with glasses and short gray hair, wearing a dull-red blouse, comes walking up to me. She looks star struck.

"Are *you* Jim Kristofic?" she asks.

"Yeah."

"Oh my God! I'm so glad I found you!"

She explains. Her husband is a doctor at Flagstaff Medical Center. He

has a patient's wife who needs to get in touch with me. She knew I was in Tucson, at the Festival of Books, but she didn't have my cell phone number. When that doctor said that his wife was at the Tucson Festival of Books and she could maybe look for me, the patient's wife just shrugged. More than 125,000 people were attending the festival in the second-largest zip code in Arizona. I was a needle in a stack of needles. The doctor rang his wife anyway, told her my name, and asked if someone could page me.

"Jim *Kristofic*?" she said into her cell phone. "I'm on the way to his panel right now!"

And so here we are, this gray-haired woman and I. She holds out her cell phone, and the doctor on the end of the line is handing the phone to his patient's wife, and that patient is Lyle Parsons.

I take the phone. The woman with gray hair and the dull-red blouse steps aside. I walk down the dimly lit hall. I talk with Lyle's wife. I learn things.

At the same time I had boarded the US Airways flight in Philadelphia to come here, Lyle and his wife and the boys got on a life flight at Page airport and flew to Flagstaff. Lyle had fallen unconscious at the foot of his bed. His body had started shutting down.

"I don't know how long he has, Jim," Julia says. "Maybe only hours."

Ken Lamberton, his curly gray hair and cowboy mustache unmistakable, walks out into the hall. He smiles, nods, and waves me inside.

I hold up my hand, letting him know I have seen him. But I'm not here right now.

"I'll be there soon," I say into the phone.

I hang up and walk inside. My brother finds a seat near the back. The room is filled, and people have to stand. Richard Shelton, that blond-gray prophet, and Alberto Ríos, that clear-eyed poet, are both seated at the front of the room. A third chair sits empty for me. People have been waiting. I find the woman with gray hair and the dull-red blouse and hand her the phone, and she touches my hand, and her face teaches me what compassion looks like.

I sit in the chair, and here it is—that moment writers dream of, after years of drafts of writing and rewriting and fights with your spouse and rejection letters that pile more than three inches high. Here the three writers sit at the table, waiting to expound upon their craft and have their egos stroked. They wait to answer questions about the things they've been saying only in their minds while sitting alone in rooms.

But only two of the writers are here. I don't know where I am, but it's

not here. I'm wishing for a rainbow I can step into that will fly me to Flagstaff—to *Dookʼoʼoosłiid*—at the speed of light.

I'm trying to say things that make sense. I'm the only writer at the table without gray hair, and I'm trying to seem the lighthearted young man from the Rez who made good. But it is the pained smile that comes after you've smashed your toe into a wall or hammered your thumb.

It's the only alternative to tears.

Ken asks the audience for questions.

The first question is for me.

"So what are you working on next?"

Getting the hell out of here.

I say something, but it's hard to focus. All of the audience members have long, thinning gray and black hair, high cheekbones, and a strong nose. They all talk in a nasal voice and laugh with wide grins that seem born to mock authority, and their name is Lyle Parsons.

As soon as they clap for us, I'm shaking hands with Richard Shelton, Alberto Ríos, and Ken Lamberton, and then I'm out the side door, and Darren is just trying to keep up with me. I need to take the rental car north. I go alone.

I'm in the wash in Ganado with the boy, walking in my Adobes, but I'm also driving the rental car north. The sun is dropping, and I have more than two hundred miles to go. I push the engine, trying not to get pulled over. I pass through the almond orchards of Casa Grande, skirt the lights of Phoenix, and drop into the Verde Valley.

In the Yellow Evening Twilight, I am descending into the valley. Sixty miles ahead, the ridged peaks of *Dookʼoʼoosłiid* shine in the ghost of the full moon rising. It would take a Diné man three days to ride there on a horse. He would have time to think about approaching that mountain. He wouldn't have to believe in Time. Time is not something to believe in.

I will be at that mountain in about an hour. I have stood there and I am there now and I am walking with Leo and Glen. And I have to believe in Time right now because Time is all I have. Lyle is at the foot of that mountain, lying in a hospital bed. He is passing into the West from the *ʼatsʼíís naałdzid* (cancer) in his yellow pancreas. It is the size of any abalone shell.

The sun has walked down behind the ponderosa pines and Folding Darkness has come when I call Julia from the car to get directions to the hospital as I pull off the highway.

"And Jim," she says. "He doesn't look good. I just want you to know that. To understand that."

I have brought the program and my author identification badge from the book festival so that Lyle can see them. I hope he can autograph them. I wouldn't have gotten them if not for him. I'm walking through the wash in my Adobes with the boy and the white poplars are shining like silver with their dark green leaves and the breeze is in our ears, but I'm also running across the tile of the hospital floor. The stink of antiseptics lingers to disguise the smell of blood and shit and mucus and rot and human death. *Eyah. Dooda.* Don't go in there.

I go in there. The elevator to the critical care wing of the hospital. Julia meets me at the door, and we fall into each other. I keep hoping that it's actually Wednesday night and Lyle and I have just talked on the phone. That this is all a bad dream.

"He's in there," Julia whispers in my ear. "I want you to have time alone with him."

I nod, and that's enough. I walk into the dark room. It's quiet. I hear a sound like my heart beating, but it's actually a machine allowing Lyle to breath. His body has forgotten how to do that.

His body lies under the soft yellow light of the desk lamp, but I know I'm not seeing Lyle. It's like someone has carved a poor, skinny imitation of Lyle out of pale wax and forgotten to add his black hair and beard.

I sit next to the body. I hold its hand. It's like touching a candle.

Put out the light, and then put out the light —

I shake away those lines from *Othello*. Goddamned Shakespeare at a time like this. No. But Lyle talked about those lines just last week. Shit. The rest of it just comes.

If I quench thee, thou flaming minister,
I can again thy former light restore
Should I repent me. But once put out thy light,
Thou cunning'st pattern of excelling nature,
I know not where is that Promethean heat
That can thy light relume.

"Hey, Lyle," I whisper. I hold his hand tighter. I rub, trying to give him some of my warmth, some of my Promethean heat.

But those strong, leathery hands—born from so many nights playing at the guitar neck and working under cars in mechanics' shops and running welding torches in smokestacks at the Navajo Generating Station—are only a memory now.

The machine whooshes the breath of life into Lyle. The nurses have daubed his open mouth with a yellow balm that looks like pine resin to keep his lips from cracking.

I don't know what to say. I am poured out like water, and the only memories left in the clay pot shine the images of driving home from football practice in the yellow evening twilight of a Utah sunset, of throwing hay to our paint horses, then watering the cottonwoods and fruit trees around my family's trailer. Near the end of the night, I sat on the tip of my mattress in the small bedroom that my brother and I shared and balanced my English textbook and my notepad over my lap. There, I started my training as a writer. I wrote to complete my English homework. I eventually wrote my own short stories. Then I'd type them in the computer lab in the high school library because my family didn't have a computer at home.

I suppose I started doing it because I'd always loved to tell stories. But I know I kept doing it because another human being of rigorous thought actually wanted to read it. I am sitting with Lyle by his pine tree while his bubbler slowly gurgles water over its roots. We are listening to Johnny Cash and talking about the tenets of Buddhism and how they relate to modern environmental policies. We both agree that George W. Bush should become a born-again Buddhist.

These were discussions I hadn't been able to have with friends my own age.

The machine whooshes. Lyle's breath is forced from his chest.

I wanted to tell stories, most of them true. I finished my master's degree in American studies. I taught American literature, creative writing, and mythology in a Pennsylvania high school that ranked among the top high schools in the country. Since high school I had written for magazines and newspapers, before I published my first book.

The machine whooshes. The answer to so many well-laid plans. So many of them started with a teacher willing to sit after school and edit the novice horror and fantasy short stories of an awkward tenth grader with crooked glasses and dirty jeans.

The machine whooshes.

It was the writing that brought me close to Lyle and his family over the years. Lyle had cautioned me against writing too often.

"What's your rush, man?" he'd say. "This book you're working on probably shouldn't come out for another ten years anyway."

Maybe I was rushing—or something was rushing me—because this day was coming.

If it had not been for the book coming out that year, I would never have been at the University of Arizona campus for the Tucson Festival of Books to receive Julia's message.

Lyle and I had said many of our parting words months before, just in case. We both sensed that each day was borrowed time.

The machine whooshes. His breath. I say something.

"Lyle. You taught me so much about life," I say. "Now you're going to teach me about death. Ever the teacher. I thank you."

I cradle the wax hand. It doesn't get warmer. I press it to my forehead.

"Thank you for being a good man, Lyle," I say. "Thank you for teaching me how to be a good man. Thank you for your life."

I stand there in the Ganado wash in my Adobes, and I also sit and hold the candles of his fingers, knowing that they're nearly burnt out.

The door cracks. Julia puts her head in. "Are you okay?"

I nod. "If there are other people outside, please let them come in."

A woman and a daughter come in. The girl is not much older than I was when I first moved to the Rez.

The girl sees Lyle's body, and she starts crying. She's sobbing and horrified. "He looks like an alien!"

I wish I could be as honest as her. I wish I could feel what she's feeling. But I don't know what to feel. My feet are not on the earth right now. I am here in the wash in my Adobes but I'm also on the mountain and I'm also walking a part of this road into the wilderness of Cancer and I'm wondering if that path can ever be walked in Beauty.

"He can't talk," Julia says, clutching my hand, "but I know he would be so proud and so happy that you're here."

"I feel like such a pilgrim in all this," I say.

Julia touches the back of my head and rubs my hair. She becomes the tender mother I never had.

"No, Jim," she says. "No. You are here. You are family."

I am in the wash in Ganado in my Adobes with the boy, but I am also driving south in the Folding Darkness, and *Dookʼoʼoosłiid* grows smaller behind me. *Tleʼhonaaʼéí* (He Who Rules the Night) has emerged from the clouds. The face of *Asdzą́ą́ Nádleehé* (Changing Woman) shines her *tsiiyeeł* from the full disk.

I get back to the hotel in Tucson at three o'clock in the morning. I lie on a mattress. I don't sleep. An hour later, I get a text message from Julia. It reads: "He's gone."

I'm in the wash in Ganado in my Adobes, but I'm also lying on that mattress in that hotel room and feeling I am on a mountain.

I shower. I get dressed in a shirt that buttons. I go to the reception for the wedding that happened yesterday afternoon while I was driving north to the mountain.

I arrive at the bride's parents' house. It's a beautiful white-plastered casa in an expansive subdivision in a Sonoran Desert now made livable by water pumped through buried pipes and air conditioners running frivolously off torched coal from *Dziłíjiin* in a power plant somewhere north of the city. Much of this water comes from the federal Central Arizona Project, a layer of concrete arteries that lift water from the Colorado River over three mountain ranges to Phoenix and Tucson with a scheme of siphons, tunnels, dams, reservoirs, and fifteen electrically powered pumping stations. When you turn on a faucet in Tucson, you are drinking some of the most expensive subsidized water in the world.

The power that runs these fifteen pumping stations is from coal ripped from the body of *Dziłíjiin*.

There are more than enough tamales and menudo to feed the hundred people who have arrived in nice clothes. Pop music fills the air, and red and yellow and blue balloons are tied to every vine and tree in the backyard.

I walk to the fence, but I can't feel the earth under my feet. I can't feel anything. Sometimes I snap my fingers just to make sure they're still on my hands. They feel molded of wax. I clench my teeth to make sure they're still in my mouth.

People walk past me and say how sorry they are. I appreciate it quietly.

The Catalina Mountains rise nine thousand feet into the air from the valley floor. These mountains hold no ferns, no aspens, no pines, no groundsel grass. They are stark and naked as the surface of Mars. I want to walk up into those mountains and never come down. But I am expected to be here, and the yearling is dying in my lap on the side of the road, and we are sitting in the snow together, and I have to get to work on Time.

I turn a chair in the corner of the yard to the desert and watch pink-footed mourning doves walk over the brown sand under green boughs of ocotillo. Lyle had looked at these mountains and birds when he was my age, when he was still healthy. When he was still alive.

I still can't feel my feet on the ground.

Later that day, I fly into the stratosphere on the US Airways jet to land back in the east. But my feet never touch the earth. I don't sleep for two

days. I don't cry. I don't mourn. Instead, I do what Lyle would have wanted me to do. I go to school the next day. I teach. Then I write draft after draft of Lyle's obituary during my lunch breaks over the next three days because I know that means that Julia won't have to. I write a letter to be read at his memorial service that I can't attend. There is no Time for it.

I survive the next few months in the suburbia of Bucks County. Then I take the job with the Park Service.

And so I am here in the wash in Ganado, the Place of Wide Reeds, and I am with the boy, and we are walking in our Adobes.

The boy notices a *na'ashjé'ii bitł'óól* (spider web) shining nearly invisible between two of the branches on the white poplar. The light of *náátsʼíílid* glows along the spun silk. The Diné say that Spider Woman taught them to weave, that she provided for their livelihood and kept them warm.

The boy asks how old the web might be. I tell him that spiders' webs usually get destroyed by birds and deer and cattle and sheep that walk through them. Spiders usually reweave them every night.

"Far out, man," the boy says. "Spiders sure don't like to give up."

"No. Maybe they don't even know how."

It's a piece of conversation I might have had with Lyle Parsons a year ago. Now I'm having it with his oldest son.

Some things carry ghosts.

The boy and I are some of those things now.

The world is full of merciful coincidences. One of these is that *hashtł'ish* sticks to human skin. And when it forms its soft pottery over your feet, you feel no pain.

Hashtł'ish is born of *Nahasdzáán*, the skin of the Earth Mother. The boy and I walk over thorns in our Adobes down to the water. I feel the earth under my feet for the first time in four months.

Maybe it is enough to understand that *Nahasdzáán* knows how to put shoes on her children's feet. And whatever we are carrying with us, we can know that *Nahasdzáán* will help share the load. She shares it with all of us.

This is what can happen when you are wearing your Adobes.

THE PEOPLE ARE THE CORN

They said they lived out there. That's why I went.

I clocked the forty-hour week at Hubbell Trading Post National Historic Site as a ranger, giving tours of the ranch, feeding churro sheep and the trading post's pet llama (the Hubbellama), catching bull snakes for the maintenance crew, helping to arrest child-abusing drunks who wandered onto the property, and watering the apricot tree in Hubbell's courtyard every morning.

I was getting paid to be myself.

It had all begun so well.

At the end of my first week, I had walked a side trail in my quiet way, through the cottonwood groves of the Pueblo Colorado Wash. About thirty yards from the trading post, a spotted gray blur shot past into one of the tall *diwhoozhí* (four-winged saltbrush).

Big damn jackrabbit, I thought. I inched closer, and the animal leaped out and landed in front of me. I could have poked it with a walking stick if I'd been holding one.

Its paws pulsed and bloomed white slits of flexing claws. The legs rippled with brown spots and black streaks running to a dark crest over its curved, sinewy back. The rising sun shimmered its honey-brown pelt and the black tufts at its ears. *Náshdóítbáí.* Bobcat.

We shared a long glance. Then the cat walked down through the rabbit-brush and into the wash. It looked back over one of its hatchet-blade shoulders, sniffed the air, and padded upstream into the willows.

That night, a kingbird sat over her two chicks to protect them from the

cool night inside her nest inside the awning of my porch. Her dark eye watched me less than a foot away. She didn't move. Kingbirds know something of that judgment of intentions we call "trust."

On my first day off, I took to the fields. Hubbell had many local workers cut rye and oats for the winter, grow peppers, corn, squash, and beans. I continued the tradition in my crappy T-shirt and black Levis that I'd worn since high school.

While I was helping weed the cornfield with the farm supervisor, he asked me if I'd been out in the canyons north of Ganado Lake.

"I'm going to try getting out there tomorrow," I said. "I've heard there are petroglyphs out there from the Anasazi."

"I heard that, too," he said. "I've never seen them. But they're out there."

The next morning, I drove to Fluted Rock, packed water and apples, and loaded my Ruger Blackhawk .357 Magnum. Wild dogs had been attacking livestock and people in the backcountry. I put my "Gone Hiking" sign on the dashboard, tipped down my cowboy hat, and walked north from the lake.

Flint and shards of petrified wood glittered in the sand at Fluted Rock's base. Dust blew through the eye sockets of six horse skulls tumbled together at the base of a hill. I inspected a loose tooth and threw it into the sagebrush.

Bees flicked their crystal wings between the bristling purple flowers of *waa'* (beeweed) and white and pink stars of *nádiznézí* (calico asters). The mud houses of *táshchozhii* (cliff swallows) emerged from the cliff walls like pottery sculpted in the hands of spirits. The wash fanned out. The grass grew thick and green along the banks. The five-fingered tracks of *tábaah ma'ii* (raccoon) pattered through mud. Half-chewed skeletons of crawdads littered the sand.

Tourists at the trading post would ask me how the Diné people raised any livestock around here. Many of these visitors had driven the sloping, juniper-spotted hills pocked with skeletal sagebrush and small sand dunes descending from the ponderosa pine forests of the Defiance Plateau. They hadn't seen any sheep, either.

I had to remind them that back in the canyons near Fluted Rock—which you couldn't see while speeding along the highway—water flowed all year. Calico asters and Indian paintbrush and Russian olive and cottonwood trees rattled at the rhythms of rain and water. In *Diné Bikéyah*, water obeyed certain extremes. You found it misting on the peaks of mountains or running along the bottoms of canyons. *Tó éí 'iiná até.* Water is Life. And Life was out there. You had to range out and find it.

I walked the pines and rolling country until I heard the first human voice in hours.

"Hah!" it yelled. Then a bulky, metallic rattling. Probably a sheepherder. The rattle probably made from a metal rod attached to a coffee can filled with rocks to keep the herd walking.

I turned the corner. Goats and sheep bleated. Dogs' running feet left a soft, rapid padding. I handled the revolver, just in case. But I am overdramatic. Sheepdogs are good to people. They've always been good to me.

Two brindle pit bull mutts ran around the corner, their tongues wagging. I opened my arms and let them jump up on me. I dug in behind their ears with my rough hands and dirty fingernails. They had probably smelled me coming from around the other bend of the canyon. I was rife with scent. I hadn't showered in many days.

"Hah!" the voice yelled again.

I turned the corner. The herd of gray sheep and white goats grazed along the base of a sheer thirty-foot sandstone cliff rising from the forest floor. A rocky slope thick with juniper led to the top of the cliff. The sheepherder thrashed in the trees and shook his coffee can rattle.

Three goats ran before him, moving along the ridges of the sheer cliff. He attempted to herd them away from the wall.

"You need any help?" I yelled up.

The sheepherder turned and walked out of the trees and down the rocky slope. The old man's white hair stuck out the sides of his Justin boots baseball cap. His torn red-plaid shirt looked like it had spent a winter in the bed of a pickup truck. He humped a Nike backpack with frayed straps. He'd tucked his .22 Ruger pistol into a small canvas holster at his side. He struggled down the slope, as though his shoes were filled with broken glass.

"Just go ahead," he gasped. "Bring them down. My knees. They're bad."

I nodded and scrambled to the top of the cliff, clinging to some boulders and flanking the ram and the ewe so they ran back down to the forest floor. But the kid wouldn't budge. He kept backing away from me, screaming, and ran to the edge of the cliff.

The little turd was going to run over the side. It was a sheer thirty-foot drop. If he didn't die, he was going to break his legs.

I shot forward, and the kid danced away, spun, and ran for the cliff again. The white fluff of his tail vanished over the edge.

Damn it.

I crawled to the edge and leaned over, expecting to see the kid splattered on the rocks.

Instead, the kid hopped off a small rock ledge near the bottom of the cliff and trotted, unharmed, toward his mother.

I shook my head. Another kid walked to the edge and pulled the same trick. He jumped face first off the cliff and hit each tiny ledge with the soft, rubbery pads of his little feet until he hopped daintily to the forest floor. Most of those steep ledges were too small to hold an apple.

I shook my head. Freaking *tł'ízí diigis*. Crazy goats. An image of Glen popped into my head. No surprise there.

I walked down to the old man. He offered his hand softly. I shook it in the traditional way, more a caress than a handshake.

"*Yá'át'ééh*," I said. "*Haa'dee la' niniya, sha kesh?*"

He laughed. "I'm coming from over there near Sawmill. Just herding today and then tomorrow, and then I have off. What's a *bilagáana* like you doing out here?"

I told him about how I'd grown up in Ganado, about how my mom had worked as a nurse at Sage Memorial Hospital, about how my brother and sister had been born there. When I told him I knew Lorinda Curly, his face lit up.

"Oh, okay," he said. "I remember your mom taking care of me one time."

He asked me why I was at Fluted Rock. When I told him I had come out here to find an Anasazi ruin and petroglyphs, he laughed at me. He informed me that there were no petroglyphs at Fluted Rock, but that farther up the canyon, toward Wood Springs, I might find some.

He looked thoughtfully to the east, his eyes flecked with yellow spots and dried by the heat. Small capillaries shone red at the edges of his nose. The alcohol's tell.

He stooped and used his finger to draw me a map in the sand. "You've got to go drive near Nazlini," he said.

Don't ask me to draw you that map. *Shahane' adiin.* I'll never tell.

I told my friend Malcolm about the place, and he wanted to see it. Malcolm and I grew up in Ganado together. His mom had been my Navajo culture teacher. When I was traveling back east to Pennsylvania to see my Anglo relatives in the summers, Malcolm was ranging up into the Defiance summit to take care of his family's sheep during their summer grazing. Many of those sheep had descended from the herd given to Malcolm's grandmother.

She was the daughter of a Navajo woman and Roman Hubbell, who took over the Hubbell Trading Post as his father, Juan Lorenzo Hubbell, aged into retirement. Juan Lorenzo Hubbell was Malcolm's great-great-grandfather.

Roman would drive up to the summit to see Malcolm's grandmother and deliver them sheep and canned goods. He would say, "*Ei awee'e bi'.*" That is for the baby. The little girl—who would someday give birth to Malcolm's mother—would cry for her dad when he left them to go back to the trading post. She'd save the fork he used to eat sardines from a can and tell her friends, "This is my dad's."

Malcolm's family had brought most of their sheep herd down from the summit six summers ago to live at Hubbell Trading Post, the place many ancestors had been born. She could barely keep herself from crying.

The family took the herd up to the grassy ponderosa pine forest on the Defiance summit two years later. All but a few were killed by wild dogs. A mountain lion finished off the rest of them the following night.

Most Diné are attached to their sheep as Anglo people are attached to their rescued dogs. His mother can't even talk about it to this day.

Malcolm and I met each other again in Ganado after the death of his family's sheep, when I came back to finish oral histories with people who lived near Ganado Lake and Round Top Hill. We went out past Ganado Lake and shot up old washing machines with Malcolm's Bushmaster AR-15 and his Glock 45 and blew up toilets with shotguns.

While we reloaded the AR-15 magazine, Malcolm adjusted the black bandana on his tall forehead. His wavy brown hair was pulled back in a traditional *tsiiyeeł* bun tied with wool yarn. His small turquoise earrings glowed from each ear. His leather and silver *k'ee'toh* (bow guard) sat comfortably on his wrist. His freckled beige skin and hazel eyes revealed his Anglo heritage from his Mormon father. But Malcolm had grown up in *Diné Bikéyah*, and I always learned from him about the place.

Later I kept some of the spent ammo shells in the center compartment of my Honda Civic so that when they rattled while I made sharp turns I could think of Malcolm, probably driving his truck on some back road near Klagetoh while I was cruising through some parking lot in the suburbs of Philadelphia.

These ammo shells were in the car when I hit the deer in the winter.

I met up with Malcolm the first weekend I came to Ganado to be a ranger. On the way to his house, summer monsoon clouds opened up over Ganado

Lake and swept the maroon hills. I got drenched and laughed when the rain woke the frogs into singing.

Malcolm chuckled from his porch when he saw my drenched T-shirt. "You've been blessed, Jim!" he said. "You've been blessed. Whoa!"

I turned up to where he pointed with his lips. A rainbow spanned over Ganado.

"*Nizhón*," he said.

"*Aoo'*." I nodded.

We visited over some *ch'il gowéhé* (Navajo tea) and cookies. I asked his four kids how they were doing in school. He and I joked about the time we'd ranged for hours along the edges of Ganado Mesa behind *Na'ashashii* to look for an Anasazi granary buried in the ground and lined with rocks and logs. We never found it.

A few days later, Malcolm and his four-year-old son and I climbed into his truck and drove up to his family's place at *Ché'chil Ha'aah'aah* (The Place of Rough Rocks) to kick back and enjoy the cool weather on the Defiance summit.

We walked through knee-high grass and small groves of scrub oak toward a comb of bright orange sandstone pocked with pebbles and slowly weathered into sharp, scalloped edges. These were the formations that gave The Place of Rough Rocks its name.

At the edge of the rocks we found the trail of a *shash* (bear). Malcolm recognized the signs: overturned rocks where the bear had been looking for worms and bugs, a few rotten ponderosa logs ripped open, a small wisp of black hair caught in a scrub oak branch.

We tracked the bear to a small muddy spring. Malcolm and I dug it out with our hands until the water ran clearer. Malcolm noticed the transparent twitching of mosquito larva in the water. He wanted to catch some dragonfly larvae in a coffee can from Ganado Lake.

"Dragonfly larvae are just vicious," he said. "They'll kill and eat those mosquitoes in no time, before they can grow and fly out of the water. I don't want those mosquitoes up here just biting everybody."

Back at the truck, Malcolm's son absently ran up to an ant hill and kicked it.

"You need to not do that, *sahn*," Malcolm said, lightly touching the boy's shoulder. The boy started crying, already reading his dad's disappointment.

Malcolm crouched and patted his back until he stopped crying. "You see those ants there? Those ants came up with us from the First World—the

Black World. They might even be the first things to have been made. You need to respect them. Those ants are teaching us when we watch them. Look how they move around. Look how strong they are! They work hard, and they move quickly. They really know what they're doing. Watch them. Don't hurt them."

I knew that one of the Diné names for ants was *Naat'ááh yiłdiighá* (The One That Walks With Leadership Again and Again). People talked about how each ant moved quickly and independently.[*]

We picked *ch'il gowéhé* in the grass, bundled each plant by folding it four times and tied it with its own stems. We left the bundles to dry on the truck's dashboard. The shoes came off and we sat in the cool pine needles. I boiled water on my small stove.

Over tea, we talked about love, about connection between men and women, about whether it could be permanent. There is the traditional story about how men and women had once separated from each other. It had started when *Áltsé Hastiin* walked into some pine forest that looked much like the one where we sat drinking tea at *Ché'chil Ha'aah'aah*. He killed a deer with his bow and thanked the deer for giving up its life to feed the people. He took it back to *Áltsé Asdzáán* at the *hoghan* and gave it to her to cook and eat.

After she'd eaten the liver and as she was licking the grease from her lips, she said, "*'Ahéhee' shajóózh*." (Thank you, my vagina.)

First Man shook his head and stepped back. "What do you mean, *'Ahéhee' shajóózh*?" he said. "What about *me*? I went out and hunted the deer! If it wasn't for me, you wouldn't be eating anything right now!"

"Yes," First Woman said, "but if it wasn't for *shajóózh*, you would never have wanted to go out and hunt for me in the first place."

With that, First Man threw his bow on the ground, and he and his woman got into it. The other men and women around them start fighting. The men sided with their bows and their hunting skills. The women sided with their vaginas.

Oh, the drama.

[*] Modern science seems to back the Diné way of thinking. Zoologist Dr. Deborah Gordon of Stanford University has posited that ant colonies actually have no hierarchy. There is a queen, but she only lays eggs. There are workers, but they only work. The queen is not an authority figure. No ant tells the other ant what to do. And yet they all get their work done. Someday we might evolve to this way of living.

If the women were going to thank their vaginas all the time, then they could live with them by themselves. So *Áltsé Hastiin* gathered the men, crossed the river, and went to live on the other side. They dug their farming fields and hunted for deer and birds and rabbits. The women lived on their side and basically did the same. But they didn't work as fast as the men. They weren't as strong. They couldn't fight away any enemies.

After four years of this, the men had plenty of food and strong houses they'd built. But they missed their women. They started getting perverted and using parts of their kills to jerk off while they thought of the warmth of their women's bodies. There is a reason there's a Diné word meaning "wife liver."

After time, men and women made peace and reunited across the river. This story is still told in the stars, where *Náhookos Bika'ii* (Whirling Man) and *Náhookos Bi'áadii* (Whirling Woman) revolve around the *Náhookos Biko'* (Home Fire, the North Star). Their revolutions are an evolution, a keeping of the fire that creates a home and harmony and a heat that doesn't fade or understand how to die.

Lyle Parsons heard this story the first time we talked about my wife and me splitting. Lyle said that in a relationship with intense, passionate highs, you were doomed to experience troughs of dark depression and jealousy. When you kept things at a more constant, nonviolent level, you didn't have any dangerous emotional wobbling. But you also had less passion and fewer sparks.

Malcolm smiled and sipped his tea. His son twisted a twig into the sandy soil and built up a small mound.

"What you're talking about is harmony," Malcolm said. "It's like music. Some music can be violent and dark. But some of the best music is violent and dark with a lot of deep harmonies. The darkness works really well with the light. They need each other. I mean, just look at Metallica. 'Fade to Black' and 'One.' Best songs ever, right?"

I threw back my head and laughed, and everything felt better sitting in the shade on the pine needles in my bare feet.

This kind of harmony in relationships—this *sǫ'ah naagháí bike'hózhǫ́* that sought to create a beauty that lasted into old age—was hard to explain to people. The television dramas and scripted MTV *Real Worlds* had destroyed most of the real world for my generation. But the stories kept this harmony alive. Malcolm and I knew there were forces trying to gnash those stories apart with their teeth.

Malcolm and his mother were both Mormon and attended Sunday services. They also practiced Diné traditions and spoke the Diné language. This made for fights in their family over the years. Malcolm's mom once told me how her father had a fox skin that he wore for *Yei Bi Chei* dances like *Tł'éé'jí* (Night Way), when the men dressed as the *yei* are summoned to heal a patient in the *hoghan*. Malcolm's grandfather and grandmother had also collected *béésh 'est'ogii* (arrowheads) in the washes after a thunderstorm, when the stories said the arrowheads shot to the earth as lightning. Her parents had collected more than fifty arrowheads and created a family heirloom by mounting them to a board in the shape of a large arrowhead.

Her sister had joined a Pentecostal church a few years earlier. One night, her sister took the fox skin and the heirloom of arrowheads to a revival tent meeting in the community where people whooped and hollered for Jesus into the night. There, the pastor lit a bonfire and called for people to make sacrifices of their false heathen traditions unto the Lord. Tradition is the Enemy of Progress. Kill the Indian to save the Man.

She threw the fox skin and the arrowheads into the fire, and verily they were consumed. Malcolm's mom cries about it any time she mentions it today. I never bring it up.

I have to raise an eyebrow when people say religion will bring peace on earth. I know I inherited that eyebrow from Lyle Parsons.

Thunder pounded to the north. The rain was coming. It had come nearly every night since I had taken up my job as a ranger. The frogs sang loud through the valley, reciting our own memories of the First World back to us.

This sort of thing had happened before. Malcolm understood this.

That's why I wanted to take him to where the sheepherder had drawn me the map.

I also took Lyle Parson's son.

We drove together and walked out toward Fluted Rock. When we reached the six horse skulls, we turned north, toward the sound of water.

A large retaining pond had filled with rainwater that now ran from the lip, carving down into a wind-ridged channel of bright pink sandstone. The brown water ponded and then blasted down in a churning crystal waterfall that dropped nearly ten feet under the shade of a searing-green cottonwood that stretched its water-drunk roots into the deep pond at the base of the falls.

"Wow," said Malcolm. "Who'd have thought this was out here? I've never seen this here."

"Yes, my good sir," I said in a lilted, mocking high-class accent, "welcome to the Falls at Ganado."

I had come to Ganado that summer after living in East Coast suburbia, where rich people were buying real estate from irresponsible builders putting up overpriced houses in what they called "developments." I lived in that place for nearly four years and still hadn't figured out what they were "developing."

They strapped on names like Pine Meadows and Fox Glen and Maple Grove and The Hunt at Warrington. Whether there were really pines or meadows or foxes or maples growing among the midsummer hum of these air-conditioned, dry-walled boxes remains to be seen. I stopped thinking about it when a person I knew bought a house in a development that had once abutted an apple orchard. Four heirloom trees grew baskets of Golden Delicious apples in his backyard.

One summer, I visited his place and saw that the apple trees had been cut down. "What happened?" I asked. "Did they get a disease or something?"

"Oh, the trees?" he said. "No, I just hated all those apples getting in the way when I would need to mow the lawn. So I had the tree guy whack them down."

I never went back to his house.

Over the years in Pennsylvania, I didn't go back to many houses. If I did, I'd have to (politely) explain to their owners the story I've read repeatedly of how if you take a *ch'al* (frog) and place it in a pot of water, it will sit, relaxed. If you heat up that pot of water, the frog will not try to jump out. Once the pot gets to boiling, the frog will stay still. Then it dies in the bubbling water. I'd have to tell them that we didn't seem much different from our First World ancestor. Most of their homes were now eating up most of the electricity produced in the country. I'd have to tell them that America held only 5 percent of the world's population but burned more than 20 percent of its resources.

Because of them, places like Black Mesa got raped and torn up and burned.

Because of them, fields got plowed up and mice went homeless and hawks went hungry and the world was on the run.

But this is upsetting. So I made jokes about The Falls at Ganado and laughed.

Malcolm and the boy and I threw the cold, rushing water onto our backs and rubbed it behind our ears to cool us. Then we walked north. I led them to where the map had led me.

The rock cliff cascaded overhead. The awning of the rock kept the sun off our backs but would give warming southern light as the angle of the sun dropped in the winter. An old Anasazi trick.

The boy saw what I had seen that day I found the place. "Wow," he said. "Wow" was right.

The petroglyphs gouged into the fragile Navajo sandstone had been spared the vandalism of the wind and rain for more than eight hundred years. Carved bear tracks walked the line of sand at the base of the panel. A snake coiled and slithered in a continuous line from one sandstone boulder to an upper panel. *Yei* figures stood with arms raised to the sky and seemed to call the rain with the crowned feathers in their heads.

On the next panel, a corn plant stretched in white etched lines. Next to the corn plant stood a man with arms and legs and body shaped identical to the plant. These people understood the truth: people have walked with *naadą́ą́* (corn) for more than three thousand years, since they bred it into existence in Mesoamerica. Maize has since walked the earth longer than any Christian or Muslim. The Diné have prayed with its pollen, ground the corn for their womanhood ceremonies, fed their relatives, cooked the meal of the blue corn to marry their wife or husband, and prayed with the cornmeal.

Díí dineʼé ei naadą́ą́ atʼé. The people are the corn.

Some of the *Diyin Diné* are named White Corn Boy and Yellow Pollen Girl. The *aniłtʼánii* (lacewing) is said to sing to the corn to grow the tassel to the sky. When traditional Diné people talk about *sąʼah naagháí bikeʼhózhǫ́,* they speak of *sąʼah naagháí* (The One Who Is Long in Life, often referring to Mother Earth) and *bikeʼhózhǫ́* (Directs Pleasant Conditions, often associated with Father Sky). The first is the proper state of femaleness (which can be experienced by the most masculine of men), and the latter is the proper state of maleness (able to be felt by the most feminine of women). *Sąʼah naagháí bikeʼhózhǫ́* is that still point between the two: harmonious, complete, beautiful perfection. A corn plant has male and female parts. When a tassel bursts with yellow pollen—that sudden expression of intense and determined life and beauty—that is *sąʼah naagháí bikeʼhózhǫ́.*

I have never seen this idea expressed on MTV.

"Wow," the boy said, "look at that."

Flat red-sandstone boulders as tall as my hip angled slightly toward the cliff face like stone armchairs. In their centers, the rock sloped into perfectly rectangular bowls as wide as loaves of bread. The people who had lived here had once ground corn on these rocks. They cooked the maize to a mush

or added it to stews or baked it as ash bread or flatbread. The Diné people weren't genetically descended from these people. But they were still their ancestors as long as they grew and ate the corn.

Malcolm had grown up here, and he had never seen this. "That's amazing," he said. "They ground it all right here. They probably stored it in different parts of the canyon to hide for the winter."

"Yeah," I said. "And I bet the Diné used those same hiding spots when they were fighting the Americans during the wars."

Malcolm nodded. The boy ran his hands inches from the bear-paw in the petroglyph panel. He had promised not to touch them when we approached, but this was almost better. You could feel the energy of their intent, despite the passing of time. The people who had created them had started leaving toward the Hopi country in the early 1300s, never to return. They had more ranging to do, and their ancestors were still restless across the Southwest to this day.

This place where we'd found the petroglyphs was probably a corn-grinding station and a storage relay.

"Lyle," I whispered. "I wish . . ."

The boy walked to the other panel. I followed.

Part of him is seeing it, I thought.

At the base of the cliff, a petroglyph of a five-fingered man stretched out his arms. His legs bent skyward like a lizard climbing a glass window. His hair crackled out from his scalp like lightning.

Above this man, flowing between his hands, was *náátsʼíílid*. A rainbow. Of course it was.

I wanted this for Lyle. The scrape of the cottonwood leaves against the rocks. The smell of wet sand after the rain. The feeling of these people, these Anasazi, learning to dance between corn and sun and water so they could be fed in beautiful harmony. They didn't wait for life to find them. They found where it already flowed and tapped in.

My literary hero Craig Childs wrote in his book *House of Rain* that he believed the Anasazi were a rain-worshiping people, moving through the Southwest along invisible spirals of climate and rainfall and establishing life where the traveling rains seemed to settle for a time. They built stone houses. They built stone granaries. They built stone kivas in the ground: the living representation of the *sipapu*, the hole of emergence from the previous world.

When archaeologists first excavated Anasazi buildings, they found the

kivas had fire-charred timbers, and many of them were collapsed. The first idea was that the kivas had been burned by raiders, much like the monasteries and churches torched by Viking pillagers in the Middle Ages of Europe.

But Childs reported that many archaeologists have a different theory. No invaders torched the kivas. The Anasazi did. When they left a village, they cleaned out all their religious artifacts and set fire to the kivas. The burning was a ceremony. When the rains shifted and they needed to move to grow their corn and have their corn grow them, they didn't hesitate.

They'd studied the patterns of water that grew their corn. Water was Life. And life was about change. These people—whoever they were—didn't fear change. They didn't fear their own restlessness.

They were counting on it.

UNTIL I SEE YOU WALKING AGAIN

I went to Hubbell Trading Post because I wanted to learn why it was important to live again. But as I got ready to leave Ganado and return to the East, I felt like I was learning to accept death. Not just Lyle Parsons's death, but my own.

It would take four seasons for me to learn what that really meant. It would take that long for me to meet the Bluebird People.

In the last week of my ranger service, I heard a whimpering in the yard of one of the Park Service houses while I walked back from the wash just after sunset. My flashlight beam found a litter of puppies abandoned, along with a small water dish, inside the fence.

The next day, someone showed up from a humane society in Gallup and picked them up. Please explain to me why these cruelties exist. Please explain these mercies that respond to them.

On the long nights, I'd walk under the constellation *Áłtse Etsoh* (The First Great One), that powerful elder walking immortally with his cane, who represents *są'ah naagháí bike'hózhǫ́*, that harmony and balance that come with time and old age. Strung from the same stars stood the great scorpion the Greeks called Scorpio, with its burning red heart star Antares.

Lyle Parsons was a Scorpio, and I didn't want him to be. I wanted his Zodiac sign to be *Áłtse Etsoh*. I want him walking into old age with a cane and teaching his sons all he'd learned.

It is all as random as any constellation. Intelligent, caring people like Lyle Parsons are taken into the spirit world, and child-abusing drunks pull up

to the front of the trading post and I have to help arrest them. These people are walking the earth just fine.

But I could forget these things while I walked a group of eighth graders from the middle school across the Ganado Valley to Hubbell Trading Post. We toured the grounds, I revealed all the places I'd shown the boy, and we walked back together through the cool breezes and rising heat of the August day.

Ken Lamberton came to visit me at the trading post. I hadn't shaken his hand since that day at the book festival. It was good to do it now. And it was easy to talk about how much I admired his book project, *Chasing Arizona*. He'd spent the year of the state's centennial covering more than 200,000 miles on the road, reporting on life from the Grand Canyon to Nogales to the Navajo Reservation.

Over a dinner of chili and tortillas, Ken asked me if I missed the West. Then comes the story.

One autumn three years before, in the middle of an outdoor sculpture garden along the Hudson River in New York, I heard a cottonwood tree rattling in the cold breeze. It was the first cottonwood I had heard in two years.

I started crying and couldn't stop for five minutes.

On my last day as a ranger in Ganado that summer, I stood under a cottonwood tree in the Pueblo Colorado Wash at Hubbell Trading Post. I clenched my fists and tried to cry. I could not.

I felt better when I walked inside the trading post and shook hands with Lennie Begay, a former Navajo Nation police officer and park ranger. He'd guided me every step of the way through my first ranger assignment at Hubbell. He'd shown me the ruins of Hubbell's first trading post at Ganado Lake.

"*Hágoónee*," Lennie said. "No Navajo word for *good-bye*. There's just 'Until I see you walking again.'"

I'd gone to visit one of my living literary heroes, Stanley Crawford, at his garlic farm in Dixon, New Mexico. We talked about the Anasazi sites discovered on the black basalt mesas surrounding the valley, about the rainfall that summer, about the guns we owned and how little we used them. Stan had moved to northern New Mexico in the 1960s, when you still heard mostly Spanish spoken on the plazas. It had felt like a foreign country. Stan said I should check out Taos.

I had heard of Taos because I had taken up reading Michael Reynolds's books about sustainable living and architecture. We'll get to that later. But I had also read of the relationship between Taos and the Pueblo Revolt,

between Taos and Kit Carson and the wars between the Americans and the Diné. The Diné name for Taos was *Tówoł*. The name refers to the stream that flows from Blue Lake near Taos Mountain down past the Taos Pueblo. It means "Gurgling Water." I spent the day in Albuquerque, then drove north toward Taos to spend the night in a sustainable house designed by Michael Reynolds.

Driving toward Taos was like traveling into a myth. I couldn't breathe when I passed out of the gorge that traces the path of the Río Grande through twists of basalt and descending slopes of sandstone. The black snake of the Río Grande Gorge wound its cracked, five-hundred-foot-deep basalt body across an ancient volcanic field gone gray and green with sagebrush. The sagebrush plain ran to the piñon and spruce foothills and then pounced to the sky in the twelve-thousand-foot peaks of the mountains. It reminded me of a Southwestern version of Gondor, the mythic country of plains and mountains in Tolkien's *The Lord of the Rings*.

If Taos is a myth, then it is retold with every sunrise. It is retold at every sunset, when *Jóhonaa'éí* walks into the border of *Diné Bikéyah* in the west and casts a purple-gold-scarlet light onto the peaks of *Mahwahlu* (Taos Mountain).

And there is something about that mountain. It is the same mountain I'd seen rising in cloud during the drive from the grave of Ganado Mucho. The soft ridges and rough lines ascending matched perfectly. A homecoming.

Who do you tell these things to?

THE BLUEBIRD PEOPLE

When I returned to the East, I'd close my eyes on every drive to a restaurant or a movie theater or a concert venue under the glow of parking lights, retail big-box stores, shopping malls, furniture stores, car dealerships, convenience stores, and other places selling things I neither wanted nor needed. Or I'd read my birding guide so I could look at kites, eagles, falcons, and *Táłtł'ááh áłééh* (The Heron Who Walks on the Bottom of the Stream). I began to imagine I was somewhere other than where I was.

Whenever I hosted a book event at a local library or bookstore for *Navajos Wear Nikes*, I knew I was back in the moment at the Tucson Festival of Books. I just wanted Lyle Parsons to raise his hand and ask a question from the audience.

The owners of a local bed-and-breakfast where I taught in Bucks County, Pennsylvania, learned they had two beavers living in the small creek on their property. The beavers—as beavers will do—built a lodge and a dam and created a small pond. When the owners of the bed-and-breakfast got a request from some people to get married on the grounds, they wanted to use a small grassy area nearby. The ground was wet from the beaver dam backing up the stream. So the owners called the Pennsylvania Game Commission. The game wardens tore apart the beaver dam, trapped the beavers, locked them in dog crates, and drove them in the back of a pickup truck to the Adirondacks in upper New York State.

Nobody checked to see that the beavers had three young kits in the lodge. These babies were left behind, abandoned. In the American affair, this is legal.

Somebody thought to call Aark Wildlife, a local wildlife rehabilitation center, to take in the young beavers. I didn't understand there was enough mercy in people that such a place could even exist.

The Aark workers built a large concrete pond in an enclosure for the baby beavers that summer. By the time I showed up for the orientation for new volunteers in the autumn, the baby beavers had all died of intestinal infections.

That Halloween, I started having dreams. I looked into a mirror and my eyes were leaking black pus.

I had more of these dreams during my Christmas break. I knew what all the Diné teachings had told me. I needed to get my hands in the earth.

That spring, I found the number of Paul Tsakos, owner of the Overbrook Herb Farm, about eight miles from my apartment. We made a simple arrangement: I would show up at eight o'clock every morning and leave by five o'clock at night. I would wear the crappiest jeans and shirts I owned. I would get my work boots resoled. I would buy a decent shade hat from the army-navy surplus store near my apartment. I would work all the gross, heavy, ass-busting jobs he had, and he would pay me with plants and fruit. I did this because I wanted to learn what the Anasazi already knew about partnering with plants. And maybe—I thought—it would stop the bad dreams.

Someone like Paul Tsakos could only wander into farming. The man grew up in Brooklyn, but his Italian grandfather ran a farm in upstate New York.

"That's where I first developed my peasant leanings," Paul would say. But Paul had drifted far from those peasant leanings in the 1960s. He earned a degree in classical languages from Boston University and then moved to Philadelphia, where he earned a master's degree in archaeology at the University of Pennsylvania. He dug for artifacts in Greece and the island of Crete. He was on the staff at the Penn Museum and helped restore pots and bowls with mud from the earth.

I can still walk through Overbrook in my mind. Behind Paul's modest stuccoed house is a small wooden shed where a reaper from the 1920s and a leather bellows hang from the rafters between tied bundles of dried garlic. A ramshackle work-shed with a tarp roof covers one of Paul's old tractors. A series of metal-frame greenhouses run toward the back of the property.

Paul has laid out his greenhouses and his gardens after his own mind. The gardens have names like Zeus, Apollo, Athena, Hera, and Hermes. The greenhouses are named Alpha, Beta, Kappa, Delta, and Epsilon. After my

first week, I can say things like, "Hey, Paul, if you're looking for that spade, I left it in Delta." And he knows right where to look.

I don't know how Paul Tsakos does this work. Paul can rise and work tirelessly all day and outpace me. I'd been lifting weights and running with weighted backpacks for six years. I'd been training in jiu-jitsu for five years. None of that mattered.

Paul had as much fat on his body as a tree. Each abdominal and forearm looked carved out of olive wood. I joked with him about it one day, and he took me out to Hera. He showed me how to use an Italian lean hoe. The Italian hoe is set on the end of a thick pole at a forty-five-degree angle to the ground, and it rips up large patches of weeds and grass when it is set to work. After a few minutes, I could feel my abs tightening like guitar strings.

"There it is!" says Paul. "The ancient abs device. Just do that for ten thousand hours, and you'll be ripped in no time!"

There was a lot of this work to be done at Overbrook Herb Farm. Paul grew everything organically, so there were no pesticides involved. Instead, you fought the weeds with your fists and your back and your patience.

Paul's wife, Betsy, was one of the most spirited women I'd met. She could work just as hard as Paul and never complain. She treasured her ragged "old lady coat" that she kept by the door. The neighbors once called the police to report a homeless woman walking down their suburban street. But it was just Betsy, taking a walk in her old lady coat.

I learned by the end of the summer how to use the digging fork, the spade, the Canterbury hoe, the scythe, the Japanese *hori-hori*, the Weedwacker, the Korean *ho-mi*, the rototiller, the machete, and my hands. This all made me feel more alive than I did in my own apartment.

I learned how to grow bull's blood lettuce, arugula, fancy rainbow carrots, broccoli, cherry tomatoes, heirloom tomatoes (oh those Brandywines), rosemary, bay, thyme, lamb's quarters, lemon verbena, parsley, garlic, onions, blue corn, eggplant, zucchini, kale, and golden beets. I wanted this knowledge. I was hungry for it.

It was a beautiful day to harvest these plants, to weight them and bag them, and to give them to Paul and Betsy. They sold the harvests to five-star restaurants in Philadelphia. Paul and Betsy couldn't afford to eat at any of these restaurants.

"We're peasant serfs!" Paul would sometimes say, laughing, while weeding or hoeing up the earth. I could also see a playful crack of tragedy in

his grin. I'd seen that crack before in my own face over the past year. I had seen it in Lyle Parsons's face.

The crown of a basil plant picked before nine o'clock in the morning and catching the strong summer light is one of the proofs of *hózhǫ́* and harmony in the world. The leaves curve out and up like the *sigul* of some desert civilization that may have birthed geometry itself.

When I leave my shift with my dirty hands and fingernails, I don't want to go home. I want to ask Paul and Betsy if I can sleep on the floor in front of Paul's bookshelf that bows with thick books on the temples of Mycenae, ancient Greek coins, the tactics of the Greek hoplites, the special variety of beetles, and French cooking. Worlds long gone.

I'm not sure there is a home to return to anymore.

Next to a row of eggplant, a pair of *dólii* (bluebirds) live in the small red wooden box that Paul nailed to the deer fence surrounding the Hera garden. These two bluebirds fly in and out all day, catching bugs and worms and grubs for their chicks they are raising in the box.

While I stack the plastic bread trays that Paul used to shade his seedling parsley and lettuce and alpine strawberries, a bluebird flashes across the sun. He flies back, pumping his wings in a crescent. He smacks a leaf on the apple tree growing next to Paul's old red shed, and I wince to think that he's had a midflight collision. But he's made no mistake.

He drops down to the fence wire and brandishes a fat green caterpillar in his beak that he's snatched from the leaf above.

The *dólii* flaps to the red wooden box and feeds the caterpillar to his two chicks. Death becomes Life in any garden.

The bluebirds watch me from the fence whenever I am weeding. They know when I'm flushing out the bugs with my strange *Nohokaa' Diné* hands. Their small shadows dart over my back as they snatch the clicking beetles and floating white cabbage moths while I weed the rows of basil and cilantro and squash and eggplant. Their short tin-whistle cries hover over me in a song.

That same week, during my Sunday shift at the Aark, I care for my first group of baby bluebirds, still gray and downy. Their nest tipped and fell in a storm. I feed them mealworms with a small hemostat.

When I go to work with Paul and Betsy the next day and help string stakes with old lengths of rubber garden hose and tomato twine for Brandywine heirloom tomatoes, I start referring to Paul and Betsy in my mind as *Dólii Diné* (The Bluebird People).

The bluebirds at the Aark become easily attached to whoever feeds them. During a certain week, whenever I walk outside to feed the great horned owls or red-tailed hawks in their enclosures, a bluebird will fly down from the roof of the clinic and land on my shoulder as though it were the most natural thing in the world.

The bluebird cheeps in my ear, and I bend over a loose, dark patch of earth, dig my fingers into the moss, and come up with an earthworm. Break it into small pieces, and the bluebird eats them one by one from my fingers. The bird cocks its head at me, breathes deeply, and then flies off to the top of the roof.

The bluebird flies down and lands on my shoulder nearly once an hour. I feed him the earthworms. We become something.

I walked into the warm summer night after showering Paul's soil from my hands and heard a scratching on the fir tree growing in front of my herb garden on my porch. Four *wóóneeshch'iidii* (cicada) had crawled up from the moist earth. The four *wóóneeshch'iidii* knew how to stay asleep in the earth and grow from egg to pupa to larva—all while tumbling through the darkness of freezing and thawing soil for more than three years, all while growing and changing and emerging from an earthbound creature into one of the winged Insect People, those travelers who bought passage for the Diné into this the Glittering World when they drove arrows through the sides of their bodies and proved by their suffering to the Grebe People that they were worthy to pass through the mudhole into this Glittering World.

I stood in my bare feet and watched the mud-caked *wóóneeshch'iidii* crawl up the brown scales of fir bark for an hour. I set my watch alarm to wake me two hours later. I could barely breath as the *wóóneeshch'iidii* cracked their muddy shells away and their bodies emerged neon-green. The cicadas arced back out of their brown skins like Olympic divers stretching into space. They clung to their own skins with their legs under the guidance of some *Nítch'i* (wind) speaking to them. Their wings unfurled like new spring leaves. The wings stretched and stiffened with liquid. After an hour, they shone like glass in the streetlight.

The *wóóneeshch'iidii* flew away by dawn.

I don't want to go back inside ever again. I never want to go back to sleep.

I take one of the muddy carapaces inside and set it on my bookshelf.

When the summer is over and I go back to school, the dreams come again. I look into a mirror, and I smile, and black pus falls out of my eyes, and my gums are yellow as cancer, and my teeth fall out.

I lift weights and train in jiu-jitsu every day. This goes on for two hours a night. The suffering is real and important.

At the end of that summer, I travel to Maine and walk up Mount Cadillac, and I know I am not really walking up a mountain. When I reach the top, I'm with my wife but I'm alone. I step around the tourists eating ice cream bars and the large men and large women who have definitely not been running in the morning, who are climbing out of their SUVs in their Columbia sportswear. They have driven up the asphalt road on the backside of the mountain to its summit, and the mountain is no longer a mountain.

The ocean is a flowing desert to the horizon with no drinkable water and extending as far as oblivion. The waves are breaking like promises.

I wish I could wake next to a smoldering campfire with sagebrush in my hair. I want to drink shit juice because I know I am a loser here.

That's when I start receiving gifts. Those compassionate coincidences.

After Hurricane Sandy, I lose power in my apartment for three days. The streetlights are extinguished. I walk outside with my dog. Orion and Sirius walk blue and brilliant across the sky. Deer walk down to nibble at the grass their ancestors had once grazed on this land that had once been a colonial farm, before the European pressures of money and population and adornment converted it into an apartment complex. We are left with a series of mortared rooms waiting to become a ruin, like the Red House of the Anasazi. *Eeyaa. Doodah.* Don't go in there.

When the power comes back on, I start having a dream. I walk under cottonwood trees, and their leaves are black against the twilit sky. I hike down to the wash. The waters tinkle over the rocks. Something is walking after me now, but I know I can't run from it because it's inside my own skin.

I fall to my knees by the water and hold two pieces of *noolyíní* (black obsidian) in my hands. Obsidian is a mineral of *sihasin*, of reverence, of the North, of the Black Road. I clack the rocks together until they splinter away into shards so sharp I could shave with them. I use these shards to cut my wrists parallel with my bones, so the turquoise blood of my veins comes flooding out and shines black against the rising moon as it finds the earth. The sand drinks, and I hear Lyle Parsons whispering in the cottonwood leaves, and I know this is the only escape.

I don't know if this is a nightmare or a clarifying dream.

I have this dream seven nights in a row.

Then I start having this dream during the day, while waiting at a stoplight where I once saw a hawk hunting from a dead oak tree in a field. That field

is gone now. Houses built for less than $200,000 that will retail for more than $600,000 now sit in muddy lots that were once fields thick with mice and rabbits and soil that Paul could have used to grow his tomatoes.

The hawk has moved on. Even he understands that it's all about location. I have not learned this lesson.

I have not cried for Lyle Parsons. I am waiting for him to teach me both.

I attended a staff training at the start of my school year and sat up in the nosebleed seats of the massive auditorium, paid for by the taxes of families descended from the culture that took the land of the Lenni-Lenape who had once fished and hunted the rocky forests of Bucks County, Pennsylvania. I sat with the wonderful people in my English department. I enjoyed them and smiled with them. It was our yearly "kickoff" session. Near the end of the session, the students entered and walked around with large papier-mâché heads designed like the masks for Mardi Gras. Most of them weren't very brightly colored, and I wondered if this was done out of respect for the BP black bleed in the gulf that had decimated the ecosystems around New Orleans.

But then the masks went away, and the spotlight came up on the stage. Our school band director and the middle school band director sat with their cello and their trombone. They were playing a melody I knew very well: the final movement of Beethoven's Ninth Symphony, "Ode to Joy." A group of a dozen students walked out from behind the curtain with brass instruments and joined the teachers playing the melody. Something was shifting in me. It was the same feeling I had in the wash with the boy when we were wearing our Adobes. A snake is swimming across whatever creek flows through my body. When the curtains part on a line of nearly a hundred students playing violins, violas, cellos, and timpani drums, I am leaning forward, and I can feel Lyle Parsons's hand on my shoulder. When the back curtain opens and more than a hundred choir students start singing the lyrics from "Ode to Joy," I feel the ice spalling something in me. I am cracking.

I had been walking up mountains looking for some easing of pain or vision of kinship with Lyle Parsons. I had never bothered to look at the species of animal to which I can most easily connect. I had never bothered to look to *Nohokaa' Diné*, playing their music with those five-fingered hands. And here they are, singing the lyrics from the poem by Beethoven's friend Friedrich Schiller, written in 1785. The lyrics are easily available. Look them up.

The students go through a final minute of the symphony. I'm bawling.

The water of my inner ocean runs over my lips. I let everyone leave ahead of me so I can finish letting it out.

I know that Lyle Parsons put me here in this moment.

That September, I spent the money for a plane ticket to visit Glen in Arizona during the long weekend of Rosh Hashanah. I had missed his graduation in May, and so I was counting my visit as his present. I brought him a small rug I had woven, a wooden spoon I had carved from a cedar tree in Ganado, and a stainless-steel lunch pail like those Betsy used to serve our crusted bread and chocolate almond butter and goat cheese. I wanted to weep when my brother Darren met me outside his rented casita in the desert north of Phoenix. We hugged, and the city lights behind him shone against the night clouds as bright and yellow as any cancer.

We drove north in a rented Toyota to Page, Arizona, back to the basin desert of the moon, where Hollywood filmmakers had recently used the Grand Staircase as a stand-in for the planet Mars in a soon-to-tank summer blockbuster film.

Hot wind burned my face as Darren and I drove my mom's new Bobcat ATV to Big Water, Utah, and toured the desert backcountry. A golden eagle followed us for miles on the way back. Her feathers bent in the thermals as the raptor slowly cycloned into the sky and hunted along Coyote Canyon.

'Atsá (golden eagles) can often live for thirty years in the wild. This could have been the same eagle who'd watched me scrambling my zit-pocked ass up that mesa fifteen years ago in search of the path of a mountain lion.

My brother Glen wanted to spend the weekend in Jerome, Arizona. Jerome is a town backhoed into the side of a five-thousand-foot mountainside overlooking the Verde Valley in south-central Arizona. The town once hosted a massive copper, gold, and silver mine. My brother wanted to stay in the historic Jerome Grand Hotel at the crown of the mountain. The hotel had once been a hospital for the miners and had also served as a mental hospital. *Eeyaa. Doodah.* Don't go in there.

We drove south, and I laughed when Glen took a Rice Krispies Treat bar as long as my forearm out of his bag. He unwrapped it and began to eat it like an oversized candy bar. He'd bought it at Walmart the night before. He and Darren and I would pick from the treat during the rest of the trip.

We reached Jerome after dark in a thundering rainstorm that lit the sides of the town as we drove up the mountain. The headlights and swishing windshield wipers set the stage for some horror film in which I was about to star.

The Jerome Grand Hotel is haunted. And I wanted to see ghosts. I hoped to see Lyle Parsons walking the halls. Perhaps I'd talk with him about my dreams. But there were no ghosts in the hotel. No horror film unfolded. Perhaps ghosts are just something we carry.

The next day, I learn that Sedona rocks become so red against the blue sky and shine bright enough that they mask the Anglo commercialism that springs up as you enter that country. Glen and Darren and I found a no-fee parking spot and hiked down to Oak Creek. We walked the green grass and shady Arizona sycamores along the muddy banks in complete silence. No people shouted or sucked water bottled in recycled plastic or out of CamelBaks strapped just above their love handles.

We found a clear green pool where trout—those finned blades—drifted in the slow current. I was the first to strip to my underwear and slide underwater. I might as well have been looking for Neil's sunglasses again—Jim Danger at the dock—as I watched my air bubbles rise to the silver surface, where air and gravity say to water, "This far and no farther."

A trout swam past, struck at my hair, and darted downstream—a flash of rainbow. I pushed to the surface. First World to Glittering World in just a few kicks.

Darren and Glen jumped in, and we swam for an hour and climbed out to the banks and into the waterfalls opposite, where a spring fed the pool. I rubbed my hand through my soaked hair and touched the back of my neck. My feet on the earth. I felt cleansed of something.

Only my brothers could do this.

We drove back to Church Wells, cooked steak and made *náneeskaadí* (tortillas), and fell asleep at the table while playing Scrabble.

We got up the next morning at four o'clock and drove toward the rising sun to Lukachukai. I wanted to take Glen to see Diné College in Tsaile. I hoped he'd attend. We took a short hike to a maroon clay hill pocked with boulders overlooking Tsaile Lake. *Gad* (juniper) spread their scaly boughs, and the tufts of grama grass and green-gray shards of sagebrush grew thick with scent.

I ran up the last fifty yards of the hill. The vein blood pumped down my neck—that *dootł'izhii* turquoise that the *Diyin Diné* invited into our bodies when they laid down the buckskin and set yellow and white corn down with eagle feathers and closed the buckskin over and summoned the wind to blow life into it and *Áłtsé Hastiin* (First Man) and *Áłtsé 'Asdzáán* (First Woman) emerged.

Glen and I laughed while running down the hill, and Darren jogged behind.

Glen and I walked back to the Diné College campus down a dirt road grown over with *ts'ah* (sagebrush) and *k'iiłtsoii* (rabbitbrush). We three turned our heads to see the sunlight reflecting off the blue-black glass of the eight-story *hoghan* at the center of the campus, the first tribal college in America. I could still remember the smell of popcorn and spilled Coke in the building when we came up here for pow-wows. Glen and Darren and I yakked and laughed as we walked.

I felt it before my eye twitched down and saw the banded scales, the edge of white near the rattle, the diamond head, the body like a thick rope woven of a deep wisdom.

Glen was laughing and looking to the west, and he flinched when I flashed my arm out in front to stop him from walking. *There.* You have read that word. That is how long this took to happen.

"Whoa!" he said.

Against a rabbitbrush in the cool morning coiled *Tł'iish 'ádaanínígíí.* The Snake That Speaks. It was at least two feet long.

This was the first rattlesnake I had ever seen. I was glad to see it here.

I crouched in front of *Tł'iish 'ádaanínígíí.* I whispered, "*Yá'át'ééh Abíní, sha'kesh.*" Good morning, my friend.

"Uh . . . Jim?" Glen said. I could tell he was worried. My face was maybe a foot from the Snake That Speaks.

Maybe I was waiting for *Tł'iish 'ádaanínígíí* to tell me something about Lyle Parsons.

Glen touched my shoulder, and I knew he was asking me to come back. The snake flicked its black lightning tongue. It had nothing to say yet. Not yet. But they say snakes know about lightning. They know about rain. And something in *Tł'iish 'ádaanínígíí* told me that a storm was coming, rain was coming. Life was coming. And after the rain, rainbows.

I turned and touched Glen's shoulder. We walked back to the parking lot, to the rented white Toyota Camry.

While we stretched outside the car, a *dólii* (bluebird) flew past, chasing a white cabbage moth, snatching it from the air in its beak.

I had to push tears away when I returned the rented car in Phoenix at one in the morning and made my flight back to the East Coast. After I landed, I read how strong storms boomed over the Reservation the day after I left. More than sixty people had to be evacuated from their homes in

Chinle and Many Farms. These homes were in the basin and the washes that collected the storm water from Tsaile and Lukachukai. *Tł'iish 'ádaanínígíí* spoke the truth.

When I returned, I learned my dog was dying of cancer. I changed her bandages and disinfected her bleeding tumor for half a year. I did not mind this. I loved my fat little black pug. And cancer and I were well acquainted at this point.

I would also say that the American affair and cancer were well acquainted. I might also say that the American affair was cancer on the body of *Nahasdzáán* (the Earth Mother).

I escaped the grief by studying more about how that cancer was growing. I learned that there were ways to stall the tumor of oil fields and the black bleeds of tanker spills and the carbon dioxide venting from our power plants, our furnace exhausts, and our tailpipes. I studied my Navajo every morning and said my prayers. But I also started working and learning about the designs of Michael Reynolds. I started to learn about Earthships.

These buildings mimic the physics of the cells of our bodies to capture energy and distribute it through the structure. How did a human being think these things up? This is not how a normal American building works. Most of these American buildings, like the hotel that hosted my senior prom, chug oil and electricity made from burning coal or splitting uranium atoms. Most of them ensure that places like Black Mesa and Church Rock get mined and destroyed again and again and again.

Earthships can heat themselves without burning any fuel. They use the heat of the sun and are so thoroughly insulated and store heat so well that their interiors can maintain a constant seventy degrees during a night when the outside temperature falls to ten degrees below zero.

These buildings made me believe that human beings can be better relatives to *Nahasdzáán*. They were mostly in New Mexico. I was living in Pennsylvania.

I moved out by the spring.

I packed my Toyota Prius and bought a plane ticket for Glen to fly out and meet me in Pennsylvania. We drove west. We passed all the paths I had migrated. It was all new, and I had been there before. We crossed the Mississippi in Mark Twain's hometown. We drifted through Colorado and down into the eagle's nest of the southern Rocky Mountains. We coasted into Taos in the middle of the afternoon.

When we pulled into the Greater World Community—the Earthship

Biotecture off-the-grid community north of Taos—and the glass of those homes shimmered in the sun, I knew I was walking down the right path.

When I drove Glen back to Arizona, I asked him whether I should try to stay in Taos for the next school year.

"Let New Mexico give you the answer," he said.

I drove back to Taos. But first I would be stopping in Gallup, New Mexico, to see a man who had built two Earthships less than an hour from my hometown of Ganado. I slept that night in the cricket silence of the Utah desert.

I did not have any dreams of slitting veins with obsidian or seabirds drowning in the black bleed of oil tankers and undersea wellheads. My dreams were forgotten by dawn.

PATH OF RENEWAL

That day I woke in my tent where I'd camped in Ganado and drove over the Defiance Summit to Gallup, the "Heart of Indian Country." Here I met one of my living heroes, and I didn't even know it.

I was driving in my red Prius to meet ER doctor John Kraker. He'd built two Earthships in Gamerco, New Mexico, and planned to get more built on the Navajo Reservation.

For the past four decades, architect Michael Reynolds has been designing and building homes that look like a cross between a space station from *Star Wars* and a hobbit-hole from the Shire. These homes collect water on their metal roofs and store it in underground tanks behind the structures. They use small solar-powered pumps and the force of gravity to circulate the water through the building. The water gets moved five times: first into the sinks for drinking; then through the shower or washing machine; then through a plant feeder, where you can grow your own food; then into a gray water tank that is used to flush the toilet; and finally into a black water cell outside the building that feeds plants .

The Earthship buildings heat themselves using an array of glass windows facing to the south. In the winter, photons from the sun spill through the glass and leap along the back walls of the building. These walls are built from old rubber tires filled with dirt pounded in by young people with sledgehammers. Each tire swallows three wheelbarrows of dirt and weighs more than three hundred pounds. The wall is usually in an arch shape, which means it can take the impact of a dump truck driving into it and

still keep its form. The tires become steel-belted, insulated rammed-earth bricks. And they store the heat of the photons running through the glass. At night, all the stored heat spills out of the tire walls through the process of convection. This creates a stable temperature without any fuel-guzzling air conditioning or expensive oil-chugging furnace.

Most people who live in these homes pay few utility bills, aside from one for propane to cook food and heat water. Many of these homes have banana trees growing in the greenhouses at the front while the air outside is ten degrees below zero and it's snowing. Let me restate that there is no heater. Earthships now cost about as much as a "normal" American home.

Based in Taos, New Mexico, Reynolds and his company, Earthship Biotecture, have been raising Earthships—meant to "sail on the seas of tomorrow"—all over the West, from Idaho to Montana to Texas. They sell plans and architectural drawings through their website so people can build them independently. They run an internship program.

The heart of Earthship Biotecture seems to beat in the Greater World Community, outside Taos, the result of Reynolds and his coworkers guiding a law through the state legislature to allow these buildings to be planned like a modern housing development. This struggle appeared in Oliver Hodge's award-winning 2007 documentary *Garbage Warrior*. Within this "Sustainable Development Testing Site," the company is trying to keep the pulse beating by starting their own school: the Earthship Biotecture Academy.

Put in motion by Reynolds and entrepreneur Ron Sciarrillo, the two men plan to use the academy to develop abandoned gravel pits in New Mexico and across the West.

Dr. John Kraker got into Earthships around the time I first moved to Ganado in 1989. I was meeting him today in Gallup to see what he'd been able to create.

I pulled up to M&R Trading along the east side of State Route 264 running into Gallup, and I had to smile. Here, we'd bought our first horse, the bay gelding Naat'áanii. I parked the car and walked to Dr. Kraker's small Nissan pickup truck. He rolled down his window and leaned out. He wore a navy blue V-neck T-shirt and red-framed bifocal glasses.

Kraker's passenger leaned into the window: a golden retriever mutt with a strong snout and soulful eyes banded with powerful color, and that color was yellow.

I petted the mutt through the window and asked his name. Gandalf.

"Why don't you just follow me up there?" he said. "Your Prius can handle the road. Probably."

We drove over a gravel washboard of a road toward Kraker's Earthships.

"So, you obviously came out here for a reason," Kraker said, stepping out of his truck. "What's your reason? Why are you here?"

I paused. I didn't know how to answer him completely, so I just did my best.

"Well . . . where I grew up, I was taught about *Nahasdzáán* and *Yah Dilhil*. Mother Earth and Father Sky. I was taught about the Emergence People, who walked up from the First World and grew stronger through all the shadows of our forgotten ancestors. We are the descendants of those people. Some of us have lived and some of us . . . some of us have died. But I owe it to the things that gave me life to help make this earth and sky as beautiful as possible. These ways of building, these Earthships here and out in Taos, are the most direct way people can do that. I don't think we can really wait for corporations or governments to change. We have to change ourselves. We can do that by learning to build a better world. These building methods I've read about could help people living out on the Navajo Reservation. So here I am."

"Well," he said, grinning, "let's check it out."

He called the first building Earthship One. The white plaster of the structure shone in the penetrating June light. We walked inside so we could sit down on a pair of sofas next to the wood stove in the corner.

From these sofas, Kraker explained how this Earthship had started as a project with a halfway house for the many alcohol and drug addicts he'd treated at the Gallup Indian Medical Center. Kraker had first seen the idea of building walls from tires in Torreon, just west of Cuba, New Mexico. So he had set up guys at the halfway house who'd been recommended by the parole officer. Some of the men had been to prison. Some had been in addiction counseling for alcohol and drugs. Kraker specialized in addictions, and he helped train counselors in addictions.

Kraker had organized his efforts around a nonprofit he named Path of Renewal. He started out with a four-man crew. And he needed to get them working. So while he was waiting for the plans for Earthship One from Mike Reynolds, Kraker just counted the number of tires from one of Reynolds's Earthship books. But the tires in the illustrations were not exactly to scale (nor were they supposed to be). So the walls ended up too far back and very steep. They actually had to double wall the tires to keep them from

walking forward. Then the work crew mounted a huge roof beam overhead on a steel pipe.

The build nearly cost Kraker his marriage. He'd maxed out his credit cards and borrowed from his and his children's life insurance fund to finish the project. His wife, a pediatrician in Gallup, had Kraker go to see a psychiatrist because she thought he might be bipolar. But once he sat down with the psychiatrist, he was diagnosed with attention deficit hyperactivity disorder (ADHD).

This didn't surprise him. "I don't know if you know that, but something like 80 percent of ER doctors are ADHD," he said.

I asked him why he was willing to pay so high a cost to finish the building. He explained the mechanics of his altruism. "I've always been sort of a tree hugger." He turned his neck and eyed my reaction to his comment. He seemed to like my response. So he continued.

"We actually used this building for the first year as a pottery business. If you notice along the walls I've got the 220-volt outlets we put in for the pottery kilns for drying. But that business ended up dying, and so we took the extra steps to finish the building as an actual residence."

I asked Kraker about some of the Earthship failings. He was happy to answer. For one, he thought Reynolds's ideas against the grid were a little misguided.

Reynolds has argued that any kind of infrastructure for power is doomed to fail. Once a corporation or a local township has invested in a power plant, it has clear incentives to use that power plant until all of the infrastructure has been paid for by its investors. Even if this means that the plant might be running on an obsolete technology, like coal or natural gas, the people will keep using it.

Dr. Kraker didn't buy that argument completely. He believed that a communal connection through power lines was essential to keep a society working. "I am for the grid," he said. "This idea that people must be totally off centralized services doesn't always benefit everyone. Having access to a tie-in to the grid also avoids costly batteries that have to be replaced or recycled or end up in a landfill."

Kraker also claimed it was better for people to live closer together in carefully planned communities. "People talk about and critique suburban sprawl," he said. "But people also need to think about rural sprawl. And that's what you have here. And you also see it in the Earthship community up at Taos. So I would also critique that."

Gandalf scooted closer and pawed at me. His mitts were huge, nearly the size of my hands if I curled my fingers closed.

"If he starts to bother you, just let me know, and I can take him outside," Kraker said. "He gets really energetic, and he scratches me up something awful."

Crusted blood had scabbed into large beads from the scratches on Kraker's forearms. Kraker rubbed his nose, patted Gandalf's head, and mentioned that the guy on the work crew who set the flagstone floor tiles got sober and actually built his own Earthship near Crownpoint.

He recalled how he and his partners at Path of Renewal used to host music nights and jam sessions in the building. Kraker had taken up the harmonica years ago and confessed to still be working out the kinks in his playing.

"The harmonica is an easy instrument to play, but very hard to master."

As we walked outside, he talked about how he'd worked with Path of Renewal until one of the board members "got rather unscrupulous" with the money. Kraker washed his hands of the nonprofit soon after.

"Now I rent the building to one of our male nurses at the hospital," he said. "He's a busy guy, and he doesn't exactly keep on top of watering everything. But that fern is still doing pretty good."

We walked out into the June sunshine, and I could feel the photons heating the back of my neck. I squinted against their dance. Sagebrush and rabbitbrush stroked our bare legs. I walked up the rocks at the side of the building and along the paths out to the rain-collecting cistern.

On the way back to Kraker's truck, he confessed that he loved Earthship One. And he'd love to live in it. But his wife would not move inside. "There's just too much baggage for her with this place. Too much weight for her to carry."

Kraker stooped over a *tsá'ászi'* (yucca plant). "I was at this sheep camp the other day near Teec Nos Pos, and we had a cookout up there," he said. "This world-class Apache chef who teaches culinary courses at Diné College made us deep-fried yucca bananas. It was the first time I ever had them."

He set to picking the small green *hashk'aan* (yucca fruit), some no larger than my big toe. When we got to his truck, he put his *hashk'aan* on his front seat.

"That's a cool paint job," I said, tapping the side of his truck. It was a bumpy surface, like black paint mixed with wood chips. Kraker told me it was actually spray-on truck bed liner. He liked going hunting in that truck

in the Zuni Mountains, and he liked that he could scratch the material and it took the damage just fine. He pointed to a scar where "three crazy Navajo women" who had come to the camp-out sat in a yurt on the edge of the truck and scratched away the paint. Kraker had asked his auto detailer to spray the liner on the truck for $750, rather than getting a $2,000 paint job.

"I'm Dutch," he said. "That means I'm careful with money. But it also just makes sense. To fix this bunch of scratches, I can just take a can of truck bed liner and spray it right over the top."

"You range up into the Zuni Mountains, huh?" I said. "What do you hunt?"

"I've done a lot of bow hunting for elk," he said. "But I'm a better hunter than a killer. I've taken shots at elk and missed. And then my partner would take the same shot and put it right through the heart."

Kraker wandered into a story of how he went on a once-in-a-lifetime hunt with his son-in-law. They hunted oryx in southern New Mexico. The oryx is that stunning antelope that emerged from the Kalahari Desert in Southern Africa, with purple-gray hair and distinct white markings on its black face. Its ribbed black horns that stretch up into the sky like bony scimitars are unmistakable when you see them moving through the desert grass. The oryxes range widely across the sands, and they are tough muthas. That's why someone had the idea to bring them to the White Sands Missile Range for people to hunt. Kraker remembered how his son-in-law shot an oryx through the lung with his .30-06 rifle. Then he had to shoot it three more times before the oryx fell over, put its tongue out, and ran into the spirit world.

Kraker opened the door to his truck and asked if I wanted to come back to his place and cook the *hashk'aan* and some oryx and stay the night before I drove on to Placitas, New Mexico. He said it was the best meat he'd ever tasted.

I followed him back to his house in the hills above town, not far from the Gallup Indian Medical Center.

We had not covered more than twelve miles, but we might as well have landed in another world. Rows and rows of Pueblo-style and stick-frame houses crowded against one another, street by street. No Earthships here. All of these houses were parasites on the earth, each a stylized, well-marketed tick sucking at the stream of oil running its heaters. Each room was lit with electrons shot over high-tension wires from power plants steaming water with vaporized coal.

We sat at his simple table nooked under a skylight. Papers collected on the counter tops. Dirty knives rested at the edge of the sink. Food wrappers sat next to old magazines. The house looked like it had been lived in by guests who'd forgotten to clean up after themselves.

"You'll have to forgive the mess," Kraker said. "My wife and I are both doctors, so we're not home much. We've tried hiring housekeepers, but they just can't keep up with us."

Kraker and I wrapped the yucca fruit in aluminum foil as we talked. We set them on a tray in a convection oven. He talked of how his father had been a missionary assigned to the region as a cook for the army. When he rolled out of the service, he worked as a cook at Rehoboth McKinley hospital. He eventually got injured on the job and fell for his nurse at the hospital, Kraker's future mother.

The conversation wandered to his work in the Gallup emergency room. I asked whether he saw a lot of drunks. He did.

Kraker had more than twenty years of hospital work beneath his answer. "Well, first of all, it's largely a misperception," he said. "The truth is that 50 percent of Navajos don't drink at all. They're teetotalers. The other 50 percent who do drink often move in a migration cycle. So they'll come into town, get good and drunk for a day or two, then go back home and be totally sober and clear and take care of their livestock. And they won't touch it for another few weeks or months. So it's not that Navajos drink any more than whites. It's just more on display."

Kraker opened the oven, and we unwrapped the *hashk'aan*. I split them open for us with my pocketknife. Kraker handed me a spoon, but I just put the pod up to my mouth and ate it straight from the husk. The small white kernels fell out like perfectly triangular pieces of white shell. I tongued their bitter taste. Their slight spice burned my throat.

"Then you have people who've learned to drink alcohol tragically from the beginning," Kraker said, spooning and chewing the white shell of the *hashk'aan*. "In the days after the wars, drinking was illegal on the Reservation. So you had to watch for the policeman or the federal agent. It was illegal to *possess* alcohol, but it wasn't illegal to be drunk. So they would drink it down as quickly as possible to get rid of it. Then there was the boarding school experience. Many children went in and had to endure a lot. Many were molested and beaten. That trauma finds its expression in alcoholism today.

"And the Long Walk is its own form of trauma," he continued. "Many

people still remember that. And then there was the federal program in the 1930s of the sheep and the livestock reduction. There you had people's livelihoods taken away, especially the men. And so they had to leave their homes, scatter up to the beet fields in Idaho and the hay fields in Colorado. Or they'd work for the railroad or in the mines. Alcohol became a way to self-medicate against the feelings of loss. The kids saw their parents do it, and so it's been passed down through the generations. Alcohol alters your mental state. And there are some bad mental states that some people have inherited."

I asked him about what my friends have said about Navajos having a genetic disadvantage when it comes to alcohol. Kraker just shook his head.

"If anything, I've seen Navajo people metabolize alcohol faster than Anglos. Someone might come into the ER and blow a .3, but within a few hours he'll blow a .08. That's rather fast."

He raised a skinny arm and ran a hand through his short hair and re-adjusted his glasses. Kraker had once run marathons, and he had kept his long hair in a ponytail. But he hadn't put on running shoes for many years, and he could feel himself growing thick around the middle. He seemed a man caught up in a restlessness he had no choice but to inherit. He paced back and forth as he spoke beside the kitchen island.

Kraker turned to the stove and made a stir-fry of carrots, snap peas, yams, and peanuts. He cooked the oryx strips separately in the oven while we talked about the reservation and being married and how the roads don't always converge and people grow apart and how the restlessness of living in a modern house can make us feel both fortunate and alone.

Kraker had grown up in Teec Nos Pos and Shiprock. He had gone to medical school in Michigan, and he'd done well. He'd had many chances at high-paying jobs in the East. But he'd ranged back into the West and found a place in New Mexico. I would have said he'd followed the rainbow to the right place. I admired him for it.

And he was right about that oryx. It was beautiful meat.

DAMN TIRE POUNDERS

Less than a week later, I was pounding tires and showering each evening with a plastic six-gallon gas can and helping to build an Earthship in the Greater World Community.

I had been paired with a roommate, Rob Dunny. Rob is a rammed-earth builder from Brisbane, Australia. He ditched the idea of going to college to become an engineer and started apprenticing to the trade as soon as he left high school. Rob takes massive metal frames and sets them up vertically, sifts the raw earth at a building site, and then pounds the earth with a pneumatic press until it forms in the frames. He works up inside the frames and rams about four feet of earth per day. It's a faster way to create a massive adobe brick wall. By the time he's finished, the wall is done in its entirety, made of the soil on which the building stands. There's very little timber used, so the building can't be mauled down to its foundations by the massive colonies of termites in Australia.

Years before, Dunny had worked as a camp counselor in Pennsylvania, where he'd taught teenagers how to rock-climb in the Pocono Mountains. This time, he's traveled to the States to be an intern at Earthship Biotecture. But he'd also ranged down through Colorado for a couple of weeks to rock-climb near Diablo Canyon. After the internship, he would travel back into Colorado and scout some more climbing walls before he returned to Australia, where he had an off-grid place out in the bush, powered by photovoltaic panels, next to his brother's organic farm.

He's a serious bloke. He likes his beer but refrains from weed. Still, he

never misses a chance to crack a joke and take a bit of the piss out of the younger interns. Few of them are older than twenty-five. Rob's just turned thirty-four. He's the old man among us.

After meeting at the Earthship Biotecture offices, Rob and I and the twelve other interns drove out to the mesa, a stretch of a half dozen roads that travel west toward the Río Grande Gorge and beyond. Buried power lines run out from Taos and give people a chance to have grid electricity. But many of the people on the mesa don't use it. Most of the homes have the slanted glass facing south that collects passive solar energy and heat. Most of the homes are built from adobe or plastered straw bales or cinder block blown with insulation. Many of them are homes built from tires sledgehammered with earth and designed by Michael Reynolds.

Reynolds came out here in 1980, when there were just a few small houses on the mesa. Teenagers still ran around in the desert with their .22 rifles and followed the coyote trails crisscrossing through the sagebrush. Reynolds used a government grant to build a house that could collect its own water from the sky, use the sun to heat itself, and grow plants for food; it used a small vertical-axis scoop to run a turbine and generate wind power. He built the structure out of old beer cans, scrap lumber, and lots of cement. Reynolds called it the Turbine House.

Some said the building was a spaceship that had just landed.

After living in that house for a few months, Reynolds realized something: he wasn't paying rent, he wasn't paying for electricity, and he wasn't paying for heating or cooling. He was independent. He didn't need money coming in every month. He could work or not work. He felt he *owned* his life.

I walked past the half dome of glass bottles matrixed in cement and got honked at the whole way by the six white geese who lived under the dome; they came crowding in to check my business. I continued to the Turbine House and knocked on the door.

A dude with a neck like a pit bull opened it. His juvenile smile, deeply tanned skin, and thick beard made his age seem immortal.

"Hey, man," he said. "What's up? You one of the interns?"

"Yeah."

"Well, right on, brother! Name's Murph. Keep up the good fight! You know where you are right now? Because this place has history, man."

"I know this is the Turbine House. I know Mike Reynolds had a lot of good visions here."

"Definitely, man. Definitely. This place is where it started."

A shadow moved behind Murph's leg. A chubby pit bull with a gray snout and cataract eyes shuffled into the doorway and sniffed my crotch.

"Hey! Bigs! Don't do that!" Murph pushed the thick dog back with his leg. "Don't mind Biggie. She's always looking for food. Do *not* feed her. I feed this big girl enough. She's already too fat." Murph said he named her after Wanda Sykes's character Biggie Shorty from the 2001 Louis C. K. film *Pootie Tang*.

I knew I would like living next to Murph.

"You want to come in and see the place?"

I nodded and walked into the triangular-framed building of dark wooden *vigas* and plank *latillas*. Sunlight flooded the kitchen from the northern triangle window. Thick patches of mint grew in a planter by the front door, next to the entrance to the shower built from glass bottles matrixed in cement and plaster. The vigas rose in a cone to a sleeping loft surrounded by triangular windows. In the corner, next to the window frame, someone had tacked a handmade sign that read: "ALL THINGS CHANGE."

Reynolds and his crew of friends had built a can dome and shaped it into a concrete pyramid. Reynolds had private theories about the power of pyramids aiding people to commune with the secrets of the universe.

I fist-bumped with Murph and rubbed Biggie's neck on the way out.

The wind tossed my curly brown hair. All things change.

Across from the Turbine House, Reynolds and his crew had set up a massive vertical-axis windmill that spun like a quarter flicked on a table-top. The huge scoop was so strong that it would sometimes lift its frame up into the air. So Reynolds had decided to build a building beneath it to anchor the windmill.

They went to work and built a three-story cylinder of cans, cement, pounded tires, and huge pine vigas. The face of the building collected southern light, and plants and herbs grew there for food and air regeneration. A cozy fireplace emerged from the north wall, with benches for people to sit in and talk philosophy, speculate on astral projection, discuss the tarot, comment on the sacredness of the Great Pyramid, for men and women to bullshit each other into a bed in some other house somewhere, to debate the best ways to prevent leaking in a south-facing roof, and to figure out how to best punish the polluting bastard plutocrats of the world. Some people just ate mushrooms and tripped out on the coals of the fire.

They called the building the Castle.

Today, that fireplace is scattered with old chessboards, books on Earthships and sustainable design, and Reynolds's treatise, *A Coming of Wizards*. I'd read the book and admired many of Reynolds's analogies. They were thoughts on how the sun and water and energy affected the phenomena of the planet. They were thoughts on how to work *with* the systems of the planet, to *encounter* the energy of the earth rather than resisting it. They were thoughts born of *doing* and *action*. Very little theory, rapid-fired through his no-nonsense Tennessee dialect. Reynolds played the philosopher-hick well, and many people had followed him over the decades.

Most of the young people would dorm in the Castle. Most nights, they would drink beer and whiskey, smoke weed, and enjoy good laughter and conversation. Most nights I walked over and talked with them. Some of them had apprenticed as carpenters in Buffalo, New York, or Scranton, Pennsylvania, the summer before. Some were in graduate school, researching how to best design systems to deal with human *chąą'* (shit), how to grow mushrooms to eliminate insect pests without the use of chemical pesticides, how to design Earthship cabins for tourists in Utah, how to build affordable buildings for schools in developing countries. Most of them were trying to get through college. Most of them had a garden waiting for them back in Wisconsin, Michigan, Illinois, Utah, Tennessee. Working to build Earthships was a bit like the summer camps some of them might have gone to when they were younger. For some it was fulfilling an Internet fantasy born in their dorm rooms late at night. For others it was a way to blow off some steam after spending damn near a year in some classroom in a college or graduate school. For some, this was a summer lark. For others, it was a way of life.

But all of them were restless. They wanted to travel. They wanted to put their muscles into something. They wanted to get dirty. They wanted to take risks.

I understood that.

Rob and I didn't stay in the Castle. We lived in a row of three domed Earthships called the Pods. My room was a circular sleeping area buried about three feet into the ground. A long tub built from cans matrixed in cement and lined with EPDM rubber, rocks, gravel, and sand, called a plant cell, ran along the front of the glass wall. A small bathroom sat to the side with a simple French drain shower. The ceiling was insulated with straw and adobe coated in plaster.

After the first two days of life on the mesa, I wondered how these young

people were able to do it. How were they going to drink and smoke most of the night and then get up early the next morning and kick ass on a construction site?

It turns out they didn't.

I stuck to my normal morning routine I'd built over the past decade: Wake at 4:30 a.m., do push-ups and sit-ups to get the blood flowing. Go for a walk. Listen to the birds and the coyotes. Feel the chill of the morning. Watch what's happening. Touch a dewy sagebrush and watch the sky turn white with predawn. Make prayers to the *Diyin Diné*. Make coffee in the blue enamel coffeepot and stir up hiker's porridge of bulgur wheat, oatmeal, flaxseed, peanut butter, dried apples, and honey. Eat and drink while writing. Drink an extra quart of water. Piss outside. Stretch. Get tools and lunch together for the rest of the day.

Rob was always up soon after. We woke our other roommates. Jacob and Jason were a pair of brothers from Tennessee. Jacob was the younger brother, but you'd never guess it. His flat-topped hair, straight back, muscled figure, and focused gait made him look like a thirty-year-old man walking in a twenty-five-year-old body. He was working through an undergraduate degree in civil engineering and wanted to see what the Earthships could offer. Jacob extended a much calmer energy, with a smooth black beard covering a boyish face unlined by worry. He'd embraced the Tennessee twang that Jason had long unlearned. He was studying horticulture at a local community college, which is code for saying that he liked "bringing the flowers," which is code for saying that he liked to smoke weed. They were some of the best people I would meet that summer.

Our fifth roommate in the Pods was Kurt, a yoga instructor from Norway, with a trim figure, hair that dangled down into his face when he wasn't tying it back into a man-bun, and inquisitive brown eyes that had probably gazed out of every window in every classroom of every elementary school he'd been shuffled through. With his thin face and smooth skin, you'd think he'd just walked out of high school. I'd later learn that Kurt was pushing thirty years and had no intention of letting that be something he cared about. But his trick of youth sprouted mostly from how he spoke to you. Kurt wanted to know about everything. *Everything.* Where were you from? Who were your parents? What did they teach you about your meaning in the universe? Did you believe it?

Kurt was also a silly bastard. He flirted with women, gave them back rubs and deep massages, listened to them, made out with them in dark corners, talked with them about different levels of meditation.

Rob smiled. "I coulda pinned that Kurt had older sisters from the start."

And Kurt did have them. He also had a mother who was a highly regarded veterinarian in animal testing labs throughout Europe. His father had innovated a biogas harvesting business after networking with local farmers in Scandinavia about ways of collecting their cows' valuable methane and bottling it for sale and distribution. Kurt had inherited their intellects, no doubt, but he also had one of the most piercing emotional intelligences I'd ever seen. He could watch you walk across a room and get a glass of water and notice something about your energy, about how you gripped the sink, and he'd ask about a feeling you were having. Then he'd ask you what you thought it meant.

He was in every moment.

And he was on time to drive to the construction site by nine o'clock. Mostly.

At the site we met our foreman, Phil Basehart. Phil had been an architecture student from New Jersey when he first came to the Southwest and learned about Earthships. They had been building an Earthship community near the valley of Valdez, on the southern slopes of Lobo Peak. They called the community REACH, for Rural Earthship Alternative Community Habitat. There, Reynolds had bought fifty-five acres on the side of the mountain. People called it "dog land." You couldn't run power, water, or sewer lines up to it. The backhoe driver Reynolds hired to excavate the site left shaking after two days. He was afraid he would tip his rig down the steep slopes. So Reynolds and his crew hung solar panels up on the ponderosa pines and ran electric jackhammers and excavated the hills themselves. They hauled bags of cement up the steep mountain "roads" in little Toyota trucks and sometimes on their backs.

"We lived like eagles up there," Reynolds later wrote in his book, *Journey*.

Phil joined those eagles when he hiked up to REACH and volunteered. They put him on a crew to mix and pour cement. After a while, Phil got tired of paying rent in Taos and started building his own Earthship in the Greater World Community. When I met him he was considered one of the veteran builders for Earthship Biotecture and had led several humanitarian builds in other countries. His humble attitude, observant eyes, Mel Gibson–esque looks, and smart-aleck good humor made him easy to talk to. There was no dumb question you could ask Phil Basehart.

That summer, we would be building an Earthship that Reynolds had named the Waybee. It was a house built with a bank loan that the company would rent to people wanting to stay the night in an Earthship. It also had

a huge attached garage, and the rumor was that Reynolds was talking with Elon Musk about getting a Tesla roadster so that the renters could drive an electric car into town and get really jazzed about solar power.

Phil organized the twenty-person crew into five groups. Each would rotate through different workstations. Some carefully built the clear-glass-bottle walls in the interior of the greenhouse, working precisely with small levels and sculpting tools to shave away the cement-earth mix so the glass shone like stars. Some pounded tires to create a perimeter wall around the exterior of the house. Some dug out and plumbed the greenhouse botanical cell running along the glass wall. Some nailed wood panels to the interior roof of the greenhouse. Some worked the metal detailing on the Pro-Panel roof. Some mixed cement and dirt and packed the tire walls on the outside of the building.

Rob, Jacob, Jason, Kurt, and I were assigned to build concrete floors. We learned how to set up a builder's level inside one of the bedrooms, how to shoot a straight line at the transom of the doorway. Using a measuring tape and the precise scope on the builder's level, we could pinpoint exactly how high we'd need to make the floor in order to keep it flat. Most Earthships have concrete floors with wooden frames built into them. The concrete holds the solar heat from the greenhouse in its mass. It can also be dyed in hues of earth, reds, and blues. Once we got the perfect level at the doorway, we mattocked and dug the floor to a straight line and knocked in rebar stakes to pinpoint the level spots. Then we cut sections of steel mesh to lay in the middle of the concrete to give it strength.

With the floor flattened, we set the frames and attached them to rebar pins in the ground so they wouldn't move once the frames were filled with concrete. We had to tap down the pins precisely until each point of the frame was level.

Then we mixed cement and ran it into the room, wheelbarrow by wheelbarrow, shovelful by shovelful. Phil stopped in every twenty minutes to check on us newbies. When we started setting the mesh in the concrete, Phil showed us how to agitate and bounce the concrete in order to settle the gravel into the bottom. "You gotta bounce it," he said. "You gotta bounce that shit."

The next day, we finished the first floor section. Phil decided we were good at it. So he took us out of the rotation and had us build more concrete floors. And then more floors.

On the first weekend, I needed to get up a mountain. I told the guys in

the Pods that I planned on going up Wheeler Peak, the highest peak in New Mexico. I asked if they wanted to come. We ascended through fields of lilies, ferns, and aspens, along the shore of Williams Lake, and up to pine forest that flattened and sloped into high mountain meadows with marmots barking at the edges of the rocky switchbacks and demanding hikers' pretzels and Doritos. We looked out to southern ridges and spotted grazing mule deer and bighorn sheep. The volcanic basalt plains stretched out to the west and dropped into the Río Grande Gorge. The rest faded into the brown and blue of mountains sketched across the horizon.

The following week, we learned how to adobe plaster the interior of the Earthship with a hawk and trowel. We learned the difference between a hard trowel and a smooth trowel. On the Fourth of July, the fireworks shimmered over Taos while my coworkers tripped on mushrooms.

We went rock-climbing at El Rito Canyon on the weekends and cooked stew for one another. Kurt burned his lentils three times. The first time, he just left them on the stove too long, and they cooked through their water and burned to the pan. Forgivable. We've all been there. The second time, Kurt put the lentils on to boil in a pan and walked away. A few minutes later, he heard a fierce steaming sound and ran to the kitchen to find the lentils scorched across the gas burner. The "pan" had actually been a plastic mixing bowl, which melted almost as soon as the blue ring of flames jumped out from the stove. The third burning of the lentils happened when Kurt got into a conversation with one of the women interns and forgot they were cooking.

That Thursday night, we all packed into our cars and drove out to KTAOS Solar Center, the home of the world's most powerful solar radio station. KTAOS played avant-garde pop and alternative rock acts like Neko Case and Birds of Tokyo, but you'd also catch the Rolling Stones and George Harrison on the airwaves. That night was lady's night, and the set was being played by local band, Katy P and the Business. And they meant business. Katy P and her band shot through covers by Modest Mouse, Donna Summers, and Gwen Stefani. They covered the opening licks of Nirvana's "Smells Like Teen Spirit" and blended it beat-for-beat with Michael Jackson's "Billie Jean." They'd start with Aretha Franklin's "Respect" and flow seamlessly into "Walk" by Pantera and then straight back into Aretha. Their drummer had serious chops, and Katy P had that silly, sexy energy and the strong vocals that put her above Gwen Stefani. She and the Business got us dancing with no problem. I was soon sweating through my green Earthship Biotecture T-shirt.

Rob, Kurt, and I met up with some of the female Earthship interns. They introduced us to their guy friends, who seemed to patiently circle them in hopes of snatching a make-out session or two.

A brawny red-headed guy who skied almost every day at the Taos Ski Valley, near the base of Wheeler Peak, pulled me aside and asked me if my name was James. When I told him it was, he said it was his name, too. He yawped that he and I were both Santiagos and that we were now *hermanos del nombre*. When he asked what brought me to Taos, I told him I was working for Earthship Biotecture as an intern.

"You're working for Michael Reynolds!?" he said. "Oh man! Another goddamn tire pounder! They say the mountain either sucks you in or spits you out. Taos is awesome. It's a great place to live. But it tests you. You have to really want to live here."

"Thanks," I said. "I'll remember that."

Rob and Kurt and I didn't get back to the Pods until one o'clock in the morning.

"Nice night," Rob said as we brushed our teeth outside. I nodded.

I stood with Rob outside the Earthship. But I was also in Glen Canyon with my brothers and sister. The *yeis* stood inside the rock, their bands of black and red clear to the eye of any who would walk that ground. The bear tracks walked up the rocks. The Rainbow Man held his five-fingered hands up toward his hair streaking to the sky like lightning. The people stood straight as corn plants, rooted to the earth.

And who would remember the people who inscribed these stories on the rock? Who sang their songs?

I knew some still told their stories. But I didn't feel they were singing loud enough to drown out the MTV stars of the world who helped the power-seeking beings sell people things that weren't helping them walk in a good way. Too many of the songs today didn't teach people to stand their ground like *yei*, to raise their hands to the sky and hold rainbows, to root themselves to the *Nahasdzáán*, the Earth Mother, like a corn plant.*

* If you think I'm exaggerating or being too much of a cranky old man, let me say this: as I wrote this passage, I took a break and looked up the current number-one hit on the *Billboard* chart. The hit was "Uptown Funk" by Mark Ronson, featuring Bruno Mars. The song is dedicated to the "ice cold" girls who look like Michelle Pfeiffer. These girls have "white gold" (this is code for the "fine ass" of a white girl with a nice, plump "ghetto booty," according to Urban Dictionary).

The frogs in a distant pond had already started singing, those *ch'al* from the First World who sing when the rain falls, who make the mud for us so we can wear our Adobes.

The frogs sang. Then came Michael Reynolds's words. They were words I'd kept with me since I'd left Pennsylvania, words I'd been learning since I was ranging through washes and canyons and mountains.

"Survival," he wrote, "is a song we sing while living."

(*continued*) These ideal women wear Chuck Taylor All-Stars shoes. They wear designer clothes from Saint Laurent. I'm sure no teenager living on the Rez or anywhere else is influenced in any way to buy these particular products.

The song praises living for the Saturday nights in a big city, drinking alcohol and handling money at the same time, and then letting the spirit of "uptown funk you up." The speaker in the song is "hot" enough to make a "dragon retire" and smoother than a "fresh jar of Skippy." I'm sure the shareholders for Skippy peanut butter love this song. It is a world where being "hot" is the same as being "cool." This is a healthy way to think and believe, of course, and a way of life that can go on forever.

But let's get this straight: the music in the song makes me want to dance until I sweat. I also think I might do this just a little better in a good pair of Chuck Taylor shoes and a hot-ass Saint Laurent tank top. Just saying.

THE SONG OF THE CELLS

After our first week, Kurt and Jacob and one of the young women, Athena, led Rob and me to visit some guy they'd met at a crafts fair in Taos. His name was Rock Ridgeway. He lived across the road from the Pods.

Rock and his partner, Judy, had set up a small oasis garden inside the metal fence of the property (which Rock had erected to stop the coyotes from eating their cats). A hoop greenhouse protected raised beds of Swiss chard and lettuce. Bonsai-manicured sagebrush spread next to small beds of cilantro and basil. A 1980s RV sat across from a simple plywood cabin painted green and turquoise. A ramshackle toolshed extended into an outhouse with a glass window to provide some heat in the winter. In the southwest corner sat a hexagonal-crystal-shaped tent covered with a heavy gold acrylic canvas.

As we approached the gate, a black border collie mutt sprinted and stopped so fast that her paws threw dust into our faces.

"Hey, girl." I held out my hand so she could sniff. Her intelligent brown eyes saw no threat and she backed off.

The familiar bright screech of a circular saw cutting lumber soared over the cabin.

"Hey, Rock!" Kurt yelled.

A blond woman with healthy skin and strong arms walked out the front door, smiled, and waved. It was Judy, Rock's partner. "He's out back," she said. "I'll get him."

Rock strode around the side of the cabin. And he really was *striding* in

his flip-flops, like an enlightened pilgrim at the edge of some promised land. His storm-cloud-colored mullet thinned at the top, but Rock still grew it defiantly long toward the back. His bushy eyebrows radiated that austere glance of a guru or wizard, but in the same moment his Texas grin and twang seemed to dispel any regality.

I couldn't stop looking at his teeth. His two front teeth grew stacked over another set of incisors directly behind them. His green sweatshirt and gray shorts looked like they hadn't been through a washer since winter. The border collie mutt raced around him with a Frisbee in her mouth.

Rock asked our names as we shook hands. He looked each of us in the eye when we answered.

"So you brought 'em?" Rock asked.

"Yeah, man," Jacob said, taking out a thick bolt of purple cloth from his backpack. The cloth looked like a canvas tent. But when Jacob opened it, he held out a hexagonal cloak with a hole in the center.

"What is that?" I asked.

"One of Rock's inventions," Kurt said. "It's a Cameleon."

"Uh-huh," Rob said. "And what do you do with it?"

"You wear it," Jacob said. "It becomes any type of clothing you want. We brought them so that Rock can show us all the folds."

Rock strode into his RV. He had created the Cameleon when he was ranging out in the Colorado mountains and realized he was carrying forty-five pounds of redundant cloth: pack, poncho, tent, parka, sleeping bag. And they were all made of nylon. He wondered if he could combine them into fewer items and cut the weight. He troubleshot the idea for three years and came up with a hexagonal shape that could be folded, zipped, buttoned, and pulled tight with drawstrings. This way, when you ranged out into the mountains, you could wear a Cameleon as a shirt and another as pants, then a third as a cape and a fourth as a backpack. When you got to your campsite, your shirt could become your pillow, your pants became your sleeping bag, your cape became your ground cloth, and your backpack unfolded into a tent.

It was part of a multiuse philosophy that Rock had been thinking about for decades after he read the works of R. Buckminster Fuller, the American designer and architect who popularized the geodesic dome and envisioned a society that used its technology to mimic the patterns in nature.

Rock walked out of the RV wearing a blue Cameleon around his waist.

"The first thing we're going to start with is the pants." Jacob and Kurt followed his lead.

"Okay. First you've got to start down here at the midsection. Now please don't look too close at my little bulge down there. You know, it's funny. I travel all over the country to Renaissance fairs. That's how I make money selling these Cameleons. And I used to do a little magic routine and move around the stage. And, well, anyway, I came down *hard* on my ankle, and I was laid up on the couch in my RV for seven weeks. And I discovered DVDs at the nearby pawnshop that you could get for just a dollar. Okay? Okay? So I sat and did the calculation that I laid on the couch and watched at least 250 hours of DVDs. And I gained more than twenty-five pounds in my gut. Since I've been back, I've just been fasting. I've only been taking in lemon tea, water, and maple syrup. And I've lost twenty-one pounds since. So I've got four more pounds to go. So what I'm saying is, don't judge my appearance just yet. So, anyway, here's how we put this together."

Rock stepped through the folding of the pants with the snappy flair of a well-rehearsed stage magician. He joked about the long piece of drawstring hanging down over his crotch.

"What about that string there?" Rob asked, looking for a good-natured way to take a little piss out of Rock's presentation.

"Well, that's your *lure*," Rock said. "You wiggle that for bait. Gives the ladies something to think about."

Athena—the only lady among us—giggled and rolled her eyes.

"Oh, I'm *bad*." Rock laughed. "I'm bad, I know. But you develop a stage routine. And I've been doing this for thirty years. I've got all my little tricks."

He saw that Jacob had tied his Cameleon a bit too loose in the back. "Now, if you don't watch out when you tie the back, you'll get dumpy butt. That sixty-year-old I-just-had-an-accident butt drop, you know? You see, I act so smooth here on my own property in Taos, but I'm really not. I was in Texas one time, up on stage. And I'd be showing people different folds, and I go through my whole act. And I'm not against gays, right? But there's this part when I'm showing off the skirt for this, and I do one little turn."

Rock did a flamboyant, limp-wrist debutante turn. "And so I'm up on this sound stage with at least seventy people watching me, and I'm doing this turn, and this huge wind comes in, like a dust devil, and just throws the skirt up over my head. I'm wearing no underwear. *Boom.* Full frontal with seventy people watching. So that's what I get for being bad."

He explained how to tie the pants up. Then he asked if someone else

wanted to try. Athena volunteered. Rock took her through how to tie a strappy sundress.

"Nice tattoo." He noticed her inked back. "Very druidic."

"It's a Celtic symbol for the sun," she said.

"It reminds me of a crop circle," Rock said. "It's the aliens and the wheat working together on those."

"You think it's the wheat pressing *itself* down?" I asked.

"No, I think it's being guided by the beings *within* it. I believe most of the processes of life are actually being dictated by a subatomic civilization. Oh, here we go. Let me just get this knot. There."

In less than ten seconds, he'd turned the strapless dress into a sweatshirt. Then a poet's shirt, like something you'd see inside the Globe Theatre in London. Then a poncho.

"You know, I have this theory that the human body was made to wear geometry," he said, securing the last knot.

Judy walked up behind the cabin where the dog had been ripping the hell out of her Frisbee. She invited us to sit out of the wind. We took shelter under their little shade house. In the center sat a small wooden shrine with a monkey figure at its center.

"Tell us about the crystals," Kurt said. "Like what you told me before."

"Oh, sure," Rock said. "Well, you know this world is set up geometrically, okay? Nature is planning all this stuff out all around us. Life is just abundantly creating *life*. And we've got our way of looking at the world. You were mostly all taught the Cartesian model in school, right? You have an x-axis and a y-axis and a z-axis, and that establishes a three-dimensional plane. You follow me? But Nature is doing *all* this stuff around us. And Nature does *not* work on that model. The architecture of life is made up of atoms. And atoms are mostly nothing. They are three-dimensional. They are *rotational*. So you've got those chains and chains of mostly nothing making up something. But they have spin. There is a tension and a compression. Those are the two true forces of Nature. Tension and compression.

"One particle repels, and the other pursues. But they're not doing it in a standard three-dimensional plane. They're chasing and repelling and spinning. That's the dance. The dance between tension and compression that creates spin. And the spin of particles creates a magnetic field. And these magnetic fields will join up together into what looks like a donut. That's the torus. You see the torus in the Olms cycle. In trees. Tension and compression from the roots up to the trunk and up to the branches. You

see it in arches. You see it in eddies on the water, that sort of spin. You see it in galaxies. You see it in the solar system.

"So the torus is a quanta. It's not a dot. It's tension and compression. And they're always spinning. If you could slow it down, it would look something like a twirling baton. When these spins join up, they create a vector. And more join up. More vectors."

Rock smiled, demonstrating it all with his hands.

"Eventually, when twelve of those vectors start coming together, there's just no more room. And so they start forming shapes. They start forming crystals. Do you want to hear more? Can I show you something?"

He walked into his RV and came back with two binders filled with pages in laminated covers. He showed us a picture of his twenty-year-old self holding up a platform the size of a pizza box on the tips of his fingers. The platform was borne up by toothpicks arranged in a crystalline configuration of isosceles triangles. In another picture, he's standing poised, and athletic, on top of the same platform. And it's holding his weight. With toothpicks. Without buckling.

Rock pointed to the pizza box platform. "You see that structure under my feet? If you took that structure down to an atomic level, you'd be looking at a diamond. And it's *strong*. That's the strength of crystals. And it's something that Nature is just building around us all the time. But we've stuck on this x-axis, y-axis, z-axis. We've built an entire civilization around that Cartesian model. And it has absolutely nothing to do with what's really going on around here. But this is Nature building. This is the sort of building that I want to tap into to create self-replicating housing."

Rock nodded, as though some silent threshold had been crossed. He grinned to reveal that reckless troublemaker. That restless, ranging mind. I'd seen that expression before on Lyle Parsons's face.

Kurt adjusted his seat on the couch. "So, Rock, you were talking about what the Creator is doing. And when you are watching what the Creator is doing, are you also talking about God? The creator of the universe?"

"I don't know what's going on with the *universe*, exactly," he said. "But I believe, by observation and inductive reasoning, that there is a subatomic civilization directing this movement of life. Different cultures have called them different things. Elves. Fairies. The kami. The kachinas. Lots of other names."

Diyin Diné, I thought. The Holy People. The Great Ones.

"But they're the same subatomic civilization who've learned to direct

and manipulate energy and matter, and they're using it to *know* us. We just need to have the vision to know *them*. When human cultures have done this, life has flourished. And that's what it's really all about. There might be a creator of the universe. But I don't think we can really *know* the creator of the universe. It's just too big for us. Some people think we can't know anything. But I don't agree with that, either. I mean, through science, I know that water will freeze at a certain temperature. I know that a triangle is structurally stronger than a square. This is the geometry and the structure of life. And we can know life. We are part of it. The universe is just too big.

"But life is probably scattered all over the universe. And they have something to do with one another. But they also might not. I don't know the universal creator, but I bow before my Creator, the Creator that gives me life. And that Creator comes from within me, within my cells and atoms. And I'll gladly give my reverence and respect to that.

"Did you ever study physics? Biology has everything to do with physics. It's based on physics. I mean, the universe is all energy. You've got light and gravity and motion. You know, the sun's rays hit the water, and it evaporates and rises, and then gravity pulls it, and it falls. And all this is going on without any organisms in mind or involved at all. What I'm saying is that there's something in life—something singing in the cells—that has 'got it' about what's going on with energy and has modeled itself off that."

The air grew colder, and the dog lifted her head. Lightning lit Rock's storm-cloud mullet. Thunder pounded the mesa. We were all staying dry in the RV. But I was also staring out the window. Which also means I was smelling the sagebrush waking to distant rain draping like dark hair over the sand. Which means I was also in my canyon of memory, and the storm was rumbling down Two Mile's dark throat. Which means that rainbows were coming, as they do after every storm.

But maybe—in the song of my cells—something was also *telling* me.

Rain fell on the roof of the RV as hard as flint arrows.

We walked to the Pods. I found one of my bags had been pulled into the greenhouse near the bathroom. My pack of beef jerky had been ripped open and all of it eaten. Nothing else had been touched.

When I walked out of the Pods, Biggie Shorty—Murph's old, chubby pit bull—lay sprawled luxuriously on the cement lid of the buried septic tank.

"You steal my jerky?" I asked.

Biggie Shorty lifted her head and farted.

How could I not laugh?

WITH OUR LANTERNS ON

That Monday, on the final week of our internship, Rob and I built one last concrete floor, and Rob swore the whole time. Rob was a professional rammed-earth builder. He kept his own clock, worked for himself, and ran a tight ship. Now he was pissed at the disorganized crew. He hated when a twenty-something would just stroll away from the jobsite so they could get a cigarette or breathe off a hangover. I helped in the swearing as we bounced the concrete into the form and knocked out the job as quickly as we could.

During our lunch break, I walked behind the outhouse and made some phone calls. A school in Gallup, New Mexico, had called me out of nowhere and asked if I wanted to interview for a teaching job. Maybe this was what Glen had predicted when he said, "Let New Mexico give you the answer."

I stepped over a black scorpion clacking its way past a sagebrush and phoned in for the interview. When we were done, the school offered me the job. I told them I would call back the next day.

Rob saw me grinning as I walked back to the jobsite.

"What do you say, Jim? You win the sweepstakes?"

"No, but either way, I'm moving to New Mexico at the end of the month. Maybe Gallup."

I called Dr. John Kraker and told him the news. I also asked if he'd be willing to rent me his Earthship. He said he'd make up a lease agreement. Things were looking good.

After work, I drove Rob and Kurt back to the Pods. I took the glass coffee-pot off the stump in front of the Earthship; at dawn I had filled it with water

and some tea bags and set out to make sun tea. I walked into the Earthship, showered with the gas-can solar shower. Then I cooked my chickpeas and lentils with olive oil, onion, and broccoli. I put on my Baja hoodie sweater and walked out to the picnic table in front of the Castle next to the green cottonwood tree in the planter built from cement and beer cans.

Every evening I had sat there, facing east, to Taos Mountain. The green leaves hissed in the cottonwoods in the planter. The reflections of clouds passed over the glass wall of the Castle. *Jóhonaa'éí* walked down in the west.

I ate the beans and the broccoli with a spoon I'd carved from a juniper branch in Ganado. The peak of the mountain turned scarlet gold with the late sun.

"If," I said to the mountain. "If you let me stay, I won't be a burden to you. I'll be useful. I'll be what I can."

The wind lifted my hair. A cloud passed over the dark peak of Taos Mountain.

They say the mountain either sucks you in or spits you out, James, *mi hermano del nombre.*

"Feel free. Do what you need," I whispered. "You know where I am."

I walked back through the sagebrush to the Pods. The pigeons living on the roof of the Turbine House flew in a scattering of purple shadows.

On the next-to-last day, I stood and talked with Tim, one of the veterans on the Earthship crew. He scratched his light gray and red beard and stretched his thin frame and well-muscled arms. His ponytail swished over his bare back like a horse's tail.

When I told him I'd like to take some of the Earthship ideas back to the Navajo Reservation, Tim nodded. He wanted to see more structures built among Native peoples. It would free them up economically.

"Not everyone is going to connect with this shape of the structure. And that's not a structural issue. It's a cultural one. But you don't have to have this particular structure to get thermal gain. We could let this design go, and we'd be fine."

He talked about Trombe walls, where people had put together a double-glazed window over an adobe surface or some kind of stone panel. The sunlight would heat the wall, and the heat would pass through and warm the inner space. He also mentioned types of thermal-mass windows, where you get a glazed window with a gel sitting in the middle of the glass to hold the heat.

I swept my hand across the Greater World Community and asked Tim what he thought of the residents living there. What sort of people could afford to buy into the Greater World?

Tim said the community was mostly made up of people with money. Either they were newly retired folks with property money, or they were younger people who'd earned their fortunes and were using the money to buy properties.

This worried some of the Earthship crew. They felt it could be holding back the development of the Earthship technology. Our foremen all had their own ideas.

Phil wanted to see more development of the concept. He wanted to see more thermal imaging. He wanted to see biogas digesters on the buildings. They hadn't done it because they just hadn't had the time. They'd been chasing the next project. They'd been chasing the next design.

After lunch, a foreman walked to where we pounded tires.

"We've got a rattlesnake over there, guys," he said. "Go catch it, and we'll get it out of here. Just go slow and be careful."

Chris, a young physics major from Utah, grabbed a shovel, and I grabbed a five-gallon bucket and a piece of plywood. We walked to the far end of the woodpile, and there she was: her scales were that beautiful yellow-sand color, and her back was covered in rows of light brown ovals flecked with white. She buzzed and flashed the lightning bolt of her blue-black tongue.

We moved the lumber aside. I set the bucket down on its side next to the buzzing snake and sat in a comfortable crouch. "*Yá'át'ééh Tł'iish 'ádaanínígíí. Ní éí ayoo' nizhon. Hadíísha' naníná?*" Hello, Snake That Speaks. You are beautiful. Where did you come from?

"What?" Chris asked, resting on his back foot.

"Nothing," I said.

"Better step back, bro!" Chris leaned the metal shovelhead in toward the snake.

"In a week, I don't know where I'll be living," I whispered to the snake. "What do you think? What do you think Lyle Parsons would say?"

Tł'iish 'ádaanínígíí flashed that purple-black lightning tongue. The brown eyes watched, unblinking.

"Uh, dude?" Chris said, a bit of worry in his voice.

I realized I was within a foot of the snake and backed up. "Thanks," I said as Chris stepped forward. He tapped the snake softly, and it slithered

into the safety of the bucket. Then Chris used the shovel to tip the bucket upright. *Badda-bing.* The snake was safely captured.

I leaned over the bucket, listening to what *Tł'iish 'ádaanínígíí* might have to say. I heard sledgehammers pounding dirt into tires back at the wall. Screws drove into sheet metal to build a roof that would catch its own water. People laughed as they slapped mud and concrete onto walls that would collect their own heat.

Maybe that was all there was to hear.

I nodded to the snake. "*Díí ayoo' baa' aheeh nisin.*" I am thankful for this.

I went back to tire pounding, and Chris drove the snake down to an old mule corral about a mile away to set it free.

After the shift, we set up a little worktable with salsa and chips and beer and pretzels. We laughed and joked and took pictures. Almost all of us were leaving that weekend. Rob was driving up into the Jemez Mountains with a climbing friend from Colorado. Jacob and Jason were driving back to Tennessee. Kurt was traveling to New York and then up to Toronto to teach some yoga seminars before flying out to Thailand and then to India. Chris was staying a few extra days and then driving back to Utah.

I didn't know where the hell I was going.

I could move to Gallup, but I wanted to stay in Taos. But I could feel that probably wasn't going to happen. The job search in the area had led to nothing but dead ends. Still, I decided to stay behind an extra two days to work on the jobsite. During that time, I could make some calls to see if any jobs opened up at the school in El Rito or whether one of the charter schools in Taos was looking to hire an English teacher. I wanted to work for Taos High School, but that wasn't happening. The district had just hired a new superintendent, and she was all about saving money. Also, the state had slapped the Taos schools with new regulations that forced them to cut more than $600,000 from their budget because of the irresponsible spending of the previous superintendent. That previous superintendent had also left the school district with a rash of legal bills from the many lawsuits he'd incurred.

Lyle Parsons would probably grin to hear this and just sigh. "Gotta love administrators."

But I still didn't know where I was going to live. If anything, I could just take my tent and camp in the mountains or somewhere in the Carson National Forest. No big deal.

On Saturday, the crew went back to KTAOS for one last night of dancing.

Katy P and the Business were playing again, and the drummer was smashing out sixty-fourth notes like they were a reflex. They shot through their set, and the crew was dancing and sweating in no time. No one was sober. But no one was drunk.

Then Katy P and the Business played a song I'd vaguely heard on the radio. The music started with a staccato ring of concert chimes; the song was part pop ballad, part slow dance tune. I didn't know the title or the band who played it. But it made the crew dance.

I knew I was standing on the KTAOS dance floor. Just as I knew that James had come by again and clapped my shoulder to say, "Hey! ¡Hermano del nombre!" Just as I knew that I would probably never meet the people on my crew again. Just as I knew that I would be homeless in less than two days.

But I was also in the parking lot of the Marriott hotel on the night of my senior prom. I was hearing the music pounding out into the desert night and hating every second of it. I had never gone to dances in high school. I'd hated the awkwardness. The pretension. The noise. The bullshit.

Yet here I was, dancing my sweat through my T-shirt and jeans. As my crew mates danced around me, I understood why. It wasn't about the music or the lights. It was about who was dancing with you.

They'd worked under the sun all week. But they were young and knew how to smile. They had just enough energy stored in the dance of their cells to move their hips and arms to this music, under this shimmer of photons.

I knew they'd leave Taos after two sunrises. They'd go back to graduate school, back to their parents' basements, back to work, back to their gardens. But they'd never leave this song.

I danced with them. And the lights flashed and burned like a rainbow.

WHERE THE BLACK LINE EXTENDS

I planned to move to Gallup, New Mexico. I had called friends and arranged for them to help me gather what was left at my old apartment, my room at the horse farm, and my classroom at the high school.

But I wanted to stay in Taos two more days. Monday and Tuesday. I knew that any teaching jobs in Taos were out of the question. But you never know.

During those two days I dreamed of seabirds drowning in black tides of oil that no pair of Adobes could withstand.

It was better to stay awake, to work under the sun, to build something, to stay restless. I would need two days to see if I could keep doing that in Taos.

Rock Ridgeway offered me the gold crystal tent at the southwest corner of the property. The plywood floor kept me dry. The prefabricated eyebolts met at the angles of the crystal and were tied together with thick cotton cord. The tent withstood the windy nights, even with the waterproof acrylic skin flapping for hours at a stretch.

Once I'd packed my things and tied up my hiking pack, Rock stepped out of his cabin wearing a yellow T-shirt and blue denim pants he'd stitched together himself. We shared coffee while Rock kept his hands busy making drawstrings for Cameleons. "I get them unfinished and then add the drawstrings so they count as 'unfinished goods,' and it slides me into a different tax bracket." He smiled.

He asked me about my application schedule, and I said I might drive out to Ojo Caliente to actually meet a school principal in person during the week. "That's a good idea. Go meet them. Make 'em look you in the eye, make 'em shake your hand."

He paused in tying the drawstrings, and I could tell he was thinking. He gave me his proposal. "I've seen that handy little Prius you have there. I know it gets good gas mileage. I've got to build an arc awning for the amphitheater out at Taos Mesa Brewing. I can do it myself, but I need some machine presses that I have up at my place in Crestone, Colorado. So how about tomorrow you drive me up there? I'll pay for gas and give you a Cameleon."

"About how far north?" I asked.

"It's about 140 miles. And it's a beautiful drive, man."

"Sounds like a good use of a Sunday."

That night, I slept in the gold crystal tent on my camping pad and sleeping bag. A summer storm pounded around the tent, and rain smacked the canvas. Frogs sang me into the dark.

I woke and stretched and exercised as the sun rose. I made coffee on the gas range inside Rock's RV and set up a breakfast of oatmeal, raisins, and apples. Rock walked into the mobile home while the clouds were still purple and pink.

I used Rock's laptop to check the school district websites for teaching jobs. No luck.

Over coffee, I asked Rock whether he considered himself an inventor or a designer or an architect.

"I'd say I'm an inventor before anything. So that means I'm mainly a fuck-up. That's the nature of experimentation, you know. The inventor's job is doing the fucking up for everyone else."

Rock buttoned his blue dress shirt and blue denim pants. Rock called the dog, "Come here, Molly!" The dog jumped into the Prius. He carried his iPad in a case slung on a thin strap over his shoulder, along with Molly's red leash. His gray hair drifted backward and his flip-flops clapped as he walked to the car with all the intention and focus of some mystic on a long pilgrimage or a wandering wizard about to set forth on a far journey.

"Oh," he said, remembering. "Let me take a quick hit before I go."

Rock was only mildly stoned as we drove north over the bridge toward Tres Piedras. We passed sandstone spires specked with pines and junipers. "They say these are the oldest rocks in the country," he said. "Old, old, old. Older than dinosaurs. Older than life."

We drove past a large compound of adobe and log buildings with tall, expensive green Pro-Panel roofs. "What millionaire owns that place? Damn," I said.

Rock explained. The place had been a school dedicated to promoting a

certain vision. A guy Rock knew named Troy had bought it and stocked it with all kinds of equipment. It had its own sawmill, cement mixer, and hydraulic lifts.

"What's the vision?" I asked.

"Vision?" Rock shrugged and shook his head. "With Troy, who knows?"

We drove north toward Bear Mountain, an ancient volcano that domed out more than two and a half miles in either direction of its 10,890-foot shield. The people of Taos Pueblo called it Bear Mountain, the sacred mountain of the North. The flat sagebrush landscape was pocked with volcanic vents of red pumice stone.

The sagebrush seemed flattened and stunted where the plain met the gradual elevation of Bear Mountain. "Not a lot of people live out here," I observed. "Does the winter keep them away?"

"Oh yeah," Rock said. "It's so cold and the wind is so intense. But the elk love it. They live up on the mountain and come down here to graze during the winters. You'll see herds of sixty of them sometimes. We're going into the San Luis Valley right now. It's a sand valley, with sand going down 22,000 feet deep. Water runs through it. It's some of the cleanest water in the world. So far, the ranchers and the farmers have kept the developers away from it."

Those ranchers and farmers had drilled more than two thousand wells into the aquifers of the valley. And they were using those wells to grow more than a thousand square miles of crops. As we drove, I tried to imagine the hataałi medicine singers who had ranged up this valley on horseback, finding water and evading hunting parties of Utes, in order to pray and gather herbs and collect the soil from Sisnaajini, the sacred mountain of the East. The mountain of Dawn and White Shell.

We drove into Alamosa, grabbed lunch, and walked Molly in the park along the Río Grande. Rock turns the talk back to crystals.

"It's like when you see a rack of pool balls. And you get 'em tight against each other." He held out his hands in a triangle. "There are fifteen racked up there. And if you pile a ball between each of those, you'd have five. And then three. And then one. And that pyramidal structure is what's creating the strength. That's the nature of the crystal. And some crystals can change, and some are fluid. Life is always shifting with energy. Right now, they're finding small algae and bacteria that are eating plastic. They're actually biodegrading the stuff and breaking it down. They're changing to fill these little niches. That's what life does. It evolves because it is life's pleasure to do so."

The Diné *hataałi* who had traveled up to the sacred mountain of the East would say that there were two rivers: *Tooh Biką'í* (Male River, or the San Juan River) and *Tóóh Ba'ááд* (Female River, or the Río Grande). It was said that no *Nahooka' Diné* could live north of the San Juan River, and none could live east of the Río Grande. The countries beyond those borders were just too vast, hunted by the Apaches and the Utes.

Now these places were farmed and herded and sold and shopped by the *bilagáana* Americans. Some of the *bilagáanas* hardly knew about the land on which they lived. They'd started hypnotizing themselves decades ago with the electronic hallucinations of color television, and the cycle of mind control hadn't let up since. It had sped up with the invention of the "smartphone" and the iPod, the thin televisions that clip conveniently to any father's belt and inside any mother's purse. You may think I'm exaggerating here, and I might be.*

But as Rock and I walked the loop in that park in Alamosa, we passed several "parenting stations" set up along the path. At one station, a circle had been painted with blue and red spirals on the sidewalk. Next to the circle was a sign spelling out a little game between the mother and the child. They were supposed to look at each other and laugh together. Other signs asked parents to put away their phones and hold their children's hands.

I asked Rock what he thought of a people and a culture who had to be taught these lessons so explicitly.

"You ever read a book called *Be Here Now*? It's by Ram Dass. You should check it out. It introduced a lot of people to Eastern philosophy back in the sixties. But that's the central message. Be here now."

I smiled and remembered Kurt. He was so good at catching me when my mind wandered out of the present. Sometimes I'd be waiting for cement to finish mixing on the jobsite. I'd start thinking about being on the mountain and about the spirit of Lyle Parsons.

"Jim," Kurt would say, "be here now." Then he and I would laugh.

"That's the trick of consciousness," Rock said. "It's so good at numbing itself. I just try to acknowledge the blessing of consciousness. I *am* some-

* If you'd like to debate, first please read Jerry Mander's book *Four Arguments for the Elimination of Television* (New York: William Morrow, 1978). Mander was an ad executive for years before he realized that the medium of television is not just bad for people's minds, bodies, and spirits—it's also unredeemable. And he was saying all this in 1978.

thing. I exist. But if I didn't know I existed, I would miss out on the whole thing!"

We drove north up the valley. The sun gleamed off the hayfields. It shimmered white along the edges of the mountains. The ground was impossibly flat, nearly curved, like the horizon of some ocean. The air was the color of my fingernails. The color of white shell.

Always it was before us: *Sisnaajini*, the sacred mountain of the East. That name means "Black Line Extending." The name comes from the volcanic soil that sits in a streaking black line right at the edge of the mountain's snowpack. You can drive up to the peaks and see the black streaks in the spring and summer.

We picked up Rock's machine presses in Crestone and made for the southern turn at Tres Piedras, and drove toward Taos. Rock contemplated leaving the presses with a friend, but his face turned bitter. "I actually can't stand that guy sometimes," he said. "One time he accused me of being a thief."

Stealing was part of the daily life growing up on the Rez. Kids stole from each other all the time. It was like a game. I got your pencil today. Let's see if you can steal my calculator tomorrow. Come on. I *dare* you. This continued until you proved you could beat up anybody who tried to take from you.

"Kids are just living that way everywhere," he said. "And then they grow to adults. But that's what I mean about experiences. They are what we make them to be. They're not who we are. That's the difference between a delusion and an illusion. An illusion is a false impression created from outside by skillful manipulation of light and space and sound. And we experience illusions all the time. We actually experience so much phenomena in the universe. I mean, to know what *this* is," he said, touching the dashboard of the car, "we don't really know what *this* is. All we get to see is this shimmer of photons flying into the wet caves of our eyes. There's lots of other sounds and frequencies we can't hear. There are types of stimuli we just can't feel. But the ones we can . . . illusions play upon that."

Many worlds revolve around us every day. We mostly live in this world, the Glittering World, the one that the shimmering photons allow us to see, the world of our bodies, made by the *Diyin Diné* when they stretched the buckskins and set the ears of *naadą́ą́'áłtsoii* (yellow corn) and *naadą́ą́'áłgaii* (white corn) in their center, when they set the eagle feathers over each and *Niłch'i* blew the life breath into the man and woman. It became our duty to walk in Beauty, to move in harmony, to range and root, then range and root again. We owed this to the *Diyin Diné* who gave us our bodies, but also to

our elders and our forgotten ancestors who passed their lives on to us. And once our elders passed, it was our responsibility to remember them as we grew into their respect and then to not speak of them once they had died.

I knew what Rock meant about illusions. But I also knew that sometimes illusions were all we had.

"Then there are delusions," he continued, "which come from inside our own minds. They are webs of thought that we create, and sometimes that way of thinking isn't even ours. It's the stuff that our parents gave us to take with us when we left. It's like, we leave the house, and they're like, 'Here. Take the garbage with you!' I call them our X-Files. And those visions come from within. Those visions cause emotion. And those emotions aren't even who we are. They aren't *us*. They are delusions we manufacture. So delusions are created from within, while illusions are created from without. And both are bad news. And it's so easy to fall into them. We're falling into them all the time.

"That's why it's good to not overthink things. Don't overthink it. And don't take it too seriously. You don't have control over it all anyway. But what you do have control over is your *perception*. Your life is this shimmering of photons. Your life is like this movie you're watching play out. But you get to decide what kind of movie it's going to be. If you want it to be a soap opera, then that's what you'll get. Do you want it to be a mystery? A romance? A tragedy? Or an adventure? I want it to be an adventure. I live my life every day happy to be part of this comedy adventure unfolding before me. I just don't overthink it. I don't take it too seriously. And I just enjoy it."

The wind rushed through the open window. My brown curls drifted across my eyes and scattered the light into auburn rainbows. We passed the rocks rising in spires out of the sand and sagebrush, those older than the journey of our ancestors between the First World and this Glittering World.

The southern Rocky Mountains spread north and south in a gleaming dark crescent in the golden light of late afternoon.

I knew Rock was right. Somewhere between the glittering illusions of sunlight and the dark delusions of our inner worlds lay the balance of our perceptions. That was where we said, "I will take this dark road" or "I will take this road to *hózhǫ́*. I will be one of the people of the Earth, of the corn, who wears Adobes and feels their feet on the skin of *Nahasdzáán*."

Where my feet would be in the next two weeks I had no idea. There was no job for me in Taos. But I knew I wasn't cold, thirsty, or hungry. I could

pay for my food. I might have a job in Gallup, New Mexico. I might stay in Pennsylvania and work another year.

Wherever I would end up, I knew I would be staring off into the distance and imagining *Sisnaajini*, Where the Black Line Extends. I understood where the line was headed. It moved around the mountain, in that reliable circle, as surely as any traveling black lines of cloud or mountains around the *ts'aa'* (wedding basket), where one enters and ranges along the band of the rainbow between sky and earth before walking out of the gap in the circle from which one had first emerged.

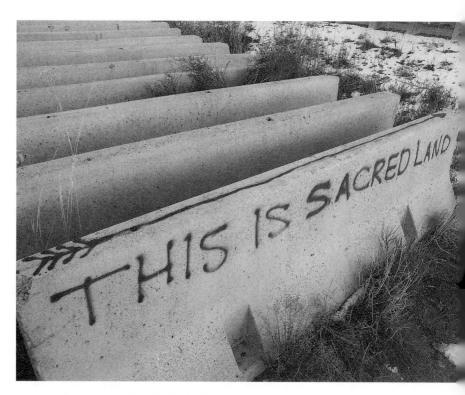

A message in spray paint from the Carrizo Mountain region.
Photo by Jim Kristofic.

EPILOGUE / THE BLUEBIRD SPEAKS

The next morning, I loaded my duffel bag, food tin, hiking pack, and ruck-sack out of Rock's crystal tent and into the Prius. I was driving back east that morning.

Water boiled for coffee while I took one last look at the concrete pyramid Michael Reynolds and his friends had built out on the mesa. On my first weekend, I had entered that pyramid and climbed up inside the loft. Deity figures—large as any *yei* carved into the walls of Glen Canyon—emerged in pieces of colored glass and mirrors in the concrete.

"These were people looking for a new way of life," I'd whispered. "A new way of walking."

I knew how they felt.

Wherever I was a year from now, I wanted to build a life on my own terms toward *są'ah naagháí bike'hózhǫ*. That lasting harmony.

But it wasn't going to be in Taos. That much I now knew.

I walked back into the RV, where Rock was checking his Facebook page. He handed the laptop to me.

"You want to check your e-mail or anything before you go?"

"Sure, man." I took the laptop and opened the Taos Municipal Schools home page to get the e-mail address for the new superintendent. I'd toured the schools twice that summer, and I wanted to write her a thank-you email. I also wanted to let her know I was interested in any future teaching positions (though there wouldn't really be any with the budget cuts the district was facing).

I wrote the e-mail and—on a whim—checked their jobs page.

There was an English teacher position open at the high school. Just like that.

"Umm . . ."

"What, man?" Rock said.

I flew into my duffel bag, unpacked my shirt, slacks, and tie, and drove down to the high school. When I pulled into the parking lot, a gang of muscled Hispano and Anglo teenagers in cutoff T-shirts and spandex football pants walked to the football field. I adjusted my tie, grabbed my portfolio, and stepped to the front door in my leather loafers.

I met one of the janitors at the front doors and waved hello. He rested his back casually against the glass door. His athletic build seemed at ease in his T-shirt and shorts. His flip-flops scraped the ground as he shuffled toward me and shook my hand.

"Good morning, sir." He grinned. "What can I do for you?"

"Oh, I'm here to talk to the principal about a job that opened up in your English department," I said.

"You want to talk to the principal?" The janitor scratched his chin. "Well, he's hardly ever here in the summer. The bum. He's probably over in some other district building. Let's go inside and see the receptionist. Maybe she can get him on the radio."

We walked into the air-conditioned building and headed for the glass windows of the main office. The janitor opened the door for me and turned around.

"Nah, just kidding," he said. "I'm Robbie Trujillo, and I'm the principal!" He laughed like a high school jock who'd just pulled off a great prank. And he had.

Trujillo invited me into his office, and we talked for more than an hour. He would try calling the chair of the English department and see if he could meet me. But he was probably fly-fishing down in the Río Grande Gorge. Trujillo asked me to call him back on his cell phone in about an hour. No problem.

I got a copy of the *Taos News* and scanned the classifieds for a place to live if the job lined up. I found what was described as a "green living" adobe cabin out near Arroyo Hondo, a rural village north of Taos. Over a cell phone call, I got directions from the landlady and drove out along a small paved road to a wooden gate topped with a pair of custom-forged iron ravens. I met with the *má sání* who owned the cabin and walked through it and the property. It had a solar room with a greenhouse. It had a Sun-Mar

composting toilet that collected poop and mixed it with sawdust or peat moss below in a drum and allowed you to compost your own poop and use it as fertilizer after a few months. It had a wood stove. It had a gray water leech-field drainage system. The viga and latilla ceiling had been rough cut with handsaws by her late husband, who had built the first roads out to the property and lived in a log cabin he'd reassembled with pine vigas and adobe mud given to him at Taos Pueblo. A stone labyrinth—aligned perfectly with the four directions—spanned with the same circling poetry of the *ts'aa'* (wedding basket) in bright white stones on the northern edge of the property. There was also a woodshop, a chicken coop, and—thank the *Diyin Diné*—an outhouse.

The *má sání* who owned the place had come to the Southwest while studying the architecture of the Anasazi at Chaco Canyon for her master's degree in architecture from a college in Boston. She'd fallen in love with the Southwest for the same reasons I had. She had seen *atiin diyinii*, those holy rainbow paths, and she had followed them.

I said I would be back. We shared a warm handshake in the cool adobe kitchen, and she said she would hold the place for a week.

I called the principal at Taos High, and he said he couldn't get on the phone with the English department chair, but that he could get me a phone interview by the end of that week.

I drove back to Rock's cabin, gave him a big hug, and drove east. I drove Interstate 40 to Pennsylvania in two days. Restless.

When I got back to Bucks County, I packed up my Prius with whatever would fit. What did not, I loaded into a U-Haul pickup truck and drove to the local Salvation Army. I spent the next day cleaning out my classroom at Council Rock with my dear friend and mentor, Joy. She and I and her husband, Paul, counseled and consoled one another while I organized my things. I left the classroom with one small tote bag of books and folders and DVDs.

When the tote bag wouldn't fit into the Prius, I had to leave that behind, too.

I spent the evenings meeting up with friends to tell them what I was doing and where I was going. A dear friend and coteacher gave me a small notebook and inscribed one of my favorite quotes from J. R. R. Tolkien on the inside cover: "Not all who wander are lost."

The next morning, I drove west. I interviewed for the job with Taos High School on the phone while driving through western Pennsylvania, where

I was born and had gone to college. The secretary for the superintendent called me back in the late afternoon and offered me the job. I pointed the car toward Taos.

On the way, I picked up my old friend, Josh, where he was working on his PhD thesis at the University of Illinois, and we drove through Kansas grasslands, spent the night in Dodge City, and headed toward the Rocky Mountains, toward that peak with its snowy top shining like white shell—*Sisnaajini*, the sacred mountain Where the Black Line Extends.

I moved into the adobe cabin owned by the *má sání*. Josh and I went fly-fishing in the mountains with my new English department chair. The next day we hiked up Lobo Peak, sat in a field of wildflowers, and looked out over the sagebrush plains of Taos to where the jagged snake of the Río Grande Gorge moved south.

The following day, we walked down into the body of that jagged snake and stepped into its flowing waters and felt the cool movements of *Tóóh Ba'ááá*, the Female River that marks the eastern border of *Diné Bikéyáh*. I knew that Diné people had ridden into this country, sometimes to trade and sometimes to make war.* Just like I knew that this water had drained from that alluvial fan of the mountains in the north and the snowmelt from their peaks. Just like I knew that the waters cooling my naked ribs had once been snow that shone like white shell on the peaks of *Sisnaajini*, Where the Black Line Extends.

I understood this even in the chuckwalla-almond brain that had seen me through summer storms and reminded me to wear my Adobes. So many other good people had done the same before me. So many people, like Lyle Parsons, had spent their lives teaching it. The builders of a better world, like John Kraker and Phil Basehart and Rock Ridgeway, had shown me a path

* After the Diné had acquired the horse, their warriors often raided the small villages of northern New Mexico for livestock. They also rode out to rescue their children from slavery. They would go to war with the people of Taos Pueblo. In 1820, Diné warriors rode into Taos and nearly burned it to the ground. People at Taos Pueblo claim that they still have Diné scalps in their kivas from those wars. When I talked with my Navajo friends about whether I should live in Gallup or Taos, they all said I should move to Taos. "We want you over there," one said. "I want a nice place to come and visit during my vacation! And we need you keeping eyes on the enemy." They were only half joking.

that would keep any more deer from dying in my lap. I was part of their path, and we all—the *Nohooka' Diné*—were part of the same Emergence story.

I was bathing in the far border of *Diné Bikéyáh*, the country I loved, in the waters of the Female River. The waters were a comfort. When I got out and sat on a rock by the current, the beads of water resting on my bare feet shone like rainbows.

I turned to Josh. "My feet are going to feel good walking here."

He nodded and didn't say anything. He knew what I meant.

I knew I would find a beauty here that I'd seen while ranging in Utah and Arizona. But I knew it would be a complex beauty. A few miles north of this spot in the Río Grande, the Chevron Corporation had carved out an entire mountainside while looking for deposits of molybdenum—that metal that softens steel for service in jet airplane wings and nuclear missile casings, for accelerating the whole American affair. I also knew that mine was closing over the next year.

In less than a week, I drove Josh south to Albuquerque and said good-bye at the train station. I knew I would miss him deeply, but—like any good friend—he would never be more than a kind memory or phone call away.

I drove back to Taos as the sunset had burned down to its purple coals and painted the southern Rocky Mountains with a gold blood light. The black snake of the Río Grande Gorge tracked the path of *Jóhonaa'éí* to the south. I couldn't keep back the tears.

That night, I slept alone in the adobe cabin for the first time. I didn't dream of slashed wrists or black blood or birds drowning in oil. I didn't dream at all. My life was the dream now.

The following morning, I brewed coffee in my blue enamel coffeepot and walked the gravel path under gray bands of dawn. A bird dipped out of the dim light and landed on the rail fence.

The bird looked familiar. I walked closer. I wanted to be sure.

"Is that you?" I asked.

The *dólii* (bluebird) hopped off the fence, flew at me, and fluttered in front of my face. He danced on his wings and hovered for more than five seconds. I could have reached out and grabbed the *dólii* if I'd wanted to. But he seemed to know I wouldn't.

The bluebird flew to the top of the nearest fence post and ran through a song. It may as well have been Ode to Joy. I could feel Lyle Parsons's presence, at least the memory of him, real as light but invisible as heat.

I wasn't sure if staying in Taos was a homecoming or a stretch of the path I was supposed to walk. But I would be willing to walk that path of Beauty every day. Who could say what rainbows waited in the next bend of the canyon?

Thank you, reader, for walking with me.